LOCKE'S THEORY OF KNOWLEDGE
AND ITS
HISTORICAL RELATIONS

LOCKE'S THEORY OF KNOWLEDGE AND ITS HISTORICAL RELATIONS

BY

JAMES GIBSON

CAMBRIDGE
AT THE UNIVERSITY PRESS
1960

PUBLISHED BY
THE SYNDICS OF THE CAMBRIDGE UNIVERSITY PRESS

Bentley House, 200 Euston Road, London, N.W. 1
American Branch: 32 East 57th Street, New York 22, N.Y.

First printed 1917
Reprinted 1960

First printed at the University Press, Cambridge
Reprinted by offset-lithography by Lowe & Brydone Ltd, London, N.W. 10

PREFACE

THIS study of Locke's Theory of Knowledge was begun as an introduction to an edition of the *Essay* upon which I have been engaged for some years, but in view of the proportions to which it has grown it has seemed better that it should appear independently. Notwithstanding the labours of Campbell Fraser and the admirable little volume by Professor Alexander, the *Essay* still suffers from the twin assumptions, that it can be understood without being studied and that its full significance can be summed up in a small number of simple propositions. In truth, few philosophical classics lend themselves less readily to such summary treatment than do its carefully guarded statements, and its complex, unstable thought positions. In the exposition of Locke's doctrine, which occupies the first half of this book, I have, accordingly, sought to indicate the grounds of my interpretation by frequent references and quotations. The relation of Locke's thought to that of his predecessors and contemporaries has hitherto received but little consideration, and that little not from his countrymen. To throw some further light upon the influences which affected his work has, consequently, been one of my chief aims. On the other hand, I have omitted all reference to the movement which culminated in Hume, to have dealt with which with the necessary fullness would too greatly have extended the length of the present work. Concerning it I can only remark that the exclusive attention bestowed upon it, as the story of the self-refutation of certain of Locke's principles, has been largely responsible for the false perspective in which the *Essay* itself is too commonly viewed. That the tendency to sensationalistic atomism was bound to work itself out is, indeed, true enough. But the significant fact that the course of the individual thought of Locke, of Berkeley, and even of Hume himself, favoured the fuller recognition of the intellectual functions involved in knowing and of the systematic character of what is known, suggests that there were other directions in which the doctrine of the *Essay* was susceptible of at least equally legitimate development.

J. G.

Bangor.
April, 1917.

CONTENTS

PART I

THE DOCTRINE OF THE ESSAY

CHAPTER I

THE PROBLEM OF KNOWLEDGE AND THE 'NEW WAY OF IDEAS'

CHAPTER II

THE POLEMIC AGAINST INNATE PRINCIPLES

CHAPTER III

THE ORIGIN AND FORMATION OF IDEAS

CHAPTER IV

THE CONTENTS OF OUR IDEAS OF MODES

CHAPTER V

OUR IDEAS OF SUBSTANCE, CAUSALITY AND IDENTITY

CHAPTER VI

THE GENERAL NATURE OF KNOWLEDGE

CHAPTER VII

THE KINDS AND LIMITS OF KNOWLEDGE

PART II

THE HISTORICAL RELATIONS OF LOCKE'S DOCTRINE

CHAPTER VIII

LOCKE AND SCHOLASTICISM

CHAPTER IX

LOCKE AND DESCARTES

CHAPTER X

LOCKE AND CONTEMPORARY ENGLISH PHILOSOPHY

CHAPTER XI

LOCKE AND LEIBNIZ

CHAPTER XII

LOCKE AND LEIBNIZ (*continued*)

CHAPTER XIII

LOCKE AND KANT

CHAPTER I

THE PROBLEM OF KNOWLEDGE AND THE 'NEW WAY OF IDEAS'

§ 1. In the popular tradition as to the contents of the *Essay concerning Human Understanding*, which for so long satisfied even the most conscientious of our historians of Philosophy, its main purport was found in a theory of the genesis of ideas which, denying to the mind both activity and the possession of any definite character of its own, derived all the contents of our knowledge from particular data of immediate experience. In virtue of this theory its author was proclaimed the founder of modern Empiricism, and if any features of his work inconsistent with the rôle thus assigned to him received any notice at all, they were treated as unintentional departures from his fundamental position. The account which Locke gives of the origin of ideas, and his view of the nature of mind and its relation to experience, will occupy us later on, when it will be found that a good many mythical elements have become embedded in the popular tradition as to his views on these subjects. For the present we are only concerned to point out that any account of Locke's work which finds its main significance in an account of the genesis of our ideas fails entirely to represent either the aim or the outcome of the *Essay*, as these were conceived by its author. Great as was the importance which he attached to his theory upon this subject, it played only a subordinate part in the scheme of the *Essay* as he designed it; and any attempt to make it central alters entirely the perspective of the whole. While he considers that it contributes towards, he fully recognises that it does not contain in itself a solution of the problem which the *Essay* sets out to solve, viz., that of determining the nature and possible extent of human knowledge. Any exposition of the thought of Locke, as expressed in the *Essay*, must therefore begin by considering what he understood by knowledge, the nature and bounds of which he sought to ascertain.

§ 2. Philosophers of an empirical tendency have generally simplified the problem of their epistemology by reducing the claims of knowledge to the level of the principles by which they have sought to explain it. Unconditional validity, strict universality and necessity, cannot, they have maintained, belong to our judgments, which are merely the cumulative result of a number of particular experiences. The appearance of rational demonstration is for them only a garb which is assumed by a form of cognition which rests at bottom upon particular data of immediate experience, and in so far as it transcends these is infected with uncertainty and imperfection. Such, however, is very far from being the position of Locke. For him, in the first place, knowledge and certainty are equivalent terms. 'With me,' he says, 'to know and to be certain is the same thing: what I know, that I am certain of; and what I am certain of, that I know. What reaches to knowledge, I think may be called certainty; and what comes short of certainty, I think cannot be called knowledge[1].' And this certainty which constitutes knowledge is an objective certainty, which must be distinguished from the highest degree of subjective assurance with

[1] Second Letter to Stillingfleet, *Works*, vol. IV. p. 145.

which a merely probable conviction may be held. In some cases, he holds, the grounds of probability are so strong that our assent is as necessarily determined by them as by a strict demonstration, but even in these extreme cases he still rigidly refuses the name of knowledge[1]. For when we have knowledge, we have something which excludes the possibility not only of doubt but of error. Now this does not merely mean that knowledge is formally distinguished from error, as the true from the false. It implies that a form of absolutely certain cognition exists, which no new facts or considerations can weaken or overthrow, and which is capable of being recognised as such by the subject. 'What we once know, we are certain is so; and we may be secure that there are no latent proofs undiscovered, which may overthrow our knowledge or bring it in doubt[2].'

Besides its certainty, there are two other general features which Locke considers that knowledge must possess, if it is to be of any serious value. In the first place, it must possess the character of being 'instructive' or synthetic, by which it is distinguished from the merely verbal certainty of the 'trifling' propositions, which only repeat in the predicate the whole or a part of the idea which constitutes the subject. And further, however subjectively conditioned and limited in its immediate range, the knowledge which Locke undertakes to investigate is regarded by him as somehow referring to and holding good of a reality which is independent of the knowing mind and of the ideas by which it is known. Besides being certain and instructive, our knowledge must be 'real.'

Nor must it be supposed that this real and instructive certainty is to be found either exclusively or typically

[1] IV. 17. 16. [2] IV. 16. 3.

in reference to particular matters of fact, of which our sense-perceptions might be supposed to render us cognisant. Such knowledge as this is distinguished by him as 'experimental' and 'historical' from the 'scientific' knowledge which consists of universal truths; and it is with the latter that he is primarily concerned. The nature and extent of our knowledge of particular sensible facts would not, in the first instance, have presented itself to him as a problem requiring serious investigation, although in the end it proved a subject for curious consideration. For, upon reflection, it appeared that this 'historical' or 'experimental' knowledge is not only inferior in its limitation to the particular, but is also deficient in the quality of absolute certainty which constitutes the essence of knowledge. The knowledge with which Locke is chiefly concerned is, therefore, that which consists in certain and universal propositions. Moreover, he holds that strictly universal statements can never be justified by a process of empirical generalisation. On the contrary, the universal proposition is one which asserts a connection which is seen to hold good from the consideration of the nature of the case. It is, indeed, only universal in its range because this connection of content is seen to be necessary. It thus possesses all the characteristics of knowledge which is logically *a priori*. Upon such universal and necessary propositions, Locke considers, the possibility of demonstration depends, without which our knowledge would be entirely without system, and could not assume the form of science.

§ 3. Now the type of such knowledge Locke, like most of his contemporaries, found in the mathematical sciences, and more particularly in geometry. The perfect intellectual transparency, which appeared to him to be possessed both by the primary assumptions of these sciences and by their demonstrations, constituted his ideal of knowledge, and formed the standard by which he tested the worth of all our intellectual possessions. His view of knowledge, like that of Descartes, is throughout dominated by his conception of the mathematical sciences, the revival and development of which constituted the most striking intellectual achievement of the age in which he lived.

In this development of mathematics, and especially in the applications which were being made of mathematics to the solution of physical problems, there was much to suggest the need of an enquiry into the nature and limits of knowledge. Descartes had already put forward a generalisation of what he took to be the method of mathematics, which claimed to represent the true method of knowledge as such, and to reveal the very nature of intelligence; although even he had found in experience a refractory element which refused to be reduced to the required form. The definite formulation of the principle of mechanical determination raised directly the question of the range of its applicability, in the answer to which the moral and religious as well as the purely scientific interests of man seemed to be closely involved. With the contemporary movement in England, of which the Cambridge Platonists were the typical representatives, which sought to place morality and the fundamental positions of Natural Theology upon a secure basis, by giving to them the form of a rational demonstration as unquestionable as any used by the mathematicians, Locke was in the fullest sympathy; and among the motives which contributed to the production of the *Essay*, the leading place must be given to his desire to serve in this way what he regarded as the highest interests of mankind.

Keen as was his interest in the scientific discoveries of his day, he leaves no room for doubt that in his opinion the knowledge which is of greatest importance for man is that which relates to his duty, and to the existence of the Divine Being, whose law he conceived this duty to be. 'Our business here,' he declares, 'is not to know all things, but those which concern our conduct[1].' 'Morality is the proper business and science of mankind in general[2].' 'Morality and Divinity' are 'those parts of knowledge that men are most concerned to be clear in[3].' And when Locke speaks of knowledge here, he means knowledge in the strict sense already explained. Least of all in matters of such weight would he be satisfied with anything short of complete certainty. The passage in the *Essay* which shows the greatest emotional warmth, in which the usually calm flow of its periods is broken by a series of almost rhetorical questions, is that in which he repudiates the idea that 'the greater part of mankind' are 'subjected to unavoidable ignorance in those things which are of greatest importance to them'; rejects with scorn the claim of the 'current opinions and licensed guides of every country' to furnish 'sufficient evidence and security,' where such great interests are at stake; and expresses his conviction that 'God has furnished men with faculties sufficient to direct them in the way they should take, if they will but seriously employ them that way, when their ordinary vocations allow them the leisure[4].' For, 'how short soever their knowledge may come of an universal or perfect comprehension of whatsoever is,' men yet 'have light enough to lead them to the knowledge of their Maker, and the sight of their own duties[5].' A note written by his

[1] I. I. 6. [2] IV. 12. II. [3] Epistle to the Reader.
[4] IV. 20. 3. [5] I. I. 5.

friend, James Tyrrell, in a copy of the first edition of the *Essay*, informs us that the discussion between 'five or six friends,' which first led Locke to formulate his problem, was one 'upon the principles of morality and revealed religion.' But such explicit confirmation was hardly needed. For Locke himself tells us that it was because he suspected 'we began at the wrong end, and in vain sought for satisfaction in a quiet and sure possession of truths that most concerned us, whilst we let loose our thoughts into the vast ocean of being,' that he was led 'to take a survey of our understandings, examine our own powers, and see to what things they were adapted[1].' It is for the security of knowledge itself, and not in its disparagement, that he would limit what he regards as the inordinate pretensions of our intellects. He would prevent men from 'letting their thoughts wander into those depths where they can find no sure footing,' because such a course can only tend 'to confirm them at last in perfect scepticism[2].'

We may now sum up our account of the primary and main problem of the *Essay*. In it Locke undertakes the investigation of the nature and conditions of a knowledge which is at once absolutely certain, strictly universal, 'instructive' or synthetical, and 'real'; the consequent determination of the possible extent of such knowledge; and the examination of its distinction from and relation to other forms of cognition, which are deficient in some of the respects enumerated. While the mathematical sciences furnish us with the typical example of such knowledge, its most important contents are held to refer to the objects of our moral and religious consciousness.

§ 4. Of the problem as thus stated, moreover, Locke

[1] I. I. 7. [2] *loc. cit.*

believed himself to have found a satisfactory solution; and it is to this solution, or some feature of it, that he draws attention on each of the occasions on which he claims originality or novelty for his work. Replying to the strictures of the Bishop of Worcester, he tells us, 'where if anywhere, that itch of vainglory was likeliest to have shown itself, had I been so over-run with it as to need a cure. It is where I speak of certainty, in these following words ..."I think I have shown wherein it is that certainty, real certainty consists, which, whatever it was to others, was, I confess, to me heretofore, one of those *desiderata* which I found great want of[1]."' Again, 'Nobody, that I had met with, had, in their writings, particularly set down wherein the act of knowing precisely consisted... If I have done anything new, it has been to describe to others more particularly than had been done before, what it is they do, when they perform that action which they call knowing[2].'

On two occasions in the *Essay* he speaks of more specific points in his theory as being in his opinion new. It is not, however, to the derivation of some complex idea from simple ideas of Sensation and Reflection that he refers us. The 'argument' which appeared to him 'new, and a little out of the way,' was one concerning 'the essences of mixed modes and relations[3],' upon which his theory of the possibility of universal knowledge in ethics will be found to depend; while it was 'the reason and foundation' of the 'clearness or cogency' of self-evident propositions which, he tells us, nobody, to his knowledge, had ever before attempted to display[4]. At the same time he is careful to disclaim the intention of offering to mankind any new

[1] *Works*, vol. IV. p. 136. The reference is to *Essay* IV. 4. 18.
[2] *Works*, vol. IV. pp. 143–4. [3] III. 5. 16. [4] IV. 7. 1.

method of attaining to knowledge. 'What I say of certainty was not to teach men a new way of certainty... but to endeavour to show wherein the old and only way of certainty consists[1].' What Locke claims, then, to have done, in answer to the question which he propounded at starting, is to have detected by a process of analysis the essential nature of knowledge, and to have shown, by a survey of the contents of our cognitive consciousness, carried out in the light of this analysis, in what regions of human thought the requirements of knowledge, in the strict sense in which he uses the term, can be satisfied, and where we must rest content with the inferior forms of cognition which he designates 'opinion,' 'belief,' or 'probability.'

§ 5. In proclaiming the possibility and necessity of undertaking such an investigation of knowledge, prior to and independently of the attempt to determine the nature of real being, Locke introduced a new point of view into philosophy; and the merits and defects of his work will be found very largely to depend upon the way in which he conceived and applied it.

Considerations concerning the nature of knowledge had, indeed, always found a place, and often an important place, in the comprehensive form of reflection which we designate Philosophy. But except in so far as these considerations had taken the direction of a search for a formal criterion, by means of which genuine knowledge might be distinguished from mere opinion, the treatment of knowledge had always hitherto been dominated by ontological considerations. Either knowledge was regarded as something to be accounted for by reference to the general principles already adopted by the system of philosophy in question for the interpretation of reality, or special

[1] Third Letter to Stillingfleet, *Works*, vol. IV. p. 459.

features of knowledge were appealed to for the establishment of ontological conclusions. In so far as the former course was adopted, the treatment of knowledge was at once secondary and dogmatic, and consisted in an attempt to comprehend its nature by means of conceptions and principles derived from some limited sphere or aspect of the known world; in so far as recourse was had to the latter method, the consideration of knowledge was only incidental and subsidiary to other interests. From the futility of a merely formal treatment of knowledge, Locke was saved by his keen interest in the varied contents of experience; while he was the first to regard the problem of knowledge as primary, and as requiring to be dealt with from its own point of view.

An investigation of knowledge, such as he proposes, is then, he maintains, a necessary preliminary to any attempt to determine the nature of real being. Apart from this, the relation in which he conceived his enquiry to stand to speculative metaphysics was a purely negative one. Such questions are to be simply left on one side. It did not occur to him that there could be any difficulty in doing this, or, again, that the enquiry upon which he was entering could yield any positive contribution towards a theory of reality. Nor did he, at the start at least, suspect that a careful examination of the contents of what claimed to be knowledge might discover a want of clearness, or even latent contradictions, in the conceptions and principles upon which its systematic structure was thought to depend. Accordingly, he began by accepting without hesitation or criticism the categories which were regarded as fundamental by the thought of his age. In the course of his enquiry, it is true, some of these, such as the idea of substance, are found to involve unexpected difficulties and perplexities, and consequently undergo a certain transformation in his hands. Such a criticism of categories, however, although an incidental result of his work, was no part of his original design, and its outcome was always a matter of surprise to him. Indeed, he often continues to write as if conceptions which he has completely undermined must still possess unquestionable validity, and furnish a key to an adequate interpretation of the real. Thus, like many other thinkers, he was destined to prove an illustration of the truth that metaphysics has a way of avenging itself on those who slight or disregard it, and that its deepest entanglements are often reserved for those who think they have discovered a path, by following which its difficulties may be evaded.

§ 6. Locke's own conception of the scope of his enquiry and its relation to other departments of knowledge is most clearly seen from his division of the sciences, in the concluding chapter of the *Essay*. He there distinguishes 'three great provinces of the intellectual world, wholly separate and distinct from one another[1],' which he names Physica, Practica, and Σημειωτική, or the doctrine of signs. Of these, Physica affords us 'the knowledge of things as they are in their own proper beings, their constitutions, properties and operations, whereby I mean not only matter and body, but spirits also, which have their proper natures, constitutions and operations, as well as bodies...The end of this is bare speculative truth, and whatsoever can afford the mind of man any such falls under this branch; whether it be God himself, angels, spirits, bodies, or any of their affections, as number, figure, etc.[2]' It is in this sense of the term 'physical' that in his account of his 'plain, historical method,' Locke rules out, as foreign

[1] IV. 21. 5. [2] IV. 21. 2.

to his purpose, 'the physical consideration of the mind,' which includes the question 'wherein its essence consists[1].' '*Toto cœlo* different' from such enquiries, he tells us, are those which constitute the subject-matter of the 'doctrine of signs,' to which the *Essay* is a contribution. As hitherto pursued, under the name of Logic, this has been chiefly concerned with words, those signs of our ideas, without which we cannot communicate our knowledge to others. It demands, however, a further and more profound treatment. If words are signs of ideas, ideas are themselves, Locke holds, signs of things, or of the reality with which the mind in its thinking is concerned. 'For, since the things the mind contemplates are none of them, besides itself, present to the understanding, it is necessary that something else, as a sign or representation of the thing it considers, should be present to it: and these are ideas[2].' It is by a more penetrating consideration of both 'ideas and words as the great instruments of knowledge,' that Locke hopes to 'afford us another sort of logic and critic, than what we have been hitherto acquainted with[3].' Leaving to others the prosecution of their 'mighty designs in advancing the sciences,' he declares that 'in an age that produces such masters as the great Huygenius and the incomparable Mr Newton, with some others of that strain, it is ambition enough to be employed as an under-labourer in clearing ground a little and in removing some of the rubbish that lies in the way to knowledge[4].'

Now it is notoriously easier to propose such absolute divisions than to carry them through; and Locke's account of the 'doctrine of signs' clearly bristles with metaphysical assumptions, the consideration of which

[1] I. I. 2. [2] IV. 21. 4. [3] *loc. cit.*

[4] The Epistle to the Reader.

would properly fall to the '*Toto cœlo* different' department of Physica. We can here only indicate their nature, leaving their fuller consideration for discussion later on. In the very exclusion of the 'physical consideration of the mind' from the purview of the *Essay*, it is implied that the mind is a substance, with its own essence, 'constitution, properties and operations.' Moreover, since a substance possesses an independent and exclusive existence, the mind and the remainder of the world of real being, which consists of other substances, stand over against each other in a way which renders impossible any direct relation between them in knowledge. It is upon this metaphysical theory that Locke bases the necessity of the mediating function of ideas, as at once belonging to the mind and referring beyond it. How axiomatic this position is for his thought appears from the fact that, although it is of fundamental importance for the whole doctrine of the *Essay*, it is only expressly formulated, and then incidentally, in its closing chapter.

§ 7. The prominence given to 'ideas' in the *Essay* at once attracted the notice of its earliest critics. It was the 'new way of ideas' which Stillingfleet undertook to overthrow in the interests of the faith which he thought was threatened by it; and it was in opposition to 'the fancies of Ideists' that Sargeant expounded the true method of 'Solid Philosophy.' Nor would it be an exaggeration to say that the larger part of the enormous mass of comment and criticism which has continued to grow up round the *Essay*, from their day to ours, has largely depended, for its cogency or want of it, upon the sense in which Locke's 'idea' has been understood. It is, therefore, of first-rate importance to determine what Locke means when he speaks about ideas; and how he conceives them to be related, on the one hand, to the knowing mind, and on the other, to the reality known. In order to place the questions raised in their proper setting, it will be advisable to consider briefly what Locke's contemporaries understood by ideas, and to notice the nature of the views and controversies which were current concerning them.

Considerable divergence existed among philosophical writers of the seventeenth century as to the signification to be attached to the term idea. By many it was employed in a way which limited its application to a medium of cognition involved in sense-perception and imagination. And even in this reference the term was ambiguous. For while it was sometimes applied to the contents of these mental functions themselves, it was also used to signify the physiological conditions upon which they were supposed to depend; whether these were still conceived as 'sensible species' or physical representations of material things, or, according to the more modern view, as consisting in some form of motion in the brain. On the other hand, by writers who had come under the influence of the revived study of Plato, the term was generally restricted to those universal notions, the apprehension of which, they thought, revealed in the most striking way the spiritual nature of the soul, and the independence of its functions of physical conditions.

In opposition to these limited and contrary applications of the term, Descartes had given currency to its employment in connection with all forms of cognition. Thus, according to him, ideas are involved alike in sense-perception and in pure or imageless thought. It is in this comprehensive sense that the term is used by Locke, to signify 'whatever is meant by phantasm, notion, species, or whatever it is which the mind can be employed about in thinking[1].' As the universal implicate of cognition, ideas are involved alike in the sensible apprehension of a colour and in the thought of an abstract object or relation, which cannot be presented to sense. For the word he disclaims any special partiality, and avows himself ready to 'change the term idea for a better,' as soon as his critics can help him to one which will bear as well the required width of denotation. His objection to the term 'notion' is not that it has been employed to signify something which is not an idea, but that it is 'more peculiarly appropriated to a certain sort' of idea, 'so that it would not sound altogether so well to say, "The notion of red" and "The notion of a horse" as "The idea of red" and "The idea of a horse[2]."'

§ 8. But what, we must now ask, is this something which is involved in all cognition? In particular, is an idea to be identified with the process of cognition or with content cognised? Or does it, perchance, include both? The distinction here implied is one which must have been familiar to Locke. In considering his relation to it, therefore, it will be well to notice the way in which it was commonly drawn, and in which he found it in the writings of the great Frenchman, to whom he was indebted both for his use of the term idea, and for his conception of the universal function in knowledge of that which it signifies.

Adopting a distinction which had been current among the Schoolmen, Descartes maintained that an idea may be regarded from two distinct points of view. It may be considered as a mode of the individual's consciousness, or as the representation of something other than itself.

[1] I. I. 8.

[2] Second Letter to Stillingfleet, *Works*, vol. IV. p. 133.

From the one point of view, it may be said to possess 'formal reality'; from the other, 'objective reality.' Thus, the 'objective reality' of my idea of a dog consists of the logical content of my idea, or the qualities which I conceive the dog to possess when I think of him. It must be observed that the recognition that an idea has 'objective reality' does not involve the assertion, or even the supposition, of an existence corresponding to it *in rerum natura*. Thus, when I think of the sea-serpent and affirm it to be a mere fiction, this fabulous monster possesses 'objective reality' in my thought.

§ 9. It will be seen at once that the nature and scope of an enquiry concerning ideas will depend largely upon its relation to the distinction thus expressed[1]. Regarded from the point of view of its factual existence, or 'formal reality,' an idea is a temporal event in the history of an individual's consciousness, which we may seek to analyse and describe, and to connect with previous conditions determining its occurrence. Such consideration of ideas, we should now say, specially belongs to Psychology, though this science cannot entirely ignore the presence of the other aspect. But by an examination of ideas we may mean something quite different from this. We may mean an attempt to define their contents more precisely, and to determine the timeless logical relations of certain of these contents to one another, in virtue of which one can be seen necessarily to imply another. We are no longer restricted to facts of mental history, but are dealing with the nature of what we cognise; and our procedure, if it be thorough enough, may pass into philosophical reflection in the form of a criticism of categories.

[1] On the bearing of the distinction on Locke's enquiry cf. Adamson: *The Development of Modern Philosophy*, vol. I. pp. 113-4.

But if the distinction was of importance for the purpose of marking off the province of an incipient psychology from that of logical and epistemological investigations, it was not free from dangers of a metaphysical kind. The distinction of aspect was liable to be treated as a difference of being, with the result that the 'objective reality,' or logical content of our ideas, came to be regarded as a kind of secondary or reflected existence of the real world in the mind, distinct alike from that world and from the subjective state of the individual. Of this danger Descartes himself affords an illustration. The most characteristic, though not the most famous, of his arguments for the existence of God, proceeds upon the assumption that the 'objective reality' of our idea of the divine being must be regarded as having an actual existence of this kind, which justifies us in treating it as an effect for which an adequate cause must be found. However imperfect, he argues, may be this manner of existence, it cannot be nothing, and cannot have nothing for its cause[1]. But since, in accordance with the prevailing metaphysics, which Descartes accepts, nothing exists but substances and their modifications, it is difficult to see what this manner of existence can be. The objective reality of an idea is by definition something other than a modification of the individual mind; the mediating function of the idea depends upon its being something other than a modification of a foreign substance. We seem, then, to be making straight for the position that in virtue of their objective reality, ideas must themselves be substances. But in that case, again, their utility as a means of mediating between the mind and other substances is destroyed.

[1] Third Meditation.

From these difficulties Descartes had held discreetly aloof, by refraining from asking what the 'manner of existence' possessed by the objective reality of an idea might be. In the subsequent development of the Cartesian School, however, the question as to the nature of the being which belongs to ideas, and their relation to the knowing mind, came to be recognised as of fundamental importance, and formed the subject of the most significant controversy which was waged within it. On the one side, Malebranche maintained that ideas were 'real beings,' possessing an existence distinct alike from the knowing mind and from the realities they represented. Against this view Arnauld contended that ideas have no being apart from the activity by which they are cognised. The terms 'perception' and 'idea,' he insisted, signify the same thing; the only difference being that the former suggests more directly the relation to the knowing mind, and the latter specially brings out the relation to that which is perceived or cognised[1]. Others, again, such as Regis, sought to establish the position that while ideas are only modifications of the thinking mind, they have an existence apart from the act of thought by which they are apprehended.

§ 10. Now although the above distinction must have been thoroughly familiar to Locke, no use of it is made in the *Essay*[2]. The nearest indication of his attitude towards it is to be derived from his remarks upon the distinction drawn by Malebranche between the 'sentiment' as subjective affection, and the 'pure idea' as object of knowledge. Upon this Locke's comment is as follows. 'If by "sentiment"...he means the act of

[1] *Des vraies et des fausses idées*, Ch. 5, Def. 6.

[2] A reference to it is involved in the Epistle to the Reader, where he speaks of ideas as 'objectively in the mind.'

sensation, or the operation of the soul in perceiving, and by "pure idea" the immediate object of that perception... there is some foundation for it, taking ideas for real beings or substances[1].' In other words, the distinction only seemed to him of importance if interpreted as signifying a difference of being, such as we have seen the distinction between the formal and objective reality of an idea tended to become. But for the supposition that ideas are 'real beings or substances' he had nothing but ridicule, while he was also convinced that they have no existence in the mind except when, and in so far as, they are perceived. For mere distinctions of reason, such as that between the two aspects of an idea would appear to him to be, he had little inclination or respect. They were apt to appear to him as merely relics of scholastic hair-splitting, which diverted the mind from its proper function, and against which the judicious thinker must be ever on his guard. And the general suspicion would not be lessened, in the present instance, by the admittedly scholastic origin of the distinction.

If, however, we turn to Locke's actual treatment of ideas, we shall find that it is implied throughout that ideas possess both aspects, although they are not always equally prominent, and confusion is apt to result from the want of a clear definition of standpoint. The idea for him is at once the apprehension of a content and the content apprehended; it is both a psychical existent and a logical meaning. The aspect of 'objective reality' appears most strikingly in the treatment in Book IV of the non-temporal relations of abstract ideas which constitute the content of universal knowledge; but it is prominent in Locke's mind throughout the discussion of ideas in Book II, since

[1] *Examination of Malebranche*, § 38. *Works*, vol. IV. pp. 232–3.

it is only as constituting 'the materials of knowledge' that he is there concerned with them. It is, indeed, a fundamental misunderstanding of his position to suppose that, in his account of the genesis of our ideas, Locke sought to derive the whole content of our knowledge from a series of psychical facts devoid of objective reference. The function of the idea is repeatedly compared by him with that of the word. Both were for him essentially representative; and he would no more have thought of forming a theory of ideas which should treat them apart from their objective reference, than he would have regarded as satisfactory an account of words which disregarded their possession of meaning. Indeed, a 'psychical fact' which is not the apprehension of an object is for him a sheer impossibility. To have admitted it would have been to run directly counter to the principle which was fundamental for his conception of mind, that 'to be in the understanding' is 'to be understood[1].'

It is the objective reality of the idea which is brought forward in its definition, as 'whatsoever is the object of the understanding when a man thinks[2]'; and it is with ideas as 'objects' of thought that the *Essay* is primarily concerned. The term 'object,' however, implies for Locke relation to and dependence upon a mind or subject. Thus while, as we have seen, he assumes throughout a realm of real being, independent of the cognitive process, but to which our knowledge ultimately refers, the constituents of this realm are not 'objects' in his sense of the term, even at the moment in which they are thought of. Like Arnauld, again, he repudiates the supposition that ideas possess an existence apart from the act of thought by which their content is apprehended. 'Having ideas and

[1] I. 2. 5. [2] I. I. 8.

perception,' he declares, are 'the same thing[1].' He is one 'who thinks ideas are nothing but perceptions of the mind[2].' Similarly, 'perception,' which is for Locke the most general name for all the operations of the understanding, is used by him to signify an act of thought by which we have explicit consciousness of some 'object' or content.

§ 11. It must be admitted that Locke's failure to distinguish between the two aspects of the idea introduces a certain ambiguity of standpoint into his work. But although he possessed quite remarkable powers of psychological analysis, and made important contributions to the development of psychology, the place occupied by psychological questions in the *Essay* is strictly subordinate. It is primarily as furnishing the contents of a new kind of idea that the fundamental cognitive faculties, perception, retention and discerning, are dealt with; while even the prolonged discussion of volition and human freedom is undertaken for the elucidation of the idea of power. In virtue of his statement that 'to give an account of the operations of the mind in thinking,' he 'could look into nobody's understanding' but his own, 'to see how it wrought[3],' his method has been identified by some of his critics with the psychological method of introspection, and it has been contended that there is in consequence a fundamental discrepancy between the problem he propounded and the method which he adopted for its solution. No such antithesis, however, can be admitted. While both Locke's conception of his problem and his method are affected by the ambiguity of standpoint which has been already

[1] II. I. 9.

[2] *Examination of Malebranche*, § 15. Cf. the still more emphatic passage, II. 10. 2, quoted below on p. 23.

[3] Second Letter to Stillingfleet, *Works*, vol. IV. p. 139.

recognised, his method is far from being that of introspection. When he looked into his mind, 'to see how it wrought,' Locke neither looked for nor found a mere flow of subjective processes, but a variety of logical contents, essentially involving a reference beyond the momentary state of consciousness in which they are apprehended; and from this reference he never attempted to abstract. It never even occurred to him to treat our cognitive consciousness exclusively, or even primarily, from the point of view of subjective process. The mind was for him essentially rational. Its 'natural tendency' was 'towards knowledge[1].' The 'natural' connections of ideas were those non-temporal relations of content, the perception of which constitutes scientific or universal knowledge. It was only in the fourth edition of the *Essay* that he noticed at all those 'other connections of ideas, wholly owing to chance or custom,' to which he gives the name association, and which subsequently assumed such an important rôle in the development of psychology in this country. And to him they are only significant as explaining the oddity and extravagance which we find in the opinions and actions of some men, a 'sort of madness' in which the mind departs from its normal, rational working.

§ 12. We must now draw attention to a further series of implications in Locke's conception of the nature of ideas and their relation to the mind. We have seen him maintaining that ideas are nothing apart from the perceptions by which their content is apprehended, and that 'to be in the understanding' signifies to be understood. While rejecting the Cartesian conception of the essence of mind, Locke derived from Descartes the principle that all mental functions are functions of explicit self-

[1] II. 32. 6.

conscious thought. And having accepted the position, he sought to develop it with a consistency which Descartes had never attempted. Indeed, several of the most important alterations in the later editions of the *Essay* are entirely inspired by this motive. It is in relation to memory that the application of the term 'object' to ideas is most likely to lead the unwary astray, by the suggestion that ideas are somehow retained in the mind, when it has no longer any explicit consciousness of them. In the first edition of the *Essay*, Locke had himself written in the customary metaphorical manner of memory as a 'storehouse' and 'repository' of ideas, expressions which were seized upon by one of his earliest critics, as involving the presence in the mind of ideas which are not objects of explicit consciousness, and as inconsistent with the grounds of his rejection of innate ideas[1]. In the later editions Locke added a passage in which he repudiated such an interpretation, and asserted in the most emphatic manner the identity of ideas and perceptions. 'Our ideas being nothing but actual perceptions in the mind, which cease to be anything when there is no perception of them, this laying up of our ideas in the repository of the memory signifies no more than this—that the mind has a power, in many cases, to revive perceptions which it has once had, with this additional perception annexed to them, that it has had them before. And in this sense ideas are said to be in our memories when indeed they are actually nowhere[2].'

Again, since ideas are 'objects' which are nothing apart from the explicit thought by which they are apprehended,

[1] John Norris, *Cursory reflections upon a book called an Essay concerning Human Understanding.* Published as an appendix to the same writer's *Christian Blessedness.* 1690.

[2] II. 10. 2.

it is impossible that an idea can be other than it is apprehended as being. To the statement that they exist only when they are perceived, we must add that their nature is exhausted in the content of this act. Each idea must be at once perceived to be what it is, and at the same time distinguished from all other ideas. 'It is the first act of the mind (without which it would never be capable of any knowledge) to know every one of its ideas by itself, and distinguish it from others[1].' Hence, ideas are, properly speaking, incapable of confusion with one another. 'If no idea be confused but such as is not sufficiently distinguished from another from which it ought to be different, it will be hard, may anyone say, to find anywhere a confused idea. For, let any idea be what it will, it can be no other but such as the mind perceives it to be, and that very perception sufficiently distinguishes it from all other ideas, which cannot be other, *i.e.* different, without being perceived to be so[2].' The solution, he finds, in reference to the name. Confusion arises when two names, which are intended to stand for different ideas, are used for the same idea; or when a single name, which is supposed to have a determinate meaning, is used for two distinguishable ideas. Accordingly, in the fourth edition of the *Essay*, Locke largely discontinued the application to ideas of the Cartesian epithets 'clear' and 'distinct,' substituting for them the expressions 'determined' or 'determinate.' But even with this revised terminology, there is, he finds, danger of misunderstanding. For, looked upon as 'some object in the mind' every idea is

[1] IV. 7. 4. Cf. IV. I. 4.

[2] II. 29. 6. Cf. *Examination of Malebranche*, § 29. 'What it is to see any idea, to which I do not give a name, confusedly, is what I do not well understand. What I see, I see, and the idea I see is distinct from all others that are not the same with it.'

necessarily 'determined, *i.e.* such as it is there seen and perceived to be.' It is only, however, to be called a determinate idea 'when such as it is at any time objectively in the mind, and so determined there, it is annexed and without variation determined to a name or articulate sound, which is to be steadily the sign of that very same object of the mind, or determinate idea[1].'

Finally, as objects of explicit thought ideas are in themselves incapable of change as well as of confusion. 'A mutable idea' is, strictly speaking, a contradiction in terms, since it is not properly 'one idea[2].' The term can only signify that at different times the same name is used to stand for different ideas. Hence, although it is impossible for any of us 'to keep one unvaried single idea in his mind, without any other, for any considerable time together[3],' there is a sense in which ideas themselves and their relations may be said to be eternal. It is here, more than anywhere else, that Locke might have employed with advantage the doctrine of the two aspects of the idea, although his own position is clear enough without it. It is only as having a meaning in which abstraction is made from temporal and subjective conditions that Locke considers that an idea can be said to be 'eternal'; and he is careful to dissociate the term from any supposition of a permanency of existence. 'What wonder,' he asks, 'is it that the same idea should always be the same idea? For if the word triangle be supposed to have the same signification always, that is all this amounts to[4].' Hence, while allowing the appropriateness of the expression *aeternae veritates*[5] to signify the propositions which formulate

[1] Epistle to the Reader, fourth edition. [2] Cf. II. 29. 9. [3] II. 14. 13.

[4] Remarks upon Mr Norris's books, § 23, *Works*, vol. X. p. 257.

[5] IV. 11. 14.

the relations between the contents of our abstract ideas, he insists that the term carries with it none of the ontological and psychological implications which had constituted its chief importance in the eyes of the Cambridge Platonists and others. If Locke failed to realise the full significance of one of the most difficult problems of the theory of knowledge, he at least freed it from its connection with the crudities of the current dogmatic metaphysics[1].

§ 13. Among the questions which the 'plain historical method' sought to lay on one side was that of the metaphysical nature of ideas themselves, concerning which, as we have seen, the followers of Descartes had found themselves in such difficulties. The initial assumption, underlying the whole procedure of the *Essay*, is that the existence of ideas may be taken for granted, and their function in knowledge examined, without entering upon the questions which may be raised concerning their nature as elements of reality, or their relation to the mind as a substance. But although these questions are excluded from the *Essay*, they did not fail to occupy Locke's thought, and form the frequent topic of his later writings. Thus, Stillingfleet is challenged to declare 'how the action of thinking is performed,' and to conceive 'how your own soul or any substance thinks[2].' In answer to the criticism of Norris, Locke traces the difficulty of explaining the mind's relation to its ideas to what he regards as its source, in the current metaphysical determination of the soul as a simple substance. 'No man,' he declares, 'can give any account of any alteration made in any simple substance whatsoever[3].'

[1] Cf. below, ch. VII. § 4.
[2] Third Letter to Stillingfleet, *Works*, vol. IV. p. 463.
[3] Remarks upon Mr Norris's books, § 2, *Works*, vol. X. p. 248.

Experience assures us of the difference between having a perception and being without it; but when we seek to penetrate below this deliverance of consciousness, and endeavour to understand the fact in terms of our assumed construction of reality, we are brought up by this insoluble problem. His *Examination of Malebranche* was professedly undertaken in order to discover whether the hypothesis of the vision of all things in God would furnish a cure for his 'unaffected ignorance' on this point, and contains his objections to the views which we have seen were current among the Cartesians. The supposition, which he thinks Malebranche's expressions imply, that ideas are themselves 'real beings' in the sense of 'spiritual substances,' is set aside as inconceivable and absurd. But equally great difficulties are found in regarding ideas as modifications of the soul. For, in the first place, the application of 'the good word modification' makes things no whit clearer than they were before, since we cannot explain in what the modification consists. All we can do is to reassert the presence of the idea. The term 'modification,' again, implies an identity between the relation of ideas to the mind and the relation of qualities to physical things, which consideration shows does not exist. 'To examine their[1] doctrine of modification a little further. Different sentiments are different modifications of the mind. The mind or soul that perceives is one immaterial indivisible substance. Now I see the white and black on this paper. I hear one singing in the next room, I feel the warmth of the fire I sit by, and I taste an

[1] This passage is immediately directed against Malebranche's account of 'sentiments' as distinguished from ideas (see above, p. 18). But it applies with greater force to the view of other Cartesians that ideas are 'modifications' of the soul. It is perhaps a consciousness of this which leads Locke to use the plural form of the third personal pronoun more than once in his discussion.

apple I am eating, and all this at the same time. Now I ask, take "modification" for what you please, can the same unextended and indivisible substance have different —nay, inconsistent and opposite (as those of white and black must be) modifications at the same time? Or must we suppose distinct parts in an indivisible substance, one for black, another for white, and another for red ideas[1]?'

From such passages as these it is apparent that the process of reflection upon knowledge from the standpoint of experience, which Locke had initiated, was already undermining the current dogmatic metaphysics in one of its strongholds. But while indicating the depth of Locke's dissatisfaction with the dogmatism of his age, they also serve to illustrate the limits of his criticism. Notwithstanding the difficulties and apparent contradictions to which the current determination of the soul as a simple substance leads us, it is not set aside as intrinsically mistaken or absurd. Locke had himself inherited the current scheme of thought, for which the categories of substance and quality expressed in an exhaustive manner the ultimate nature of reality, and he never thought of questioning either its general validity or its applicability to the subject of experience. Accordingly, he still continues to think of the soul as a substance, possessing a nature of its own independent of experience; and only concludes that the manner of its existence, and the way in which it performs the functions revealed in experience, are beyond the reach of our knowledge. The question of his relation to the assumptions of the traditional metaphysics will, however, be discussed in a later chapter.

[1] *Examination of Malebranche*, § 39.

CHAPTER II

THE POLEMIC AGAINST INNATE PRINCIPLES

§ 1. There existed a wide-spread tendency, among writers upon philosophical subjects in the seventeenth century, to rest the validity of what they regarded as the fundamental principles of knowledge and conduct upon a vague and often unexplained appeal to Nature. By 'Nature' they generally understood the universe of reality, material and immaterial, in its orderly and universal modes of activity; and from it they commonly distinguished the arbitrary and occasional exercise of human powers which, depending upon an undetermined faculty of free-will, could not be brought within this ordered system. Thus the objective and universal validity of the principles of knowledge and morality was identified with their naturalness. The evidence of reason was the 'light of Nature'; and those who held that moral principles could be established without appealing to revelation, maintained the existence of a 'law of Nature' binding upon all. From this identification of objective and universal validity with naturalness a further step was commonly taken, by which our recognition of the truth of propositions possessing these characteristics was referred in some way to the operation of Nature, or of God acting through Nature, upon our minds. There thus came to be widely accepted, in various forms, a theory of natural and innate principles, upon which those who differed most in other respects often found themselves in substantial agreement. For the many who still held by the scholastic method of formal deduction, the theory supplied the starting point of which their procedure stood so obviously in need, now that the authority of Aristotle and the Church could no longer be appealed to as final. Innate ideas occupied a prominent position in the philosophy of Descartes; while in England innate principles were proclaimed by almost all of those who were seeking to find a rational basis for knowledge and conduct, among whom Lord Herbert of Cherbury and the writers known as the Cambridge Platonists were the most important.

When we enquire more particularly as to what Nature was supposed to have contributed towards our knowledge of the principles in question, or in what their innateness was conceived to consist, it is difficult to obtain an intelligible reply. The supposition that innate knowledge is explicitly possessed from the earliest dawn of consciousness was expressly repudiated by all writers of repute, although such a view was sometimes attributed to Plato and his followers[1]. Lord Herbert of Cherbury and the Cambridge Platonists are as clear upon this point as Descartes himself. But these writers differ from one another in the account which they give of the meaning of the latent or implicit presence of ideas and principles in the mind prior to experience. According to Lord Herbert, the mind is like a closed book, which opens upon the presentation of an object and reveals the characters already contained within it[2]. Descartes explained the innateness of ideas as consisting in a natural bias or predisposition to their formation,

[1] Cf. Culverwell, *An elegant and learned discourse of the Light of Nature*, p. 89; Cumberland, *De Legibus Naturae*, Introduction, § 5.

[2] *De Veritate*. Edition of 1656, p. 68.

which he compared to an inherited tendency to certain diseases[1]. More, who connected the theory with the Platonic doctrine of reminiscence, maintained that even while implicit, this knowledge is both active and actual, like the skill of a sleeping musician[2]. Cudworth wrote vaguely of 'an innate cognoscitive power,' which the soul possesses, 'a power of raising intelligible ideas and conceptions of things from within itself[3].' Glanville, the acute critic of all forms of Dogmatism in Philosophy and Science, maintains that the principles of religion are 'those inbred fundamental notices that God hath implanted in our souls; such as arise not from external objects, nor particular humours and imaginations, but are immediately lodged in our minds; independent upon other principles or deductions; commanding a sudden assent, and acknowledged by all sober mankind[4].' It is true indeed he maintains, that innate principles 'do not lie in the minds of all men in the formality of such propositions; yet they are implicitly there, and in the force and power of them every man reasons and acts also. They are the seeds of reason[5].' If a representative of the modern spirit, such as Glanville, could use such expressions, we may be sure that the theory assumed still cruder forms in the pulpit, and in the conversations upon philosophical subjects, in which every educated gentleman was then expected to be capable of taking a part.

§ 2. Two things are necessary to enable us to appreciate the aim and historical significance of the polemic

[1] Reply to the 'Programme' of Regius, Article 12.

[2] *An antidote against Atheism*, bk I. ch. 5, §§ 2–3.

[3] *A Treatise concerning eternal and immutable Morality*, bk IV. ch. I.

[4] *Essays upon several important subjects in Philosophy and Religion*, 1676. Essay V. pp. 5–6.

[5] *op. cit.* Essay II. p. 50.

against this vague and confused theory, which occupies the first book of the *Essay*. We must abstain from reading into the controversy points of view which have only been rendered clear by the discussions which it has directly or indirectly raised; and we must take into account its relation to the ultimate problem which Locke had set before himself, viz. the determination of the nature and possible extent of certainty or knowledge. The conception of a purely logical priority of first principles was as foreign to Locke's opponents as to himself. Although, as we have seen, they were not agreed as to the nature of the existence which pertained to innate ideas and principles prior to experience, they all held that in some real sense they were already 'in the mind' of the individual, and that their presence served as a natural force or bias determining the temporal development of consciousness. Nor shall we read Locke's argument aright if we suppose that the question at issue is that of the activity or passivity of the mind in relation to its experience. The upholders of the theory he opposes commonly employed the metaphor of the stamp and its impression in describing the source of innate principles, and even Descartes regarded it as essential to the objectivity which he claimed for innate ideas that their apprehension should be freed from dependence upon any subjective activity. Innate ideas, he considers, are ideas which the mind simply finds in itself, as distinguished both from those which it receives from without and those which it makes for itself. Indeed, so far as the question of mental activity is involved in the controversy at all, one of Locke's objections to the theory he opposes is that it represents certain truths as merely given to the mind, apart from the exercise of that active comparison and examination, which he holds to be involved in all human knowledge. The question of the activity of mind, in any more abstract or speculative sense, does not enter into his purview throughout the discussion, and its consideration would not have been regarded by him as relevant to his purpose, or as a necessary preliminary to the constructive part of his work.

§ 3. Again, the first book of the *Essay* is not simply designed to prepare the way for an account of the temporal rise of ideas in and through experience. Locke does, indeed, consider that the theory of innate principles stands in direct conflict with the manner and order in which experience shows that ideas first occur in consciousness. His account of the way in which the mind comes by its ideas will, he thinks, render his rejection of innate principles 'much more easily admitted[1].' But he refers us, for the positive complement of the argument of Book I, not to his theory of the derivation of ideas from experience but to his account of the way in which we may attain to certainty or knowledge. 'It would be sufficient to convince unprejudiced readers of the falseness of this supposition,' *i.e.* of innate principles, 'if I should only show (as I hope I shall in the following parts of this discourse) how men, barely by the use of their natural faculties, may attain to all the knowledge they have, without the help of innate impressions, and may arrive at certainty without any such original notions or principles[2].' In particular, he would have us consider his novel account of the nature of the self-evidence which is possessed by certain so-called maxims or axioms, such as the Laws of Identity and Excluded Middle; since, in the absence of any satisfactory theory upon this point, an innate origin has been claimed for these truths with exceptional con-

[1] II. I. I. [2] I. 2. I.

fidence. While, in fact, the denial of innate principles receives confirmation from our ability to show that all our ideas can be traced back to an origin in experience, since without innate ideas there can be no innate principles, the prolonged examination of the theory is rendered necessary by its forming the basis of an erroneous view of the nature of certainty or knowledge, and of the way in which it is obtained. 'Truth and certainty' were, he tells us, 'the things pretended' by the upholders of the theory[1], and it was on account of these pretentions that the theory was so emphatically challenged by him.

§ 4. Before proceeding to examine Locke's arguments, or to consider more closely against whom they were directed, or how far they constituted a relevant objection to the theory of innateness as it was set forth by its principal exponents, it will, I think, be well to endeavour to gather from Locke's own expressions what he conceived to be the rival theory of certainty, of which innate principles formed the foundation. The theory asserts, in the first place, a special origin for our knowledge of the principles which it claims as innate. This knowledge is not to be ascribed to 'the use of our natural faculties,' exercised upon the data of experience, but to the direct action of Nature or of God, by which these principles have been 'stamped' or 'imprinted' upon the mind 'in its very first being[2].' They form 'a distinct sort of truth[3]' from the rest of our knowledge, which is designated as 'adventitious.' Besides and in consequence of this difference in origin, they possess a peculiar value for knowledge. They have a certainty and an authority which no knowledge with a different origin can claim. Left solely to the use of 'our natural faculties' we should be condemned to an 'uncertain,

[1] I. 3. 13. [2] I. 2. I. [3] I. 2. 5.

floating estate[1]' from which we are only saved by this 'bounty of Nature[2].' But the 'self-evidence' which is claimed for these principles seems to be independent of any rational consideration. They are 'sacred[3]' and are protected from critical examination by 'The principle of principles—that principles must not be questioned[4].' Not only is it claimed that these principles are certain in themselves, but that they are 'the foundations of all other knowledge[5].' By this is meant that all other certain knowledge is the result of formal deduction from them. For, according to their supporters, reason is 'nothing else but the faculty of deducing unknown truths from principles or propositions that are already known[6].' Or, in the language of the Schools, all reasoning proceeds '*ex præconcessis et præcognitis*[7],' and innate principles form the starting point, independent of experience, presupposed by such a method. Besides furnishing the 'foundation of knowledge,' innate principles contain 'the rules of living' by which men are required to conduct their lives. For, it is urged, it would be inconsistent with the goodness of God to suppose that He had left men to find these out for themselves[8]. In innate principles we must therefore find the philosophical basis of Religion and Ethics, no less than the source of the certainty of scientific knowledge.

Seeing that they constitute 'a distinct sort of truths' of such supreme importance, it might have been expected that their adherents would have furnished us with a complete list or 'catalogue' of them. This, however, they have not done[9]. And when we ask for the grounds upon which these principles are declared to be innate,

[1] I. 3. 13.
[2] I. 2. 10.
[3] I. 3. 21; I. 3. 25.
[4] I. 4. 24.
[5] I. 2. 21; cf. I. 2. 25.
[6] I. 2. 9.
[7] IV. 7. 8.
[8] I. 4. 12.
[9] I. 3. 14.

or for a means of distinguishing them from propositions of a more lowly origin, we are merely referred to the general consent of mankind. Universal agreement is the great argument for their existence[1], and the only 'mark' or criterion of innateness which is produced[2]. Universally admitted, therefore innate; innate, therefore certain and beyond the reach of criticism—so runs the argument.

§ 5. Such a theory, it is clear, did much more than run counter to Locke's view of the origin of our ideas and the temporal order of their formation in consciousness. By seeking to rest the certainty of its first principles upon the extraneous support of an incomprehensible matter of fact, and by its acceptance of universal consent as the ultimate criterion of truth, it violated his fundamental conviction, that truth must make good its claim by an appeal to the intellectual faculties of the individual. Too often, especially in its application to theological and practical questions, it only replaced the appeal to the authority of Aristotle and the formulated dogmas of the Church by an appeal to a general agreement, which was in practice equivalent to the authority of current opinions and ecclesiastical prejudices. It not only gave a false account of the nature and source of certainty, but it served as an encouragement to the greatest of all hindrances to knowledge, viz. the lazy acquiescence in the opinions of others, by which men avoid the trouble and exertion involved in the right use of their intellectual powers. Throughout the discussion Locke opposes to the theory of innateness the view that knowledge is only to be won by the active employment of our faculties, in 'the consideration of things.' It is only by this means that we can distinguish the evidence of truth from the mere influence

[1] I. 2. 2. [2] I. 3. 27.

of irrational custom. Without this labour the characteristics of genuine knowledge are wanting, even though our assent may be given to that which is in itself true. 'The floating of other men's opinions in our brains makes us not one jot the more knowing, though they happen to be true. What in them was science is in us but opiniatry....In the sciences anyone has so much as he knows and comprehends; what he believes only and takes upon trust are but shreds, which, however well in the whole piece, make no considerable addition to his stock who gathers them. Such borrowed wealth, though it were gold in the hand from which he received it, will be but leaves and dust when it comes to use[1].' In this insistence upon the necessity for an active appropriation of truth by the individual, we have, I believe, the deepest motive of Locke's polemic.

§ 6. We must now turn to the consideration of the arguments which Locke urges against the theory of innate principles. If the statement that certain principles are implanted in the very nature of the mind is taken in its strict and literal sense, it implies, Locke urges, that all men possess from birth a knowledge of the truths in question. This follows at once from the identification of existence in the mind with existence as an object of self-conscious thought. Hence, while universal consent, if it existed, would be no proof of innateness, unless it could be shown that this agreement could not have arisen in any other way[2], it must be the 'necessary concomitant of all innate truths,' should such exist[3]. Any exceptions to the alleged universality of consent amount, therefore, to a strict demonstration of the falsity of the theory[4]. And experience assures us that such exceptions exist, since

[1] I. 4. 23. [2] Cf. I. 2. 3. [3] I. 2. 5. [4] I. 2. 4.

young children, idiots and savages have no knowledge of the principles for which this origin is claimed[1].

Locke is aware, however, that the defenders of the theory have sought to guard it against so easy a refutation. They talk about a knowledge which is at first only 'implicit'; by which, he insists, they can only mean a capacity for knowledge[2]. 'The capacity,' they say, 'is innate, the knowledge acquired[3].' Now the existence of an innate 'power' or 'capacity' for knowledge Locke had no intention of calling in question. He assumes throughout that the mind has 'inherent faculties' which it brings into the world with it[4]. 'I think nobody who reads my book can doubt that I spoke only of innate ideas and not of innate powers,' is the comment which he wrote on the margin of Burnet's 'Remarks on the *Essay*.' But to apply the term innate to certain ideas or principles merely because the mind is capable of forming them, appeared to him a 'very improper way of speaking, which, while it pretends to assert the contrary, says nothing different from those who deny innate principles[5].' From such a misuse of language, he considered, nothing but confusion and misunderstanding could result.

Moreover, such a line of defence, he points out, is fatal to the claim that innate principles constitute 'a distinct sort of truths,' differing from others in their origin and possessing a peculiar certainty and authority. 'If truths can be imprinted upon the understanding without being perceived, I can see no difference there can be between any truths the mind is capable of knowing in respect of their original. They must all be innate or all adventitious; in vain shall a man go about to distinguish them[6].' And

[1] I. 2. 5. [2] I. 2. 22. [3] I. 2. 5.
[4] I. 2. 2. [5] I. 2. 5. [6] I. 2. 5.

the admission that innate principles are not 'a distinct sort of truths' is regarded by Locke as equivalent to the abandonment of the theory. For with their distinct origin, their claim to be regarded as possessing a peculiar certainty, and as constituting the foundation of all other knowledge, falls to the ground. Locke's argument, then, assumes the form of a dilemma. Either the theory signifies that certain ideas and principles are explicitly present from the earliest period of consciousness, or it merely asserts the existence of a general capacity for knowledge. In the former case, it is admittedly false. In the latter case, it is totally unable to support the theory of certainty which has been reared upon it.

§ 7. Before bringing our account of Locke's polemic to a close, it is necessary to consider, more definitely than has yet been done, who were the opponents he had chiefly in mind. The answer to this question can only be obtained by a process of inference. Lord Herbert of Cherbury is the only writer to whom he refers by name, and in doing so he informs us that he only consulted the *De Veritate* when his own first book was already far advanced[1]. The question is one which has puzzled most recent commentators upon the *Essay*, owing to the supposed necessity of finding in the writings of his contemporaries a defence of an explicit innateness. For, as we have seen, none can be found. Such a doctrine is, indeed, occasionally referred to as having been held. Culverwell and Cumberland, as we have seen, attribute it to 'The Platonists,' and Norris is careful to explain that there is little that he can accept in any literal sense in 'that grey-haired venerable doctrine of innate or common principles[2]'; while Samuel Parker argued much in the manner of Locke against an

[1] I. 3. 15.

[2] *Cursory Reflections*, p. 21.

actual universality of consent. But while the doctrine of an explicit innateness was one against which other writers besides Locke thought it worth while to protest, no actual representative of such a view is forthcoming. It must not, however, be supposed from this, as has sometimes been done, that Locke has merely set up and overthrown a man of straw. In attacking a position the practical strength of which depends upon an absence of clear definition, it is necessary to place the alternative interpretations of which it is susceptible in as searching a light as possible; and the enterprise cannot be held to have failed of its object, if the result is to show that even in the opinion of its defenders no part of the ground is tenable. Locke's argument, as we have seen, assumes the form of a dilemma, of which the theory of explicit innateness is only one of the horns. That it is the one he presses first is due to the fact that it seems to him to be the interpretation which expresses the proper signification of the terms used, and the only one which can even pretend to bear the weight of the theory of knowledge which is reared upon it.

We shall, I think, succeed better in localising the special direction in which Locke's polemic is aimed, if we start from the theory of certainty, of which he regarded the theory of innate principles as furnishing the foundation. That theory, as we have seen, held that all other knowledge was derived by syllogistic deduction from certain first principles, which it declared must be accepted as themselves beyond both proof and questioning. It was, in fact, the contemporary representative of the scholastic method. It is true, of course, that a theory of innate ideas had formed no part of the orthodox doctrine of the Schools, and was at variance with the view of its chief representatives. It was not, however, against any leading exponents of scholastic thought that Locke wrote, but against the actual tendencies which he found around him. And among the men with whom Locke was brought into contact the scholastic modes of thought survived, though in a weakened form, to an extent which is not generally realised. At Oxford a diluted form of Scholasticism held almost undisputed sway during the whole time of Locke's connection with the University, and to one who had suffered from the formal aridity of its instruction in the classroom, it would bulk much more largely than to those who now judge of the thought of the age by its written expression. It was just in these circumstances, when the insufficiency of the appeal to the verbal authority of Aristotle had come to be recognised, but the purely formal deductive method which had been wrongly read into Aristotle's logical writings was still maintained, that the theory of innate principles, partly suggested by the wider study of another ancient writer, would naturally find a ready welcome.

An examination of Locke's references to his opponents fully bears out the suggestion that, in attacking the theory of innate principles and the theory of knowledge which rested upon it, he conceived himself to be engaged in conflict with the current procedure of the Schools. He anticipated that his denial of innate principles would 'seem absurd to the masters of demonstration[1]'; that he would be censured for departing from 'the common road[2],' and for 'pulling up the old foundations of knowledge and certainty[3].' He took as the chief examples of innate speculative principles 'those magnified principles of demonstration[4]' the Laws of Identity and Contradiction,

[1] I. 2. 28. [2] I. 2. I. [3] I. 4. 23. [4] I. 2. 4.

which his opponents regarded as the 'first principles of knowledge and science[1].' In view of these facts, it is clear that the defence of innate principles was in his mind closely connected with the abuse of maxims, and the use of faulty methods of demonstration, against which he protests in the concluding book of the *Essay*. Indeed, we even find him there referring to the maxims upon which the rest of knowledge was alleged to depend as 'these innate principles[2].' But if the opponents he has chiefly in view in Book I are the upholders of maxims of Book IV, his designations of the latter leave no room for doubt as to whom he had in mind. It was 'scholastic men' who indulged in 'a great deal of talk' about 'sciences and the maxims on which they are built[3].' It was 'the beaten road of the Schools' to lay down 'principles as the beginnings from which we must set out, and look no further backwards in our enquiries[4].' It was 'the rules established in the Schools' which declared 'that all reasonings are *ex præcognitis et præconcessis*[5].' Nay, Locke even declares that it was only where the Peripatetic Philosophy had been introduced that men regarded the Laws of Identity and Contradiction as what the upholders of their innateness declared them to be, 'the foundations on which the sciences were built' and 'the great helps to the advancement of knowledge[6].'

§ 8. While it is maintained that the first book of the *Essay* is primarily directed against what its author conceived to be the final refuge of the old scholastic ways

[1] I. 2. 28.

[2] IV. 7. 10. Cf. Third Letter to Stillingfleet: 'It is plain, out of the same place, that by maxims I there mean general propositions which are so universally received under the name of maxims or axioms that they are looked upon as innate.' *Works*, vol. IV. p. 369.

[3] IV. 7. 10. [4] IV. 12. 1. [5] IV. 7. 8. [6] *loc. cit.*

of thought, it is not of course suggested that the polemic had no further bearing, or that Locke had not this wider reference in mind. A theory of innate ideas had occupied a prominent place in the Cartesian philosophy, and an appeal to the innateness of certain ideas or principles is, as we have said, to be found in a large number of contemporary English writers who claimed to have definitely broken with the older methods and positions. It is not improbable that it was the consciousness that he was at the same time dealing with this larger circle which led to the vaguer and less direct indications in the first book of the opponents he had chiefly in mind. The influence of the writings of Descartes, in particular, appears in the thrice repeated use of the term 'adventitious' as opposed to innate[1]; but it is certainly not against Descartes that the argument of Book I was primarily directed[2]. In so far as he and others, who claimed to represent the modern spirit, fell back upon a theory of innate ideas or principles, they seemed to Locke to be only incompletely emancipated from the scholastic mode of thought, with its faulty method of demonstration; in so far as the innateness and consequent unquestionableness of certain principles was supposed to be guaranteed by an appeal to 'universal consent,' he thought the gates were opened to a flood of reactionary tendencies, by allowing to current prejudices the stamp of 'sacred' and unchallengeable validity. At the bar of the understanding itself, and there alone, he was convinced, could the claims of truth be justified; for the understanding, as he says, 'can own no other guide but reason[3].' But while, in the view of reason itself, 'the

[1] I. 2. 5; I. 3. 20; I. 4. 21.

[2] Cf. below, chap. IX. § 19, where the bearing of Locke's argument upon Descartes' position is considered.

[3] IV. 16. 4.

general consent of all men in all ages, so far as it can be known,' must be allowed to contribute to the degree of probability of matters of fact, such as 'the stated constitutions and properties of bodies, and the regular proceedings of causes and effects in the ordinary course of nature[1],' it was not by such means that the foundations of science, or of what Locke regarded as the still more important truths of religion and morality, could be secured.

[1] IV. 16. 6.

CHAPTER III

THE ORIGIN AND FORMATION

§ 1. The ground having been cleared by the refutation of the Theory of Innate Principles, which Locke regarded as the basis of the only theory of knowledge fundamentally opposed to his own, the way would seem to be open for a direct attack upon the main problem of the *Essay*, the determination of the nature and extent of human knowledge or certainty. Instead of making such an attempt, however, Locke proceeds, in his Second Book, to discuss at considerable length certain questions concerning our ideas, the consideration of which he regards as an essential preliminary to the solution of the problem of knowledge.

That ideas cannot of themselves constitute knowledge, Locke is perfectly aware. The unit of knowledge, he maintains, is the proposition or judgment, which is alone capable of being true or false. When, contrary to strict propriety, ideas are spoken of as true or false, it is always, he points out, in virtue of some secret or tacit proposition, in which an affirmation or denial is made[1]. But if ideas, taken as such, fall short of the requirements of knowledge, it is also true that apart from ideas there can be no knowledge. Although certainty cannot be 'placed in any one single idea, simple or complex,' it must be 'grounded on ideas[2].' Ideas form, indeed, 'the materials of knowledge,'

[1] II. 32. 1.

[2] First Letter to Stillingfleet, *Works*, vol. IV. p. 57.

their different varieties and special contents must be taken into consideration, if our account of knowledge is to proceed beyond a formal definition of the act; while the possible extent of human knowledge will be, at least in part, determined by any limitations which may be found to exist in this material. Accordingly, what Locke proposes in his Second Book is to take a survey of our ideas, in abstraction from the knowledge into which they enter, as a preparation for the consideration of 'the use which the mind makes of them in knowledge.' That the attempt to carry out such an abstraction should break down at certain points need not surprise us.

We must be prepared to encounter, moreover, the ambiguity of standpoint and consequent confusion which result from Locke's failure to distinguish between the idea considered as a psychical occurrence, or 'perception of the mind,' and the idea regarded as a content of thought, or 'object of the Understanding.' Speaking generally, it may be said that, while here as elsewhere the objective aspect of the idea is that with which Locke is primarily concerned, the subjective point of view obtrudes itself more frequently in the Second Book than in the remainder of the *Essay*.

§ 2. In the forefront of his investigation of ideas Locke places the question of their origin. Now an enquiry into the origin of our ideas may be understood in several different senses. It may represent an attempt to ascertain the primitive form of our cognitive consciousness, and to trace the history of this consciousness from its earlier to its later stages; or, seeking to pass behind ideas, it may signify an attempt to show the dependence of some or all of our ideas upon causes which are not themselves ideas. But, while both of these lines of thought find a place in Locke's theory, we shall not understand his position if we regard it primarily from either of these points of view. For him, as for his contemporaries generally, the whole historical aspect of experience possessed little significance and no intrinsic interest. On the other hand, the attempt to connect ideas with real causes is recognised by him as strictly transcending the limits prescribed by the 'historical plain method.' The truth is that the whole enquiry into the origin of our ideas, and the manner of formation of those which are complex, is in Locke's mind inextricably connected with the logical determination of their content. To understand why this should be so, and to comprehend the significance of the Second Book of the *Essay*, it will be necessary to consider certain presuppositions with which he approached the subject.

For thinkers of the seventeenth century, to whom all ideas of development were entirely foreign, the place which is now filled by the conception of evolution was occupied by the idea of composition, with the implied distinction between the simple and the complex. A complex whole being regarded as the mere sum of its constituent parts, these latter were not thought to undergo any modification as the result of their combination; similarly, the whole was supposed to be directly resolvable into its parts without remainder. The whole temporal process containing nothing but different combinations of the same simples, out of which nothing genuinely new could emerge, the historical point of view from which we trace development in time, and seek to comprehend the new determinations which arise in its course, was without significance. To comprehend a complex whole, all that was required was a process of direct analysis by which the simples contained in it were distinguished. Then, starting with the simples, thought could retrace with perfect adequacy the process by which the whole had originally been constituted.

The widespread influence of this mechanical *schema* appears from the fact that it meets us in different forms, and in different connections, in systems of thought which have little else in common. The assumption that each natural body is capable of being resolved into a number of 'simple natures' forms the primary presupposition of Bacon's view of nature, and underlies his whole conception of inductive method. The theory appears in Descartes in a form which more closely resembles its application by Locke. The objects of our thought are divided by him into the 'simple natures,' which form the content of our innate ideas, and the complexes which result from their combination. With reference to the latter alone is error possible; and in order to avoid this we must begin with the simple and proceed step by step to objects of increasing complexity, making sure that we admit no element which does not possess the inherent clearness and distinctness of the absolutely simple data of knowledge. Finally, the theory appears in a still more developed form in Leibniz. Not only are all other notions and truths declared to be reducible by analysis to certain simple or primitive ones, as to the letters of an alphabet; but the distinction between the simple and the complex is explicitly applied to reality, which is resolved into 'simple substances,' which have no parts, and compound substances which are nothing but collections of these.

It was, then, with this current scheme in his mind that Locke approached the consideration of our ideas. In order to understand their nature, we must, he thought, first ascertain the 'original,' 'primary,' or 'simple' ideas, which form the 'material' of which all others are composed. Until we have analysed our complex ideas into their elementary constituents, with 'pains and assiduity,' we shall not, he assures us, be able to put off the 'confused notions and prejudices,' which we have 'imbibed from custom, inadvertency and common conversations,' but shall be doomed to build upon 'floating and uncertain principles[1].' Accordingly, the first step in our survey of the contents of our ideas must consist in detecting these ultimate cognitive data, and showing how they come to be apprehended by the mind. The simple constituents of all our ideas having been thus exhibited, nothing remains to be done but to show how by their combinations the complex ideas of which they are the elements arise. But, on the assumption that the elements undergo no modification in their combination, the analysis of the complex and an account of its generation from the simples which make it up are strictly complementary to each other. It was for this reason that the question of the determination of the logical content of our ideas came to be so closely connected in Locke's mind with an investigation of their origin and manner of formation. To set forth the simple ideas of which a complex idea is composed is to perform a process of logical analysis, without which we cannot determine its value for knowledge. But this process being also virtually an account of the generation of the complex idea from the simple elements, the question as to 'what' an idea is becomes inseparable from the question as to 'how the mind comes by it.'

But while Locke began by accepting the current composition theory as a matter of course, and while its

[1] II. 13. 28.

distinction of simple and complex professedly underlies his whole discussion of ideas in the Second Book of the *Essay*, he makes no attempt to carry out a strict application of its implications, or to force its *a priori* scheme upon a refractory material. When, as soon happens, it proves inadequate for the comprehension of the content of our ideas, it is tacitly abandoned, though never formally withdrawn. We shall find that alike in the way in which he distinguishes 'simple' and 'complex' ideas, in his recognition of different kinds of 'complex' ideas, and in his account of the operations of the mind by which they are formed, Locke is forced to depart from the presuppositions of the theory; while its inability to adapt itself to the specific nature of our different ideas becomes more evident the further he proceeds. Even, however, when its insufficiency forces itself upon his attention, and leads to formal contradiction, it is never expressly repudiated.

§ 3. According to Locke's formal definition, a simple idea is one which 'being in itself uncompounded, contains in it nothing but one uniform appearance or conception in the mind, and is not distinguishable into different ideas[1].' It must be noted that, as an 'appearance in the mind,' the simple idea possesses the objectivity which we have seen belongs to every content of thought as such. Like all other ideas, it may, if we like, be said to be 'subjective,' in the sense that it has no existence apart from the perception or apprehension of the mind to which it is present; but its presence to the mind is the presence of a specific object of thought. It must, therefore, on no account be identified with the elementary sensation or feeling of some modern psychologists, conceived as a purely subjective

[1] II. 2. I.

modification, without any objective reference. So far was Locke from attempting to derive all the contents of our knowledge from data of sensibility so conceived, that the mere possibility of such an abstraction never occurred to him.

The simple idea consisting, then, in an objective content of thought, its simplicity is declared to lie in the unanalysability of this content. It cannot, however, be said that Locke made any serious attempt to apply this criterion, in order to determine the ideas which are to be accepted as simple, or even made clear to himself the precise sense in which this incapacity for analysis is to be understood. This appears most clearly from his treatment of our ideas of extension and duration. These seemed to him to have an indefeasible claim to a place amongst the ultimate data of our cognition, or our 'original' ideas. But he finds that while they are 'justly reckoned amongst our simple ideas, yet none of the distinct ideas we have of either is without all manner of composition; it is the very nature of both of them to consist of parts[1].' Such an admission could not escape criticism, and the ambiguity of Locke's standpoint comes out still more clearly in his attempt to explain and defend his position. On the one hand he replies, that if extension essentially consists in having *partes extra partes*, this of itself constitutes the idea a simple one, since 'the idea of having *partes extra partes* cannot be resolved into two other ideas[2].' On the other hand he suggests, more tentatively, that the least perceptible portions of extension and moments of duration might fitly be regarded as the simple ideas from which all other spacial and temporal ideas are obtained by composition. It is evident that the appeal is made in

[1] II. 15. 9.

[2] *loc. cit.* note in Coste's French edition.

the one instance to a logical simplicity of conception, in virtue of which Locke maintains that like all other simple ideas the idea of extension is indefinable[1]; and in the other to a supposed simplicity of sensible presentation. But if neither plea will suffice, Locke refuses to be bound by his own formal principle of division, to which, as to all devices of classification, he attributes only practical importance. 'It is very common,' he remarks, 'to observe intelligible discourses spoiled by too much subtilty in nice divisions. We ought to arrange things as well as we can, *doctrinae causa*; but after all there will always be plenty of things which cannot be made to fit in exactly with our conceptions and ways of speaking[2].' In the same way, we are told, that our ideas of the powers possessed by substances may be regarded as 'simple' constituents of our ideas of substances, though the idea of power involves a relation and does not conform to his definition of the simple idea[3].

§ 4. It is evident, in fact, that the attempt to determine our 'original' or 'primary' ideas by the criterion of abstract simplicity is not seriously pressed. Locke proceeds, instead, to draw attention to two other characteristics of these elementary data of cognition, viz. their relation to experience on the one hand, and to our mental activity on the other. (1) We cannot make any 'simple' idea for ourselves. The mind's relation to them is accordingly declared to be one of passivity. (2) Our simple ideas are all apprehended in the first instance as contents of actual experience. We shall consider first the latter of these two propositions. Of the experience in which our simple ideas originate, Locke distinguishes two kinds, Sensation and Reflection. The former yields

[1] II. 13. 15; cf. III. 4. 7 and 11.
[2] II. 15. 9 note in Coste's edition.
[3] II. 23. 7; II. 21. 3.

us ideas of the various determinations of external things, as these are presented to our senses; while by the latter we obtain ideas of the operations of our own minds. The use of the term Sensation, and the fact that the examples which Locke first brings forward, of ideas received in this way, are ideas of sensible qualities, such as 'yellow, white, heat, cold,' must not mislead us as to the range assigned by him to this source of ideas. The above 'ideas of one sense' are to him no more immediate than our ideas of 'space or extension, figure, rest and motion,' which he holds are directly furnished to us both by sight and by touch; while Sensation as well as Reflection is conceived as yielding the ideas of 'existence' and 'unity.' That such different determinations should be regarded as equally immediate is an indication of the small progress which had as yet been made in psychological analysis. But it also serves to show how far Locke was from professing to derive all our ideas from data of sensation in the modern sense of the term.

Further, it must be observed that as these original data of experience are not to be identified with subjective modifications, so neither are they to be regarded as apprehensions of a merely logical content divorced from reality. They are, on the other hand, regarded by Locke as revelations or appearances to mind of real existences. The ideas of Sensation are, from the first, ideas of the qualities of material things; ideas of Reflection are, similarly, ideas of the operations of our own minds. A fatally easy method of transition is thus opened up, from a descriptive account of the primary contents of experience to a theory of their causal dependence upon real things. Ideas 'of' the qualities of external things come to be treated as ideas received 'from' them, and the experience in which the simple idea originates is treated as depending for its existence upon the operation on the mind of an extra-mental material cause. We must briefly notice the way in which Locke regards the reception of ideas by Sensation and Reflection as taking place.

§ 5. Turning, then, from the nature of our simple ideas of Sensation to the conditions of their reception, we find that they are dependent, in the first place, upon the affection of our bodily organs by external things. Like most of his contemporaries, Locke at times applies the term sensation to this bodily affection. It must not, however, be supposed, on this account, that there is any tendency on his part to confuse or to identify the physical process and the state of consciousness, which are as sharply distinguished by him as by Descartes. While Locke is not hampered by the special difficulties of the Cartesian theory of mind and body as distinct substances, he accepts from Descartes the antithetical nature of the distinction between consciousness and the phenomena of the external world. The connection between body and mind is, he maintains, one of the things which we must recognise on the ground of experience, but which we cannot understand. 'Impressions made on the retina by rays of light, I think I understand; and motions from thence continued to the brain may be conceived; and that these produce ideas in our minds I am persuaded, but in a manner to me incomprehensible. This I can resolve only into the good pleasure of God, whose ways are past finding out[1].'

But while the actual experience of an idea of Sensation must be regarded as in some inscrutable way dependent upon a bodily affection, its existence is not regarded by

[1] *Examination of Malebranche*, § 10.

Locke as entirely determined by physical conditions. Sensation is a 'mode of thinking[1],' and the mere reception of the simple idea involves an operation of the understanding by which its content is 'noticed' or 'perceived.' Nor does this mental function of perceiving invariably follow upon the completion of the physical conditions. It may be withheld, as the result of the concentration of attention in some other direction; and in that case no idea of sensation can arise, although all the requisite physical conditions are present. 'How often may a man observe in himself, that whilst his mind is intently employed in the contemplation of some objects, and curiously surveying some ideas that are there, it takes no notice of impressions of sounding bodies made upon the organ of hearing with the same alteration that uses to be for the producing of the idea of sound?...Want of sensation, in this case, is not through any defect in the organ, or that the man's ears are less affected than at other times when he does hear; but that which uses to produce the idea, though conveyed in by the usual organ, not being taken notice of in the understanding, and so imprinting no idea in the mind, there follows no sensation[2].' Locke would doubtless have been puzzled to explain what it is that is not noticed in such cases, but it is at least clear that he recognises the need of a co-operative function of the mind for the experience of these simple ideas of Sensation.

§ 6. We must now turn to the consideration of the other form of experience and source of ideas, which Locke designates Reflection. This term had been applied by many writers before Locke's time to the peculiar function by which the mind becomes aware of itself, and of its own

[1] II. 19. 1. [2] II. 9. 4.

actions. This function was conceived metaphorically as a turning back of the mind upon itself, as distinguished from its direct action in apprehending external things. By the Schoolmen, who used the term in this sense, the reflex action of the mind in cognising itself was regarded as an intellectual function, differing from sense-perception in its intrinsic nature as well as in its object. Others, before Locke, however, had sought to institute a parallelism between Sensation, as yielding cognition of external things, and an analogous form of inner experience, or 'Internal Sensation,' by means of which the mind becomes aware of its own actions. But if it is necessary to be on our guard against reading more recent views into his use of the term Sensation, it is still more necessary to avoid attributing to him a developed theory of the 'inner sense,' such as we find, for instance, in Kant. For while Locke must bear some share of the responsibility for the origin of that misleading conception, it is far from representing unambiguously his own doctrine. Although he holds that Reflection 'is very like Sensation' and 'might properly enough be called "internal sense,"' there are essential respects in which his view of the nature and function of Reflection differs even from his own conception of Sensation.

In relation to external things, as we have seen, he holds that ideas are needed to serve as signs, since these things cannot themselves be present to the understanding. But in his statement of the general position of the representative theory of knowledge, Locke makes an exception in favour of the mind itself. This, and this alone, of 'the things the mind contemplates,' is 'present to the understanding[1],' and does not, consequently need to be

[1] IV. 21. 4.

represented by an idea as sign. Hence, again, it is that he holds, that of the existence of self, and of no other existence, we have an intuitive knowledge. But although ideas are not required to perform a representative function in the case of self-knowledge, they are none the less involved in the content of this, as of every other, kind of knowledge. Now the presence of the mind to itself not only renders possible, but essentially involves an awareness of itself and its own operations. All mental functions are for him functions of thought, and 'thinking consists in being conscious that one thinks[1].' Hence 'the operations of our minds will not let us be without at least some obscure notions of them[2].' A special act of 'notice' or attention is, however, required to enable us to form definite ideas of specific operations, and it is this which constitutes Reflection. Such 'notice,' we saw, was an essential condition of the reception of simple ideas of Sensation; in the case of Reflection it is at once of greater importance and of greater difficulty. Although operations are constantly being performed by the minds of children, 'yet, like floating visions they make not deep impressions enough to leave in their mind clear, distinct, lasting ideas, till the understanding turns inward upon itself, reflects on its operations, and makes them the objects of its own contemplation[3].' Hence, while the simple ideas of Sensation which men possess are limited by the 'greater or less variety' afforded by 'the objects they converse with,' they receive simple ideas 'from the operations of their minds within, according as they more or less reflect on them[4].'

§ 7. But if, as we have seen, a mental operation of 'noticing' is involved in the acquisition of all our simple

[1] II. I. 19; cf. II. 27. 9. [2] II. I. 25. [3] II. I. 8. [4] II. I. 7.

ideas, how, it may be asked, are we to understand the repeated statement that in the reception of these ideas the mind is merely passive? In order to understand this contention, which is undoubtedly regarded by Locke as of fundamental importance, it will be necessary both to consider the nature of the distinction which he draws between mental activity and passivity, and the precise respect in which passivity is here attributed to the mind. Speaking generally, he maintains that a thing can only be properly said to be active in so far as it brings about an effect without being determined by anything beyond itself. To be active the 'substance or agent' must 'put itself into action by its own power[1].' Now, of such self-determined initiation of change, we have experience, he considers, in volition, and nowhere else. From this position two consequences follow. On the one hand, we have, strictly speaking, no idea of activity taking place in the physical world. On the other hand, mental activity is restricted to voluntary action. Thus, we are told, that the mind can only be said to be active in thinking 'when it with some degree of voluntary attention considers anything[2].' Or, to take a particular kind of thought, we find that 'the mind is oftentimes more than barely passive' in remembering, since 'the appearances of those dormant pictures' depends sometimes on the will[3]. The identification of mental activity with volition is, indeed, only a particular application of the view that all mental processes involve self-consciousness. I cannot *be* active without recognising the active process as having its source in myself, or as voluntarily determined.

The mind's activity being identified with voluntary action, its passivity in the reception of its simple ideas

[1] II. 21. 72. [2] II. 9. 1 [3] II. 10. 7.

does not imply that these ideas are wholly determined from without, irrespective of any co-operation from itself. It is, on the contrary, quite consistent with the recognition that in the mere reception of such ideas a mental operation of 'noticing' or 'perceiving' is involved, an operation of one of the powers which are 'intrinsical and proper' to the mind itself, so long as this operation is not conceived as one which we can perform or withhold at will. A mental function such as this, which is only elicited by the presence of an external stimulus, is for Locke only an indication of a 'passive power' in the mind, to the exercise of which it would be incorrect to apply the term activity. No special importance, again, is to be attached to the use of the traditional metaphor of 'impression.' While this is the term which Locke most frequently employs, when he is insisting upon the non-voluntary character of the contents of our simple ideas, at other times he speaks of these as 'suggested' and 'furnished' to the mind. It has been held[1], indeed, that the use of the term 'suggestion' implies the tacit recognition of a less directly sensible and more intellectual source of ideas than Sensation. But it is certain that no such distinction was intended by Locke, who writes of simple ideas without distinction as 'suggested and furnished to the mind[2].' The most that can be said is that, while the term 'suggested' brings out more definitely the implication of an operation of mind in the acquisition of the idea, the term 'impressed' indicates more emphatically its independence of our volition.

§ 8. Further, it must be observed that it is only the determination of the nature of these primary contents of our

[1] Cf. Webb: *The intellectualism of Locke.*

[2] II. 2. 2; cf. II. 3. 1; II. 12. 2.

cognition which Locke places entirely beyond the control of our will, and it is only in this respect that he pronounces the mind to be entirely passive. Thus he recognises that the actual process of experiencing ideas of Sensation or Reflection may involve the presence of an active factor, even in his own limited sense of the term activity. While our ideas are to be regarded as 'only passions of the mind when produced in it, whether we will or no, by external objects,' they must be conceived as 'a mixture of action and passion when the mind attends to them, or revives them in the memory[1].' And upon the importance of this act of attention, Locke strongly insists. 'Sometimes the mind fixes itself with so much earnestness upon the contemplation of some objects, that it turns their ideas on all sides, remarks their relations and circumstances, and views every part so nicely, and with such intention, that it shuts out all other thoughts and takes no notice of the ordinary impressions made then on the senses, which at another season would produce very sensible perceptions; at other times it barely observes the train of ideas that succeed in the understanding, without directing and pursuing any of them; and at other times it lets them pass almost quite unregarded, as faint shadows that make no impression[2].' Attention, moreover, is recognised by Locke as the chief factor upon which the revivability of our ideas depends. Now this function of attention is regarded by him as normally controlled by the will, and as accordingly a form of mental activity. All, then, that is signified by the passivity of the mind, in relation to its simple ideas, is that the nature of these primary contents is independent of our will. We can neither make them for ourselves, in the first instance, nor

[1] *Examination of Malebranche*, § 15.   [2] II. 19. 3.

refuse to receive them, as they are presented to us in experience.

§ 9. If it be asked, why Locke attached so much importance to this doctrine, the answer is that he conceived this passivity as a guarantee, and, indeed, the only possible guarantee, that there is nothing arbitrary in the ultimate data of our cognition. The need for such a guarantee was, in fact, one of the commonplaces of the thought of his age. In the same way, and for the same purpose, Descartes had insisted upon the passivity of the Understanding, or the faculty by which ideas are apprehended, declaring that it is 'a passion of the mind to receive such and such an idea, and that only its volitions are actions[1].' But while the positive counterpart of this view is for Descartes a theory of the innate character of the ultimate cognitive data, Locke insists upon their derivation from experience, and thus obtains, as he thinks, a guarantee, which Descartes' theory does not afford, that they in some way correspond to real existents.

§ 10. As distinguished from our simple ideas, all other ideas are spoken of as in some sense 'the work of the mind.' That is to say, while the mind is 'wholly passive in respect of all its simple ideas[2],' it 'uses some kind of liberty in forming those complex ideas[3].' It is not to be supposed, indeed, that the formation of complex ideas is in all cases voluntary and deliberate, or that it proceeds in entire disregard of any guidance from experience. Simple ideas, Locke remarks, may be 'observed to exist in several combinations united together[4]'; and when this is the case the complex idea which comprises them

[1] Cousin's edition of Descartes' Works, vol. IX. p. 166.

[2] II. 12. 1.

[3] II. 30. 3.

[4] II. 12. 1; cf. II. 22. 2.

is said to be obtained, like the simple ideas themselves, 'by experience and the observation of things themselves[1].' What Locke has chiefly in mind is that in the case of none but simple ideas are we justified in asserting such an origin in experience from the nature of the case. The mind has a power of connecting at will simple ideas which have not been experienced together; hence the mere existence of a complex idea is no evidence that the same combination of elements has ever occurred in actual experience. Nor, consequently, would we be justified, apart from special considerations, in assuming that the complex idea has, like the simple idea, an existing counterpart in the real world.

§ 11. But while, as we have seen, experience may supply us directly with the plurality of contents contained in a complex idea, and thus furnish a clue to its formation, it is important to notice that the mere presentation together of a number of elements is not of itself sufficient to constitute them a single complex idea. For the complex idea involves the recognition of a unity which does not belong to the plurality of simple ideas as such. In order that these may constitute a single complex idea, it is necessary that the mind should exercise its 'power to consider several of them united together as one idea[2].' That this is no merely nominal function appears from the doubt which Locke throws upon the capacity of brutes for complex ideas. Brutes, he is confident, 'do not of themselves ever compound them and make complex ideas' apart from the guidance of experience. And even when experience presents them with several simple ideas together, as the 'shape, smell and voice of his master' may be presented together to a dog, Locke considers it probable that these

[1] II. 22. 9. [2] II. 12. 1; cf. II. 22. 4.

may rather constitute 'so many distinct marks whereby he knows him,' than form a single complex idea. In confirmation of this surmise, he appeals to the apparent absence from the lower animals of ideas of numbers, which are regarded by him as the most obvious and readiest products of composition. But if the animal fails to attain to a complex idea, although the plurality of constituents necessary to form it is presented by experience, this can only be because it is unable to perform the unifying function which is needed to enable us to 'consider' the various data as elements in a single whole.

§ 12. The operation of the mind upon its ideas by which it 'puts together several of those simple ones it has received from Sensation and Reflection, and combines them into complex ones,' is named by Locke 'compounding[1]'; the more specific term 'enlarging' being applied when the composition is of ideas 'of the same kind,' as in the generation of our ideas of quantity. It is evident that the composition theory, strictly interpreted, breaks down even in relation to the complex ideas which are so formed; since it cannot account for recognition of the unity of the whole, which they have been found to involve. The complex idea, accordingly, cannot be regarded as resolvable without remainder into the simple ideas which enter into its constitution. The failure of the composition theory becomes, however, much more conspicuous when we find that 'compounding' is not the only mental operation which gives rise to complex ideas. For, according to the theory in question, the mind being once supplied with the elementary data of cognition, the only elaborative function which it can perform is that of combining them

[1] II. II. 6.

into different complexes, unless we would add a further operation by which it merely undoes the result of its previous labour. Under the influence of this conception of a quasi-mechanical composition, we find Locke at times writing as if all our non-simple ideas were complexes of this kind, and as if what he calls 'compounding' together with a complementary process of 'decompounding' were the sole operations by which the mind deals with its ideas. 'The dominion of man in this little world of his own understanding,' is, he declares, 'much what the same as it is in the great world of visible things, wherein his power, however managed by art and skill, reaches no further than to compound and divide the materials that are made to his hand[1].' But when he comes to deal with the actual nature of our secondary or 'complex' ideas, the inadequacy of the composition theory at once shows itself, and its presuppositions are abandoned still more completely than was the requirement of an absolute simplicity in the simple idea. For, in addition to its power of compounding, the mind is declared to possess powers of comparing and abstracting, the products of which cannot be represented as mere complexes due to a composition of elements. As distinguished from compounding, comparing consists in 'bringing two ideas, whether simple or complex, together, and setting them by one another, so as to take a view of them at once, *without uniting them into one*[2].' In this way a distinct kind of ideas is formed, consisting of apprehensions of relations between the terms compared. And although at times Locke may vaguely refer to abstraction as a process of 'decompounding,' he is led to recognise that something more than the inverse of the process of compounding is involved in the

[1] II. 2. 2. [2] II. 12. 1. Italics mine.

formation of the 'general ideas' which he refers to this source.

But although ideas of relations and general ideas were never treated by Locke as mere results of composition, it was only in the fourth edition of the *Essay* that they were definitely distinguished from these; while no attempt was made, even then, to bring his treatment of the subject as a whole into line with the view there put forward. In an addition made to the twelfth chapter of the Third Book, the three operations of compounding, comparing and abstracting are described. To the first of these, *all* our complex ideas are ascribed, complex ideas being thus treated as merely co-ordinate with, and not inclusive of, our ideas of relations and our general ideas. Notwithstanding this, the heading 'of complex ideas' is still retained for the chapter as a whole, and the term 'complex idea' continues to be used as a designation for all ideas which are not 'original,' 'primary,' or 'simple.' If we continue to follow Locke's more frequent usage, it must at least be recognised, that just as we previously saw that a simple idea may, according to Locke, involve a certain complexity of content, so it now appears that the complex idea, with which it is contrasted, need not involve a composition of elements, but may be instead a product of comparison or abstraction.

It appears, in fact, here again, that the distinction which Locke has in mind, throughout his discussion of ideas, is one between ideas which are 'primary' or 'original' and those which we may call our secondary or derivative ideas, rather than between the simple and the complex; the two principles of division being identified under the influence of the composition theory. Whether they involve composition or not, Locke is at all events clear that our ideas of relation and the products of abstraction can claim no place among our 'primary' or 'original' ideas. For comparison presupposes that the mind is already cognisant of the ideas compared; and the process of abstraction can only be performed if the content to be abstracted is already before the mind, in a certain context from which abstraction is made. By whichever of these operations an idea is obtained, it presupposes, therefore, the possession by the mind of the elementary data of Sensation and Reflection, and their subjection to a mental operation which is not entirely independent of our will.

§ 13. As Locke's views concerning our ideas of relations and our general ideas are of cardinal importance for his whole theory, it seems necessary to call attention here to some further features of his treatment of these topics. In the first place, it should be noticed that an idea of relation is, according to Locke, the product of overt comparison. Hence, as he himself explains, an idea may be absolute, or non-relative, although it is the idea of a whole involving relations between its parts. 'Thus a triangle, though the parts thereof compared one to another be relative, yet the idea of the whole is a positive absolute idea[1].' Indeed, it turns out that, 'when attentively considered,' all ideas whatsoever are found to include in them 'some kind of relation[2].' Relations in this sense are involved, as we have seen, even in simple ideas of Sensation and Reflection. These relations remain 'secret,' however, until an overt act of comparison is performed, by which we acquire for the first time an idea of relation. Further, we must notice the bearing upon Locke's account of our ideas of relations of his general theory of the ultimate dependence of all our ideas upon experience. It is clear

[1] II. 25. 6. [2] II. 21. 3.

that, according to Locke, an idea of relation cannot itself be a content of Sensation or Reflection. Neither can any mere combination of simple ideas either constitute or give rise to such an idea. Its formation depends upon the peculiar mental act of comparison, and when formed it is for the mind a distinct object of thought, over and above the terms from the comparison of which it results. But while this is true, it is also true that the mind can perform no act of comparison unless it is already supplied with the terms to be compared, and these terms can have no positive content which has not been experienced through Sensation or Reflection. Therefore, although our ideas of relation cannot be directly resolved into data received from these sources, as a strict interpretation of the composition theory would require, they all 'terminate in,' or are 'ultimately founded upon,' such simple ideas[1]. In this sense, and in this sense alone, does Locke maintain that all our ideas are dependent on the simple contents given in immediate experience.

§ 14. The part played by general ideas in Locke's theory of human knowledge is one of first-rate importance, since the universality which characterises scientific knowledge would be impossible without them. Their possession, moreover, he holds, is 'that which puts a perfect difference between man and brutes[2],' the vast superiority of the human to the animal mind being ultimately dependent upon this 'proper difference.' For the present, we are only concerned with the preliminary questions as to the nature of general ideas and the way in which they come to be formed by the mind. In the first place, then, it must be noticed that general ideas, like ideas of relation, can never be presented as such in experience, the objects

[1] II. 28. 18. Cf. II. 25. 9.

[2] II. 11. 10.

of which are always concrete and particular. Thus, the idea of white, as given in sense-perception, is experienced as the quality of this piece of chalk, or of this mass of snow. In other words, it is presented along with others as an element in a concrete whole. Further, even when the mind has attained to the possession of general ideas, the characteristic of universality does not attach to these ideas considered as psychical existences. It is only in its significance, Locke maintains, that an idea is capable of generality; as an existent it retains its particularity, though that which it represents is universal. This distinction, between the particular existence and the universal signification of our general ideas, is repeatedly emphasised by Locke, although it has often been ignored by his critics, from Berkeley onwards. The question of the manner of the formation of our general ideas is, accordingly, for him, the question as to how ideas, which are and must remain particular in their existence, come to be invested with this universality of representation. Locke's answer is that their universality is dependent upon a two-fold mental function. The content to be generalised must, in the first place, be considered apart from its original setting in our experience, by a process of abstraction. Further, it must be thought of as standing for, or representing, all other particulars of the same kind. 'Thus, the same colour being observed to-day in chalk or snow, which the mind yesterday received from milk, it considers that appearance alone, makes it a representative of all of that kind, and, having given it the name "whiteness," it by that sound signifies the same quality wheresoever to be imagined or met with[1].' Locke's account of the process of abstraction has, however, often been misunderstood;

[1] II. II. 9.

while his recognition of any further activity of mind, in the formation of general ideas, has commonly been ignored.

For the misconception as to what Locke meant by abstraction, the representation of his view given by Berkeley, in his famous polemic against abstract ideas, must be held in the main responsible. Interpreting the term 'idea' as signifying a content of sense-perception or imagination, Berkeley supposed Locke's account of the abstract general idea to imply that the common features of the members of a class were presented in the form of an image, apart from all the particularising circumstances with which these are presented in experience. Locke's idea, however, cannot be understood in this narrow sense. It includes in its denotation the 'notions' which Berkeley was subsequently obliged to introduce, as well as that which is capable of being presented in sense-perception and reproduced in imagination. Nor .does Locke claim to be able even to think of as separated, elements which are inseparable in experience. All that his theory of abstraction requires is that we should be able to single out, and consider apart from its context, the content which is to be generalised. But such 'partial consideration' does not, as he points out, imply that we think of this content as separated, or as capable of separation, from all others. 'A partial consideration is not separating. A man may consider light in the sun without its heat, or mobility in body without its extension, without thinking of their separation. One is only a partial consideration, terminating in one only; and the other is a consideration of both, as existing separately[1].'

But abstraction, however understood, does not of itself yield the general idea. Locke does not suppose

[1] II. 13. 13.

that the universal can be discovered by the application to the contents of experience of any mere process of analysis. Universality consists in a relation, the apprehension of which, like the cognition of all other relations, must have its source in a comparing activity of the mind. For the formation of a general idea it is not enough that the mind should single out a certain content, as the object of its consideration. It must consider this content in a determinate manner, viz. as representing all the particular things in which the same quality may be found. The mind must 'take' or 'set up' the content abstracted as the representative of all other ideas of the same kind, before it can become general. The generality which we ascribe to certain ideas is, in fact, 'nothing but the capacity they are put into by the understanding of signifying or representing many particulars[1].' Although there is considerable vagueness as to the psychological processes involved, Locke appears to recognise the necessity of a relating activity, by which the abstracted content is thought of in distinction from, and at the same time in relation to, its particular exemplifications.

[1] III. 3. 11.

CHAPTER IV

THE CONTENTS OF OUR IDEAS OF MODES

§ 1. Having dealt in our last chapter with Locke's general theory of the origin of our ideas in the simple contents of Sensation and Reflection, and the formation of complex ideas from these elements, we must now proceed to examine, in more detail, his treatment of some of the more important ideas which enter into the constitution of our knowledge. In doing so, it will not be possible to separate completely the point of view of content from that of origin and manner of formation, with which, as we have seen, it is so intimately united in his thought. Indeed, it is precisely in the attempt to apply to some of our most fundamental conceptions the principle that the positive content of all our ideas must be drawn from experience, that what is primarily a descriptive survey of ideas tends to pass over into a criticism of the current categories.

The predominantly objective and logical point of view, from which the investigation of ideas is undertaken, shows itself in the classification of complex ideas, which forms the framework of the greater part of the Second Book of the *Essay*. Instead of a division based upon the diverse mental operations involved in their formation, complex ideas are divided according to the nature of the content apprehended, into ideas of modes, substances and relations. Ideas of modes are defined as 'such complex ideas which, however compounded, contain not in them the supposition of subsisting by themselves, but are considered as dependencies on, or affections of substances[1]'; while 'the ideas of substances are such combinations of simple ideas as are taken to represent distinct particular things subsisting by themselves, in which the supposed or confused idea of substance, such as it is, is always the first and chief[2].' So far, our classification has only followed the distinction of the two ultimate forms of being recognised by the current metaphysics. But now that we are dealing with ideas, and not with things as they are in themselves, a place co-ordinate with these is assigned by Locke to the relations which we apprehend as existing between the other objects of our thought. To ideas of modes and substances, he adds as a distinct category, ideas of relations.

§ 2. Our ideas of modes are further divided into ideas of simple and mixed modes. Simple modes are formally defined as 'variations, or different combinations of the same simple idea, without the mixture of any other[3].' Although they are a species of complex idea, these modes are called simple, we are told, 'as being contained within the bounds of one simple idea.' What Locke appears to have primarily in mind is the product of a composition, formed of repetitions of the same content, such as he thinks is involved in the generation of our ideas of numbers, and in the 'enlarging' of our ideas of spacial and temporal distance. If, however, we ask, what we are to understand by the identity of the content which is repeated, we at once raise a question which is fatal to the view that all universals are derivative. In the definition of mixed modes a difference in *kind* among the simple ideas combined is insisted upon[4], and

[1] II. 12. 4. [2] II. 12. 6. [3] II. 12. 5. [4] II. 12. 5. Cf. II. 22. 1.

such a wide interpretation is given to what constitutes sameness of kind that ideas such as that of a tune are included among simple modes, on the ground that the ideas concerned are all of the same kind. But if 'the same simple idea' means an idea of a certain kind, and if being 'contained within the bounds of one simple idea' merely means being of a certain kind, the simple idea is explicitly recognised as a universal.

The same result emerges, if we ask, with reference to the definition of simple modes, what is meant by '*variations*, or different combinations of the same simple idea'? It is not improbable that, under the influence of the composition theory, Locke would have replied that different 'variations' are nothing but different combinations. As a matter of fact, however, he includes among simple modes ideas which can only be regarded as 'variations' of the simple ideas, of which they are said to be modes, in the sense that they are different specifications of the same universal. We shall, indeed, find throughout Locke's treatment of the subject a constant alternation between his professed view, that the simple idea is a unit from which ideas of simple modes are obtained by composition, and the tendency to treat the simple idea as a universal, of which the modes are so many different species or alternative determinations.

§ 3. The ideas which Locke cites as typical illustrations of his definition of our ideas of simple modes, are those of 'a dozen' and 'a score'; and it is with regard to our ideas of numbers that the conception of a combination of identical elements to form a complex idea seems to work most smoothly. The 'idea of unity or one' being accepted as a simple idea, which 'every object our senses are employed about, every idea in our understanding, every thought of our minds brings along with it[1],' these units are thought to receive no further determination from their summation than the fact that they are summed. Locke recognises, indeed, that for the formation of an idea of a number something more is required than the bare repetition of our idea of unity. As we have seen, it is necessary for the formation of any complex idea that the elements which constitute it should be considered as constituting a single whole. Hence, in the case before us, besides repeating the idea of a unit, we must *add* these repetitions together[2]. Moreover, Locke finds that for the formation of such ideas, and their further manipulation, it is peculiarly necessary that the combination should be fixed for the mind by means of a name. 'For the several simple modes of numbers being in our minds but so many combinations of units, which have no variety, nor are capable of any other difference but more or less, names or marks for each distinct combination seem more necessary than in any other sort of ideas. For, without such names or marks, we can hardly well make use of numbers in reckoning, especially where the combination is made up of any great multitude of units; which, put together without a name or mark to distinguish that precise collection, will hardly be kept from being a heap in confusion[3].' But in so far as our ideas of numbers involve the act of adding unit to unit, and the fixing of the whole thus formed by means of a name, the process of their formation clearly transcends that of a mechanical composition.

§ 4. We have already noticed the apparent contradiction in the inclusion of the idea of space among our simple ideas, in view of the fact that every portion of space, however small, must be thought of as involving a plurality

[1] II. 16. 1. [2] II. 16. 2. [3] II. 16. 5.

of parts and at least what Locke calls 'secret' relations between these parts. It being once admitted, that a simple idea may contain a complex of relations within itself, the idea of space seems to Locke to possess all the other characteristics which he seeks in our 'original' ideas. Like all simple ideas, it is indefinable[1]. It is an idea which the mind could not make for itself, but which it is compelled to accept as an ultimate constituent of its experience; although containing parts, it cannot be generated by a composition of parts. While Locke had at one time accepted the view that extension is merely 'the relation of distance between parts of the same thing,' in the *Essay* he definitely rejects this purely relational theory of space. Distance he finds is involved in duration as well as in extension; but duration and extension clearly are not identical. That the specific nature of spacial relations is dependent upon a peculiar characteristic of certain objects of experience and is unanalysable, is, then, an important part of what Locke has in view in his insistence on the simple nature of our idea of space[2]. If we enquire further concerning the origin of this idea, Locke has no hesitation in ascribing it to Sensation. The origin of the idea in our visual and tactual experiences seems to him 'so evident, that it would be as needless to go to prove that men perceive by their sight a distance between bodies of different colours, or between the parts of the same body, as that they see colours themselves; nor is it less obvious that they can do so in the dark by feeling and touch[3].' Indeed he finds that every visual experience, and most of those of touch, furnish us with this idea[4].

[1] II. 13. 15.

[2] For the development of Locke's views concerning space see below, h. x. §§ 6–7.

[3] II. 13. 2.

[4] II. 13. 25.

The idea of space being thus accepted as an original datum of experience, or simple idea, 'each idea of any different distance, or space, is a simple mode of this idea[1].' Thus, experience having once furnished us with the idea of spacial distance, ideas of an indefinite number of distances can be fashioned by the mind, without further resort to experience. For this it is only necessary that we should have settled in our mind a definite idea of some stated length, which can be 'repeated' as often as we like, and the repetitions 'added' to one another. Hence our ideas of space, after those of number, furnish Locke with his readiest examples of what he regards as ideas of simple modes formed by a process of 'enlarging.'

In describing the process by which a greater length is generated from a less as one of mere 'repetition' and 'addition,' Locke appears to ignore the difference between a spacial and a numerical whole, and the consequent difference in their manner of construction. Incidentally, however, the difference between a numerical sum and a spacial or temporal whole receives some amount of recognition. Our idea of the infinity of space and time is, he tells us, 'nothing but the infinity of number applied to determinate parts of which we have in our minds the distinct ideas[2].' By this we must understand him to mean, that any units which we may take of space or time possess a qualitative character of their own, by which they are distinguished from the featureless units of Arithmetic. 'Every part of duration is duration too, and every part of extension is extension[3].' Further, we are told that expansion and duration resemble each other in that they involve 'this common idea of continued lengths, capable of greater or less quantities[4]'; and in being 'continued lengths,' it is

[1] II. 13. 4. [2] II. 17. 10. [3] II. 15. 9. [4] II. 15. 1.

implied, they differ from number or discrete quantity. Locke does not, however, recognise that corresponding to these differences in the contents dealt with, there must be a difference in their manner of combination. Still less does he realise that in all cases of ideational construction there is involved a special form of combination, at once relative to and distinguishable from the materials combined.

Besides our ideas of different distances, or quantities of linear space, our ideas of the simple modes of space include, we are told, 'all the variety of particular figures.' The idea of figure itself, like that of space, is regarded as a simple idea which we receive from sight and touch[1]. That is to say, the objects of these senses are experienced as possessing definite boundaries, as well as the vaguer characteristic of extendedness. But this idea of figure, or bounded space, having been once derived from experience, the mind is able to fashion for itself different modes of this idea, or figures which have never been presented in experience. Indeed, Locke finds that this idea 'affords to the mind infinite variety. For, besides the vast number of different figures that do really exist in the coherent masses of matter, the stock that the mind has in its power, by varying the idea of space, and thereby making still new compositions, by repeating its own ideas, and joining them as it pleases, is perfectly inexhaustible[2].' Under the influence of the composition theory, Locke proceeds to describe this power of free construction as dependent upon our ability to repeat or divide our ideas of linear distance, and to join the lengths thus obtained at any angle, until a portion of space has been enclosed. It is evident, however, that the advance, from the generation of a greater distance by repetition of a less, to the free

[1] II. 5. 1. [2] II. 13. 5.

construction of figures, has placed a further strain upon the theory which it is still less able to bear. When length is joined to length in the same direction, we merely obtain a greater length in that direction. But when line is 'joined' by the mind to line, 'with what inclination it thinks fit[1],' until a portion of space has been enclosed, the product is a figure and not a line. And that a figure cannot be regarded as the result of a mere process of compounding lines or lengths is implied in Locke's insistence upon the need of an actual experience of figure, as the indispensable basis of free figural construction. What is clearly needed is the recognition, that in 'varying the idea of space' the mind is performing an operation which is essentially different from that of mechanical composition[2].

§ 5. The idea of distance, or of 'continued lengths,' is, as we have seen, common to our spacial and temporal ideas. But whereas in the one case we are dealing with 'lasting distance, all whose parts exist together, and are not capable of succession,' in the other we are concerned with 'perishing distance, of which no two parts exist together, but follow each other in succession[3].' Since our ideas of both are simple, these statements are not to be regarded as definitions, but as indications of a certain community of nature in our spacial and temporal ideas, notwithstanding the uniqueness of each. The idea of duration, or of this peculiar kind of 'perishing' distance, is regarded by Locke as the simple or original idea, of which our ideas of particular durations and periods of

[1] II. 13. 6.

[2] On the nature of ideal construction as the discovery of possible alternatives admitted by the nature of some universal cf. Stout, *Manual of Psychology*, 3rd edition, bk IV. ch. 2, § 5.

[3] II. 15. 12. Cf. II. 14. 1.

time, of time itself, and of eternity, are so many simple modes. This idea of duration and the idea of succession, apart from which he finds duration inconceivable[1], are regarded by Locke as simple ideas of Reflection, which arise as the result of our 'notice' of the passage of a train of ideas through our mind; such a constant succession of ideas being an invariable feature of our waking life. It must not, however, be supposed that the experience in which these ideas originate is that of a mere flux, without any contrasting permanent. I cannot, Locke holds, have an idea which is not apprehended as mine. Throughout the sequence of ideas, I have, consequently, a constant perception of my own existence. The successive ideas are, therefore, from the first apprehended as successive perceptions of a permanent self, while the perception of this continued existence of myself, in contrast with the changing ideas, is that which first affords me the idea of duration. 'For whilst we are thinking, or whilst we receive successively several ideas in our minds, we know that we do exist; and so we call the existence, or the continuation of the existence of ourselves, or anything else commensurate to the succession of any ideas in our minds, the duration of ourselves, or any such other thing coexistent with our own thinking[2].' The idea of duration having been originally obtained from Reflection, or as a determination of our own being, it can be 'applied' to the objects of the outer world, our apprehension of the temporal character of which is in this sense secondary or derivative.

While holding that no idea of duration can be formed without the consciousness of a definite contrast between an enduring self and its changing ideas, Locke is led to make what he calls an 'odd conjecture' concerning the

[1] II. 15. 12; II. 17. 16.

[2] II. 14. 3.

experience upon which this consciousness depends. He surmises that 'there seem to be certain bounds to the quickness and slowness of the succession of those ideas one to another in our minds, beyond which they can neither delay nor hasten[1].' Accordingly he defines an instant as a part of duration which takes up 'the time of only one idea in our minds, without the succession of another[2].' As lacking any 'sense of succession' the experience of such an instant could not, indeed, of itself give rise to the idea of duration. But the limit thus imposed upon the rate of flow of our ideas, constitutes, Locke considers, the ultimate condition upon which all our measurements of duration depend.

In maintaining the subjective origin of our ideas of duration and succession, Locke directly controverts the view then generally accepted that our temporal consciousness is essentially dependent upon the apprehension of movement in space, and is directly determined by its objective occurrence. Motion, he insists, can only give rise to an idea of duration if, and in so far as, it occasions a constant succession of ideas; and such a succession may be experienced without the apprehension of movement. He recognises, however, that the perception or 'sense' of duration, as directly measured by the flow of our ideas, is only the most elementary form of temporal cognition, which stands in need of correction and further elaboration. For such a consciousness a period of dreamless sleep is non-existent[3]. Further, duration as thus cognised is relative to our state of attention; for, 'one who fixes his thoughts very intently on one thing, so as to take but little notice of the succession of ideas that pass in his mind, whilst he is taken up with that earnest contemplation, lets slip out of his account a good part of that duration, and

[1] II. 14. 9. [2] II. 14. 10. [3] II. 14. 4.

thinks that time shorter than it is[1].' Moreover, until we have obtained a more objective measure of duration, there is an inevitable want of distinctness in our apprehension of the order in which events occur. Accordingly, 'having thus got the idea of duration, the next thing natural for the mind to do, is to get some measure of this common duration, whereby it might judge of its different lengths, and consider the distinct order wherein several things exist; without which a great part of our knowledge would be confused, and a great part of history be rendered very useless[2].'

This further development of our cognition of duration depends upon the discovery of certain physical phenomena, which constantly recur at apparently equal periods and are observable by all, and the acceptance of them as our standard of reference and measurement. The required conditions are best fulfilled in our actual experience by the movements of the heavenly bodies, which furnish us with units of duration which are approximately uniform and universally observable. The consideration of duration as thus measured out into days and years and hours, constitutes what Locke understands by *Time*. We cannot, however, in this way, escape entirely from the relativity and subjectivity which attach to our whole temporal consciousness. For, not only is time, by its definition, relative to the movements of the heavenly bodies, but there is no way in which we can assure ourselves that any two lengths of duration, however measured, are really equal. Since 'no two portions of succession can be brought together, it is impossible ever certainly to know their equality. All that we can do, for a measure of time, is to take such as have continual successive appearances at seemingly equidistant periods; of which seeming equality we have no

[1] *loc. cit.* [2] II. 14. 17.

other measure but such as the train of our own ideas have lodged in our memories, with the concurrence of other probable reasons to persuade us of their equality[1].' 'Duration in itself' must, therefore, be distinguished both from duration as immediately experienced and from time, or objectively measured duration, since it is 'to be considered as going on in one constant, equal, uniform course[2].'

§ 6. In Locke's treatment of our spacial and temporal ideas he is led to recognise that the mind has the power of forming ideas which are essentially incapable of being presented in our experience. For, while extension and duration are directly presented as attributes of material things and our own thoughts respectively, the ideas once obtained are capable of being used independently of their original setting. Notwithstanding its origin, we can 'apply' our idea of space where no matter is or is conceived to be, and our idea of duration to periods in which we experience no succession of ideas[3]. While we can only have a 'sense' or actual perception of extension or duration as involving a variety of discrete qualitative differences, the 'pure' space and duration, of which we form ideas, are apprehended as uniform and continuous. While the parts of body are capable of separation, and the flow of ideas is broken by periods of unconsciousness, the parts of pure space and duration are incapable of separation even in thought[4]. Again, although the extension and duration of actual perception are finite in magnitude, and possess sensible *minima*, space and duration are regarded as in themselves boundless or infinite, and as infinitely divisible. Finally, while extension and duration can only be experienced as attributes of particular bodies or of our finite

[1] II. 14. 21. [2] *loc. cit.* [3] II. 14. 5. [4] II. 15. 10.

minds, our thought mounts to the recognition of 'the boundless invariable oceans of duration and expansion, which comprehend in them all finite beings, and in their full extent belong only to the Deity[1].' We find, then, in Locke, at least an implicit recognition of the distinction between perceptual and conceptual space and time; the latter being regarded as resulting from a process of mental elaboration performed upon the materials afforded by perception. To account for the profound transformation which he describes, he can, indeed, only appeal to our powers of abstracting and enlarging. But the inevitable inadequacy of his account of the processes, by which the constructions in question are effected, does not destroy the value and originality of his general position. The only aspect of the question upon which Locke dwells at any length is the nature and manner of formation of our idea of infinity. His ability to exhibit the origin and constitution of this idea forms, he considers, the greatest achievement of the theory of the empirical derivation of our ideas.

§ 7. Infinity is, for Locke, primarily a quantitative conception. 'Finite and infinite,' he writes, 'seem to me to be looked upon by the mind as the modes of quantity, and to be attributed primarily in their first designation only to those things which have parts, and are capable of increase or diminution by the addition or substraction of any the least part; and such are the ideas of space, duration and number[2].' He holds, indeed, that it is not merely in this quantitative sense that infinity can be predicated of the Divine Being, and his attributes. We 'cannot but be assured' that God is 'incomprehensibly infinite[3].' We must recognise that his attributes 'do, without doubt, contain in them all possible perfection[4].'

[1] II. 15. 8. [2] II. 17. 1. [3] *loc. cit.* [4] *loc. cit.*

But by thus using the term in a non-quantitative sense, we do no more than indicate that we are in the presence of that which transcends our powers of comprehension. We can form no definite idea of that to which our 'assurance' refers. As soon as we endeavour to fix the meaning of the term as thus employed, we find that we can assign none but a figurative one. The only idea which we can form of the infinity which we ascribe to the power, wisdom and goodness of God, is one which 'carries with it some reflection on, and intimation of, that number or extent of the acts or objects of God's power, wisdom and goodness, which can never be supposed so great, or so many, which these attributes will not always surmount and exceed, let us multiply them in our thoughts as far as we can, with all the infinity of endless number[1].' By such means, however, we cannot truly represent 'how these attributes are in God.' We have here, for the first time, an example of the contrast, which Locke institutes, between the ideas which we are capable of forming and the nature of the reality which we seek to represent by means of them, but for the comprehension of which they prove to be inadequate.

We must turn, then, to the consideration of infinity in the only sense in which it can be exhibited as the content of a definite idea. Starting with the idea of a numerical unit, or with the idea of any finite distance in space, or period of duration, we can, as we have seen, 'repeat' the idea, and produce the idea of a larger whole of the kind in question by 'adding' these repetitions together. Now, not only is this process never brought to an end by the intrinsic nature of that with which it deals, but, however far it has been carried, one finds, 'he has no more reason to stop, nor is one jot nearer the end of such addition, than

[1] *loc. cit.*

he was at first setting out[1].' Further, we are not only unable to find, but we are unable to conceive such an end[2]. We are thus led to form ideas of the number series, of space, and of duration, as endless or infinite. In the same way, if, instead of 'repeating' and 'adding' our units, we regard our initial quantities as divisible into parts, we are led to recognise that the process of mentally dividing a given extension or duration is also one to which there can be no limit. We thus form an idea of the infinite divisibility of space and duration.

It is evident that the idea of infinity obtained in this way is both what Locke calls 'negative' and 'comparative.' It is the idea of an absence of limits, of something greater or smaller than any assignable quantity of which we can form a definite idea. It is thus involved in all 'the indeterminate confusion of a negative idea[3].' We find, indeed, that the very characteristics of quantity upon which the formation of the idea depends, render it impossible for us to frame a positive idea of an infinite quantity. The attempt to form such an idea involves the absurdity of seeking 'to adjust a standing measure to a growing bulk[4].' In the confusion which is involved in the supposed but impossible idea of an infinite quantity, Locke finds the source of the antinomies which affect our reasonings concerning infinite space and duration. 'Let a man frame in his mind an idea of any space or number, as great as he will, it is plain the mind rests and terminates in that idea; which is contrary to the idea of infinity, which consists in a supposed endless progression. And therefore, I think, it is that we are so easily confounded, when we come to argue and reason about infinite space or duration, etc. Because the parts of such an idea not being perceived to be,

[1] II. 17. 3. [2] II. 15. 2. [3] II. 17. 15. [4] II. 17. 7.

as they are, inconsistent, the one or other always perplexes whatever consequence we draw from the other[1].'

But, even although this source of our contradictory reasonings be recognised, a further difficulty awaits us when we consider the relation of our idea of quantitative infinity to reality. We can only lay to rest, in the region of ideas, problems which break out afresh when we consider them with reference to the world of real being. For, on the one hand, we seem forced to regard quantitative infinity as a characteristic of the real world. Consideration of the nature of space not only leads us to form an idea of its infinity, but makes us 'apt to think that space in itself is actually boundless[2]'; nay, on further reflection, Locke finds that we 'must necessarily conclude it, by the very nature and idea of each part of it, to be actually infinite[3].' And the same holds good of duration, since 'he that considers something now existing must necessarily come to something eternal[4].' But if infinity is a characteristic of real being in its quantitative aspect, a serious discrepancy is revealed between our idea of this infinity and that which we seek to cognise by means of it. Our idea is 'negative' and 'comparative'; whereas, according to the current view, the correctness of which Locke assumes, only predicates which are positive and non-relative can be ascribed to reality. Here, again, Locke merely draws attention to the contrast, between the ideas of which we are capable and a reality for the comprehension of which they announce their own insufficiency. The negative nature of our idea of infinity is declared to be a 'defect,' which is due to a 'disproportion' between our finite minds and the reality which we seek to understand. Although, then, we must regard a quantitative infinity as a positive

[1] II. 17. 8. [2] II. 17. 4. [3] II. 17. 4. [4] II. 17. 5.

characteristic of reality, it is as 'incomprehensible' when so considered as we have already found a non-quantitative infinity to be. Our minds are 'overlaid by an object too large and mighty to be surveyed and managed by them[1].' And here, as before, this object is for Locke none other than the Divine Being, of whom infinite space and duration must somehow be attributes.

§ 8. Passing from our ideas of the simple modes of quantity to our ideas of those of quality, we shall find that although the treatment of the latter is slight, it contains points of considerable importance as regards Locke's general position and his relation to the composition theory. To begin with, he finds that although our ideas of qualities, such as 'whiteness' and 'sweetness,' can be 'repeated' as readily as those of 'a yard' or 'a day,' these repetitions are not capable of being 'added' to one another so as to 'enlarge' our ideas of these qualities. Our ideas of qualities, not consisting of parts, are incapable of being increased by the addition of parts. Thus when we repeat the idea of whiteness, and seek to 'put together' these repetitions in our mind, we find that 'they embody, as it were, and run into one, and the idea of whiteness is not at all increased[2].' We have already seen, although Locke does not himself definitely recognise it, that the nature of the process of construction, which he calls the 'addition' of ideas to one another, varies with the nature of the content with which we are dealing. We now have an explicit statement that the possibility of performing the process at all is dependent upon characteristics of the content.

If, as appeared at the outset, our ideas of simple modes are confined to those obtained by 'compounding' repetitions

[1] II. 17. 21. [2] II. 17. 6.

of the same content, the above consideration would force us to the conclusion that there can be no ideas of simple modes of qualities. In the short chapter[1] upon 'other simple modes,' which follows the discussion of our ideas of quantity, Locke, however, recognises the existence of simple modes of qualitative ideas. For, although these ideas do not consist of parts, and consequently cannot be 'enlarged' by addition, they are capable of being 'compounded' with other ideas of the same kind; while, as we have seen, Locke treats 'ideas of the same kind,' by which he understands ideas belonging to the same sense, as equivalent to the 'same ideas,' when considering them for purposes of compounding. In this way we obtain such ideas as those of 'compounded tastes and smells,' or of words as auditory complexes. But the most interesting of these ideas are the ideas of 'different degrees, or as they are termed, shades, of the same colour.' Their inclusion among complex ideas implies that they are ideas which the mind is able to make for itself, without resort to specific experience. We are, however, warned that these ideas of quality 'cannot be augmented to what proportion men please, or be stretched beyond what they have received by their senses[2].' The mind is, therefore, restricted to supplying intermediate 'shades' or 'degrees' between the ideas of colours derived from experience. Thus, we cannot form the idea of a purer white than we have received by Sensation, though we can make for ourselves ideas of a less degree of whiteness than this, which may never have been experienced[3]. It was in such ideas that Hume, who regarded them as simple because unanalysable, subsequently found the 'one contradictory phenomenon, which may prove that it is not impossible for ideas to go

[1] II. 18. [2] II. 17. 6. [3] *loc. cit.*

before their corresponding impressions[1],' or, in Locke's terminology, for the mind to make for itself a new simple idea.

When we come to our ideas of the simple modes of thinking, pleasure and pain, not only is no attempt made to apply the composition theory, but the sense in which these ideas are termed ideas of 'modes,' and the grounds for their inclusion among complex ideas, are by no means clear. We are indeed told that the idea of 'perception or thinking,' in the wide sense in which these terms cover all forms of cognition, is a simple idea of reflection, of which 'remembrance, discerning, reasoning, judging, knowledge, faith, etc.' are modes[2]. But although thought is a universal of which these 'modes' are specifications, our ideas of its modes cannot be formed by 'varying' the idea of thought, apart from experience. On the contrary, in the chapter which deals with the ideas of these mental functions, they are spoken of as modes of thinking which the mind observes in itself[3]; while discerning and remembrance are elsewhere treated, along with perception, as operations of the mind by the performance of which we obtain simple ideas of Reflection[4]. And similarly, in order to obtain ideas of the passions, which are regarded as simple modes of pleasure and pain, we are told we must observe how pleasure and pain, 'under various considerations, operate in us—what modifications or tempers of mind, what internal sensations (if I may so call them) they produce in us[5].' In the face of such statements, we cannot suppose that Locke regarded these as ideas which the mind could make for itself, without resort to specific experience. Still less can it be held that the various 'modes' of consciousness are formed

[1] *Treatise*, Book I. Part I. Section I. [2] II. 6. 2.
[3] II. 19. 1–2. [4] II. 10 and II. [5] II. 20. 3.

by a mere composition of the simple ideas of thinking, pleasure and pain. No attempt, in fact, is made to account for them by the composition theory. The simple idea is here most plainly not a unit of composition, but a universal, of which the modes are particular determinations, the nature of which can in these cases only be learned from experience.

Little need be said of the treatment of our ideas of mixed modes, which is slight and perfunctory. Each mixed mode consists of ideas of different kinds, combined by the mind, and considered as forming a single complex idea, which is consolidated and fixed by means of a name. The only condition of such combination which is mentioned, is that the different ideas must be 'consistent.' The ideas which Locke has chiefly in mind here are ideas of human actions, for the analysis of which he would apparently have been satisfied with the enumeration of the marks which make up the connotation of a name, and the derivation of these marks from simple ideas of Sensation and Reflection. It is, to say the least of it, unfortunate that Locke did not examine more closely the nature of the construction involved in such ideas, and their relation to experience, in view of the connection which he subsequently seeks to establish between ethics and the mathematical sciences.

CHAPTER V

OUR IDEAS OF SUBSTANCE, CAUSALITY AND IDENTITY

§ 1. In following Locke through his treatment of our ideas of modes, we have been chiefly concerned in watching the gradual breakdown in his hands of the composition theory. The ideas of substance, causality and identity, which form the subject of the present chapter, raise problems, and involve difficulties, of a different kind. Causality and identity are for Locke ideas of relation, and such are admittedly not the result of composition. And while adhering to the current view that substance is in itself an absolute, unaffected by relations, he reaches the paradoxical conclusion that the only idea we can form of this absolute is a relative one.

The possibility of ideas of relation being once admitted, Locke is, therefore, no longer under an obligation to make his account of our ideas of these specific relations square with the presuppositions of the composition theory. We shall find, however, that in dealing with our ideas of substances, Locke's thought is constantly hampered by the strictly analogous assumption of the current metaphysics. For, just as the composition theory, in the form in which it was put forward by him, sought to resolve the contents of our ideas into a number of separate and self-identical units of experience, so the metaphysics, which he inherited, held that reality consists of a number of separate and self-identical substances, or units of being. To Locke's analysis of the fundamental category of this metaphysics we must now turn.

§ 2. 'The ideas of substances,' we are told, 'are such combinations of simple ideas as are taken to represent distinct particular things, subsisting by themselves; in which the supposed or confused idea of substance, such as it is, is always the first and chief[1].' This 'supposed or confused idea' is that of a 'support' or *substratum* to which the simple contents in question are referred, and in which they are thought to inhere. For the origin of these contents and for their union in certain combinations, it is sufficient, Locke thinks, to appeal to experience. Simple ideas which are constantly experienced together are for this reason united by the mind, and designated by a single name. The problem of substance centres, therefore, round their reference to something which is not itself a simple idea or content of experience. The idea of such a *substratum* is not only the central constituent of our ideas of particular substances, but constitutes, when abstractly considered, the idea of 'pure substance' in general, which is 'the same everywhere.' What then is this *substratum* to which we refer the contents of our experience? How does the idea of it arise? What is the justification of the reference?

§ 3. That substance cannot be experienced as a particular content of Sensation or Reflection, Locke is perfectly clear. As distinguished from such elements of immediate experience, it is spoken of as something which we 'suppose.' The supposition, however, is not one which is merely suggested by these elements, but is from the first implied by them. For, all 'simple ideas, all sensible qualities,

[1] II. 12. 6.

carry with them a supposition of a *substratum* to exist in, and of a substance wherein they inhere[1].' In fact, the simple idea, being avowedly conceived as the cognition of a quality, all that is required is to draw attention to the relation to a substance which it implicitly contains. If any further justification of the 'supposition' is asked for, Locke declares that it rests upon a necessity of thought. It is 'because we cannot conceive how' these simple ideas 'should subsist alone, nor one in another,' that 'we suppose them existing in and supported by some common subject[2].' The same point is expressed more positively in reply to Stillingfleet. 'All the ideas of all the sensible qualities of a cherry come into my mind by Sensation; the ideas of perceiving, thinking, reasoning, knowing, etc., come into my mind by Reflection. The ideas of these qualities and actions, or powers, are perceived by the mind to be of themselves inconsistent with existence....Hence the mind perceives their necessary connection with inherence, or being supported; which being a relative idea superadded to the red colour in a cherry, or to thinking in a man, the mind frames the correlative idea of a support. For I never denied that the mind could frame to itself ideas of relation, but have showed the quite contrary in my chapters about relation[3].'

§ 4. It seems clear from such passages as these that it is in a necessity of thought that Locke finds an explicit justification of the 'supposition' of a *substratum*, which he assumes as implicit in the simple ideas of Sensation and Reflection themselves. A more modest claim, and an account of the origin of the idea more in keeping with the development which his principles subsequently received

[1] First Letter to Stillingfleet, *Works*, vol. IV. p. 7.

[2] II. 23. 4.

[3] First Letter to Stillingfleet, *Works*, vol. IV. p. 21.

at the hands of Hume, has been thought to be contained in the opening section of the chapter of the *Essay* which deals with the subject. Writing there of our ideas of particular substances, he tells us that 'we accustom ourselves to suppose some *substratum*' of the qualities we experience together. This has been taken to imply that the idea of substance itself is merely a product of custom. It is clear, however, that it is not the idea of substance which is placed upon this insecure basis, but the assumption that certain qualities are to be regarded as belonging together, and referred to the same substance. When we find that 'a certain number of these simple ideas go constantly together,' they are presumed to belong to one thing, and called by one name[1]. In the formation of the particular combination custom is the determining principle; for, as Locke elsewhere maintains, no necessary connections can be discovered between the elements which enter into it. But Locke never intended us to understand that our recognition of the dependent nature of these elements, as 'qualities' or 'modes,' and their consequent reference to a substance, can be accounted for by constant experience, or referred to custom.

§ 5. It has frequently been objected that Locke's account of substance as something which we 'suppose,' but do not experience, is in any case glaringly inconsistent with his general theory of the origin of our ideas, since the supposed *substratum* is admittedly not a content of Sensation or Reflection. The objection, as thus stated, fails, however, to take account of Locke's general theory of our ideas of relation. For, as we have seen, no idea of relation can be a content of Sensation or Reflection. All that the empirical theory of the origin of our ideas maintains, in

[1] II. 23. I.

reference to them, is that these ideas must be 'founded in,' or 'terminate in,' ideas derived from one of these 'channels.' The difficulty which really confronts Locke is not that of admitting an idea which is not itself a datum of immediate experience, but that of bringing the idea of substance into line with his general account of our ideas of relation. For, an idea of relation, we are told, can only arise as the result of an act of comparison between two distinct terms; whereas, in the case we are now dealing with, only one term of the relation is given. The difficulty is, however, hidden from Locke by his initial assumption that our simple ideas from the first involve a reference beyond themselves.

§ 6. While Locke had no misgivings about either the origin or the validity of the idea of substance, there is one feature of this idea which caused him great perplexity. He finds that we can attribute no definite nature to that which serves as a support of qualities. It remains for our thought an indefinite something, 'a supposed I-know-not-what,' of which we can form no positive idea. We talk, then, like children, when we speak of substance; our intellectual position in its regard may be likened to that of the Indian, who held that the earth rested on an elephant, the elephant on a tortoise, and the tortoise on —something, he knew not what. Our idea of substance, in fact, turns out to be no more than that of an unknown *x*, to which we refer the contents of experience.

In order to appreciate what seemed to Locke the startling nature of this result, we must bear in mind the position assigned to substance in the metaphysics which he inherited, and from which he never succeeded in entirely breaking away. For it substance, and substance alone, possessed an absolute and indefeasible reality. While reality was held to consist of substances and their qualities, the former were thought to possess an ontological superiority, since qualities depend upon substances for their existence, and indeed 'flow' from them in some mysterious way. A substance must, therefore, be thought of as possessing a being of its own, apart from, and prior to, the qualities which we refer to it. As Locke remarks, it is 'supposed always something besides the extension, figure, solidity, motion, thinking, or other observable idea, though we know not what it is[1].' For, as he urges, a support 'cannot be nothing[2]'; nor, more generally, can a relation 'be founded in nothing, or be the relation of nothing[3].'

From the implications of this unhappy conception Locke never succeeded in completely freeing himself. In view of the unknowableness of the substrate of qualities, he could, upon occasion, write satirically of 'the very great clearness there is in the doctrine of substance and accidents,' and disparage the use of the distinction 'in deciding of questions in Philosophy[4].' It never occurred to him, however, that the substance, apart from its qualities, is a mere abstraction, and as such incapable of existence; or, that the conception being a relative one, a contradiction is involved in treating it as an absolute; or, finally, that having been set over against all its qualities, it cannot, *ipso facto*, have a determinate nature of its own, whether known or unknown. While, therefore, the effect of Locke's examination of the conception is to show that it is destitute of all positive value for our knowledge, he is far from abandoning it. He maintains, instead, that we are here in the presence of the most signal instance of the necessary

1 First Letter to Stillingfleet, *Works*, vol. v. p. 7.
2 *loc. cit.* p. 29.
3 *loc. cit.* p. 21.
4 II. 13. 20.

imperfection of human knowledge. 'We may be convinced,' he declares, 'that the ideas we can attain to by our faculties are very disproportionate to things themselves, when a positive, clear, distinct one of substance itself, which is the foundation of all the rest, is concealed from us[1].'

§ 7. We must now turn from Locke's treatment of substance in general to his account of our ideas of material and spiritual substances. In doing so, we find at once that his general analysis of the idea of substance carries with it an important consequence. Since the only idea of substance which we can form in either case is that of 'a supposed I-know-not-what,' which underlies the qualities revealed to us in experience, it is impossible for us to determine the innermost nature of either matter or mind. By a material substance we can only mean the unknown '*substratum* to those simple ideas we have from without'; and by a mental or spiritual substance the equally unknown '*substratum* to those operations we experiment in ourselves within[2].' The Cartesian dualism of finite substances is, therefore, seen to be an entirely unfounded piece of dogmatism. In its place we have a distinction within experience between two kinds of ideas, and a confession of entire ignorance concerning the nature of the substrate which is implied in each case. Being thus in the dark, concerning that which lies beyond or beneath experience, we cannot even know whether the substance which thinks in us is material or immaterial. Indeed, we find that the attempt to conceive it as either lands us in insoluble difficulties. For, 'he who will give himself leave to consider freely, and look into the dark and intricate part of each hypothesis, will scarce find his reason able to determine him fixedly for or against the soul's materiality.

[1] IV. 3. 23. [2] II. 23. 5.

Since, on which side soever he views it, either as an unextended substance, or as a thinking extended matter, the difficulty to conceive either will, whilst either alone is in his thoughts, still drive him to the contrary side. An unfair way which some men take with themselves; who, because of the inconceivableness of something they find in one, throw themselves violently into the contrary hypothesis, though altogether as unintelligible to an unbiassed understanding[1].' Therefore, along with the Cartesian dualism, we must also abandon all attempts to demonstrate the immortality of the soul on the ground of its immateriality. Nor does he consider that this conclusion involves any sacrifice of moral or religious interests, holding, as he does, that 'all the great ends of morality and religion are well enough secured without philosophical proofs of the soul's immateriality[2].' We shall find, however, that Locke is not prepared to apply the same principle in the case of God, or to admit the possibility of his being other than a purely immaterial thinking substance.

If we abandon the fruitless attempt to determine the nature of the *substratum* of body or mind, and consider what is definite in the ideas which we are capable of forming of them, we shall find, Locke maintains, that in each case our idea is clear and distinct, or more properly 'determinate,' in so far as it consists of contents which have been presented to us in experience; but that we meet with insuperable difficulties as soon as we endeavour to comprehend how and why these determinations exist. Before following out the comparison here suggested, in detail, it will be necessary to consider Locke's view of the characteristics which constitute the knowable natures of matter and of mind.

[1] IV. 3. 6. [2] IV. 3. 6.

§ 8. To begin with, Locke rejects the Cartesian view, according to which extension constitutes the essence of material substance[1]. In addition to its extension, he maintains, every body possesses the fundamental quality which he calls solidity, in virtue of which it fills a certain space, to the absolute exclusion of all other bodies from the space thus occupied. It is evident that solidity thus conceived, as involving a power of resistance 'so great that no force how great soever can surmount it[2],' is a highly intellectual conception. It is, however, regarded by Locke as a simple idea of the sense of touch. 'The bodies which we daily handle,' he tells us, 'make us perceive that, whilst they remain between them, they do by an insurmountable force hinder the approach of the parts of our hands that press them[3].' But while the exigencies of his theory seemed to require such a derivation of the idea from bodies of sensible bulk, solidity is in reality regarded by Locke as strictly speaking belonging to the insensible particles which form the ultimate constitution of matter, rather than to its sensible appearances. 'The mind, having once got this idea from such grosser sensible bodies, traces it further, and considers it, as well as figure, in the minutest particle of matter that can exist; and finds it inseparably inherent in body, wherever or however modified[4].'

Solidity, conceived in this absolute sense, and attributed to the minute insensible particles which form the hidden nature of body, is distinguished from hardness, which is declared to be relative to the constitution of our bodies, and to consist in 'a firm cohesion among the parts of matter making up masses of a sensible bulk, so that the whole

[1] Cf. below, ch. IX. § 11. [2] II. 4. 3. [3] II. 4. 1.
[4] *loc. cit.*

does not easily change its figure[1].' Now to those who, like Locke, favoured the revival of the old theory of the atomic constitution of matter, this cohesion, which is exemplified, though in a less degree, by a soft as well as by a hard body, presented a source of serious perplexity. There being nothing in the nature of an atom to lead to its attachment to another, some explanation of their union had to be sought outside the atoms themselves. The nature of this principle of cohesion, accordingly, formed a favourite subject of speculation among those who rejected both the scholastic and the Cartesian conceptions of matter. Rejecting as untenable the various contemporary hypotheses, the cohesion of the parts of matter is declared by Locke to be one of those indubitable matters of fact, revealed in experience, the comprehension of which seems to be beyond our powers[2].

Upon the solidity of body, again, depends its capacity of communicating motion by impulse. But here, too, we are in the presence of a matter of fact which, though obvious in experience, is incomprehensible. The difficulties which Locke finds here, however, will best be considered when we are dealing with his treatment of causation.

§ 9. The distinction, which we have noticed above, between the solidity, which every portion of matter, however minute, possesses in itself, whatever may be the condition in which it exists, and the hardness, which is relative to our organs, and only indicates a temporary state of the insensible particles of which a body of sensible bulk is composed, is expressed in Locke's terminology by saying that, while the former is a primary quality, the latter is only a secondary quality of body. The famous doctrine

[1] II. 4. 4. [2] II. 23. 23–5. Cf. IV. 3. 29.

covered by these terms had had a long history before its appearance in the *Essay*. Originating among the Greek Atomists, the theory had been revived by Galileo, and given an extended currency by Descartes; while the terms used by Locke, to mark the distinction, were first employed for the purpose by his friend Boyle. What, then, we must ask, were the presuppositions and significance of the theory as it was formulated by Locke?

Behind the theory, as Locke understood it, lay the metaphysical assumption that the qualities which really belong to a substance must belong to it 'in itself,' apart from any relation in which it stands to anything else, including our organs of sense and the perceptions which are mediated by them. Further, since such intrinsic determinations must either constitute, or flow from, the essence of the substance, they must belong to it at all times and in all conditions. Thus, the 'real, original and primary qualities' must exist 'in the things themselves,' and this 'whether we perceive them or not'; moreover, they are 'always in them,' and are 'utterly inseparable from them in what estate soever they be.' On the other hand, any apparent characteristics of a thing, which it possesses at one time but not at another, cannot be attributed to the thing as it is 'in itself,' but are merely indications of accidental and temporary relations in which it stands to other things, or to our minds. As such they are not strictly speaking qualities of the thing at all; if, however, we so far accommodate ourselves to popular usage, as to speak of them as qualities, we must add the qualification 'secondary.'

As primary qualities of matter Locke enumerates 'solidity, extension, figure, motion or rest, and number[1].'

[1] II. 8. 9.

That our ideas of these qualities are identical in content with the determinations of real things is simply taken for granted. 'A circle or square are the same, whether in idea or existence'; this, he thinks, 'everybody is ready to agree to[1].' The whole weight of the discussion is accordingly directed to the refutation of the view that our ideas of the sensible or secondary qualities, as well as those of the primary qualities of body, are 'exactly the images and resemblances of something inherent in the subject[2].' The argument upon which Locke chiefly relies is the supposed impossibility of distinguishing in this respect our ideas of secondary qualities from ideas such as that of pain, the content of which, he thinks, must be admitted to be incapable of directly qualifying a material thing. Appeal is also made to such facts as the dependence of colour upon the presence of light, which Locke thinks can obviously make no real alteration in the body itself[3]; and to the relativity of sensations, such as those of cold and heat, to the temporary condition of our organs, in consequence of which the same water may appear hot to one hand and cold to the other[4]. That all colours, sounds, etc., 'as they are such particular ideas,' only exist in the act of Sensation, apart from which they 'vanish and cease, and are reduced to their causes, *i.e.* bulk, figure and motion of parts[5],' is merely a statement of his position, and not an argument for it. But while these sensible qualities cannot belong to material things as they are in themselves, our ideas of them must be attributed to the agency of real things. There must, then, be something in the things themselves which, upon occasion, gives rise to these ideas. As powers in the things to produce ideas in us, the secondary qualities

[1] II. 8. 18. [2] II. 8. 7. [3] II. 8. 19.
[4] II. 8. 21. [5] II. 8. 17.

can, however, be nothing but the primary qualities of the insensible parts of matter.

§ 10. Having seen the way in which Locke conceives the nature of matter, as known in and through experience, we must return to the comparison which he institutes between the ideas we are able to form of mental and material substances. Here we find at once a further divergence from the position of Descartes. Not only does Locke reject the view that extension is the essence of body, but he refuses to divest minds themselves of all spacial determinations. 'Where and when,' he declares, 'are questions belonging to all finite things[1],' to minds as well as to bodies. And since experience assures us that a mind may operate in different places at different times, mobility must also be attributed to minds. The characteristics which are at once primary and peculiar to material substances are (1) the cohesion of solid extended parts, and (2) the communication of motion by impulse; the remaining qualities of body being either dependent upon these, or common to body and spirit. But, as we have seen, while experience assures us of the factual reality of these attributes, we are unable to form any conception of the *modus operandi* of the one or the other. The fundamental and distinctive characteristics of what we call mind or spirit are (1) thinking, and (2) the ability to initiate movement by willing. Now, while the manner in which the mind performs these functions is incomprehensible, they are as solid and obvious facts of experience as the equally incomprehensible characteristics of body. Accordingly, our ideas of material and spiritual substances are equally clear, and equally defective. In both cases the *substratum* is unknown, while the distinctive qualities of body and spirit are equally conceivable and

[1] II. 15. 8.

equally inexplicable. 'To conclude:—Sensation convinces us there are solid extended substances; and Reflection that there are thinking ones: experience assures us of the existence of such beings, and that the one hath a power to move body by impulse, the other by thought; this we cannot doubt of. Experience, I say, every moment furnishes us with the clear ideas both of the one and the other. But beyond these ideas, as received from their proper sources, our faculties will not reach. If we would enquire further into their nature, causes and manner, we perceive not the nature of extension clearer than we do of thinking. If we would explain them any further, one is as easy as the other; and there is no more difficulty to conceive how a substance we know not should, by thought, set body into motion, than how a substance we know not should, by impulse, set body into motion[1].'

In view of its importance, and of the place assigned to it in contemporary theories of innate ideas, the account which Locke gives of the nature and origin of our idea of God is remarkably slight, its formal treatment only occupying three short paragraphs. The content of the idea, we are told, consists of those qualities and powers which we experience in ourselves by Reflection, and which it is 'better to have than to be without,' each enlarged by our idea of infinity. The scholastic identification of reality and perfection is implied, though it is not explicitly enunciated, and of course no attempt is made to explain or justify it. Nor is Locke prepared to draw the same consequence, from the unknowability of the *substratum*, as he drew in the case of finite minds. Although the Supreme Being is 'incomprehensible' and cannot be known 'in his own essence,' we must, he maintains, conceive him as immaterial. The

[1] II. 23. 29.

reason which he gives for this greater definiteness in our idea of God, than in our idea of finite spirits, is that all the qualities of the Supreme Being must be 'essentially inseparable' from him, whereas thinking is not of the essence of matter. The possibility that matter may think in us is merely the possibility that God may have bestowed upon certain portions of it a power which forms no part of its essential nature.

§ 11. As the data of immediate experience, or the simple ideas which we receive by Sensation and Reflection, serve to suggest to the mind the idea of substance, which we find ourselves compelled to recognise as implied by them, though not included among them; so, the changes which we experience as taking place in these data can only be understood by means of a further set of ideas, which consideration shows to be similarly necessary. These are the connected ideas of active efficiency, power and causality. Locke's view of the relation of these ideas to one another is somewhat obscured by the exigencies of his exposition. Since our ideas of different substances are found to consist largely of ideas of the powers which they possess of altering other substances, the idea of power is treated, for convenience, as a simple constituent of these ideas, although it is admitted to involve a relation. The idea of power thus obtains priority of treatment to that of causality, which is regarded as an idea of relation between substances or their modes, and as consequently presupposing ideas of substances, in which the relation must be grounded. The order of ideas here implied was of course in agreement with the fundamental position attributed in the metaphysics of the time to the category of substance, and with the connected tendency to interpret activity and causation as merely the actualisation of pre-existing potentialities. Nevertheless, in the account which Locke gives of the two ideas, it is implied that the idea of causation is logically prior to that of power, since we only come by the latter idea when we consider 'in one thing the possibility of having any of its simple ideas changed, and in another the possibility of making that change.' For this we only do when we have been led to conclude, as the result of reflection on the constancy of our experience, that 'the like changes will for the future be made in the same things, by like agents, and in like ways[1].'

§ 12. When closely examined, moreover, the ideas of both causality and power are found to involve the idea of active efficiency. For Locke, as for Descartes, the innermost significance of the idea of causality is that of the active initiation of change. And while accepting from Scholasticism the current distinction between active and passive power, he holds that the former is 'the more proper signification' of the word[2]. Accordingly, neither causality nor power can be understood until we have tracked the idea of activity to its source and exhibited its content[3].

While holding that 'whatever change is observed,' whether in outward things or in ourselves, 'the mind must collect a power somewhere able to make that change, as well as a possibility in the thing itself to receive it[4],' Locke maintains that a clear idea of the nature of activity can only be derived from our experience in willing. For if, in the first place, we examine closely the qualitative changes

[1] II. 21. 1.

[2] II. 21. 4.

[3] For other implications of Locke's conception of causation, see below, ch. VIII. § 11.

[4] II. 21. 4.

which take place in physical things, we find that they convey no idea of the nature of any activity by which they are effected. All that we can observe in such cases is the effect produced, and not the action by which it is brought about. 'When a countryman says the cold freezes water, though the word *freezing* seems to import some action, yet truly it signifies nothing but the effect; viz., that water that was before fluid is become hard and consistent; without containing any idea of the action whereby it is done[1].' Locke had come, however, to regard such qualitative changes as the result of movement among the minute particles of which bodies are composed, and in movement Hobbes had already declared all active power to consist[2]. In order to carry our analysis further, we must, therefore, enquire whether the facts of movement in bodies, as observable by our senses, contain any element which can be regarded as the source of our idea of activity.

We have already seen that 'the only way we can conceive bodies operate in,' is by impulse or impact[3]; and that although the way in which motion is communicated by impulse is incomprehensible, the fact is undeniable. When, however, we examine the facts from this new point of view, for the purpose of discovering an element of experience answering to our idea of activity, no such element is discoverable. 'For, when the ball obeys the stroke of a billiard-stick, it is not any action of the ball, but bare passion. Also when by impulse it sets another ball in motion that lay in its way, it only communicates the motion it had received from another, and loses in itself so much as the other receives; which gives us but a very obscure idea of an active power of moving in body, whilst we observe it only to transfer but not produce any motion.

[1] II. 22. 11. [2] *Elements of Philosophy*, Part II. ch. x. § 6. [3] II. 8. 11.

For it is but a very obscure idea of power which reaches not the production of the action, but the continuation of the passion[1].'

The production of movement by willing is, it is true, as incomprehensible as its communication by impulse. But we have in the former case, what we have not in the latter, an experience of its active initiation. 'The idea of the beginning of motion we have' then 'only from Reflection on what passes in ourselves, where we find by experience that barely by willing it, barely by a thought of the mind, we can move the parts of our bodies which were before at rest[2].' This experience of activity we have, again, in the voluntary control of our own thoughts; but of thinking, and the activity involved in it, it is obvious that external perception can give us no idea at all. In willing, then, and nowhere else, have we an actual experience of the efficiency which Locke regards as the essential constituent of our concept of causation.

§ 13. The idea of activity having been traced to a subjective origin, what, it may be asked, is our justification for applying the conceptions of causality and power, in which it is essentially involved, to unwilled changes in the external world, seeing that these cannot afford us the experience from which this idea could be derived? Locke replies that, whatever their origin, the ideas of causality and power can be seen to be necessary for the comprehension of these changes. 'Whatever change is observed, the mind must collect a power somewhere able to make that change[3].' Again, '*Everything that has a beginning must have a cause* is a true principle of reason, or a proposition certainly true; which we come to know by the same way, *i.e.* by contemplating our ideas, and perceiving that the

[1] II. 21. 4. [2] *loc. cit.* [3] *loc. cit.*

idea of beginning to be, is necessarily connected with the idea of some operation, and the idea of operation with the idea of something operating, which we call a cause; and so the beginning to be, is perceived to agree with the idea of a cause, as is expressed in the proposition[1].' The changes which we experience but do not initiate must, therefore, be referred to causes which are thought of as efficient in producing them. Our discovery of the subjective origin of the idea of efficiency is regarded, however, by Locke, as capable of throwing some light upon the real nature of these causes. As exercising activity, must they not be minds or spirits? It is, at least, he maintains, 'worth our consideration, whether active power be not the proper attribute of spirits, and passive power of matter.' And allowing himself one of his few indulgences in speculation, he proceeds to make the suggestion which Leibniz subsequently found so much to his taste: 'Hence may be conjectured that created spirits are not wholly separate from matter, because they are both active and passive. Pure spirit, viz. God, is only active; pure matter is only passive; those beings that are both active and passive, we may judge to partake of both[2].'

§ 14. It will be observed that, throughout Locke's treatment of the subject, there is no suggestion that the idea of causality essentially involves that of uniformity, or necessary connection according to law, which is now often regarded as its primary implication. The term 'law of nature' still retained for him the theological implications to which, indeed, we must ultimately trace the attempt to unite in a single conception the ideas of active efficiency and uniformity of behaviour. The regularities

[1] First Letter to Stillingfleet, *Works*, vol. IV. pp. 61, 62.

[2] II. 23. 28. Cf. II. 21. 2.

which we discover in the outer world are regarded as the expression of laws imposed upon nature by its Author, which consequently partake of the immutable constancy of the divine will. Since, however, we cannot penetrate to the divine decrees themselves, the universality of any particular kind of factual connection cannot be deduced from this general assumption. Nor can we perceive any intrinsic necessity in the connections of natural phenomena as revealed by experience. When we pass beyond the particular matter of fact, and frame empirical generalisations, we leave the realm of knowledge in the strict and proper sense. 'The things that, as far as our observation reaches, we constantly find to proceed regularly, we must conclude to act by a law set them; but yet by a law that we know not: whereby, though causes work steadily, and effects constantly flow from them, yet their connections and dependencies being not discoverable in our ideas, we can have but an experimental knowledge of them[1].' And experimental knowledge, when the attempt is made to transcend the facts of actual experience, yields only probability. While, therefore, we may 'conclude' from what we have 'so constantly observed' that 'the like changes will for the future be made in the same things, by like agents, and in like ways[2],' the inference is not of a necessary character, or capable of finding a place in the system of demonstrative truths which constitutes science. The problem, however, in this form, is not one which greatly occupied Locke's thought. The justifiability of assertions of necessary connections among matters of fact, which is for Hume the central crux of the question of causation, presented itself to Locke, as we have seen, as the question of the possibility of a

[1] IV. 3. 29. [2] I. 21. I.

knowledge of the necessary coexistence of attributes in the same substance.

§ 15. The last of the special conceptions treated by Locke, which calls for our notice, is that of real or individual identity. The chapter in which the subject is discussed at considerable length was only added in the second edition, at the suggestion of Molyneux, who desired an amplification of the 'touches' upon the *principium individuationis* which had occurred in the *Essay* in its original form. The ideas of real identity and diversity are regarded as ideas of relations, the terms of which are objects which we experience as existing at different times. Concerning the origin of the idea of identity Locke has little to say, beyond its assignment to an act of comparison which has reference to 'the very being of things.' For the rest, the chapter is devoted to the consideration of the conditions under which it can be affirmed, especially in the case of personal identity, which Locke finds to raise at once the most difficult and the most interesting problems.

§ 16. Beginning with that which he regards as the simplest case, he finds that when the existents which we compare are indistinguishable in content, individual identity can signify nothing but a continuity of existence, by which that which is experienced at one time is thought of as having occupied a given position in space on some former occasion. 'That, therefore, that had one beginning, is the same thing; and that which had a different beginning in time and place from that, is not the same, but diverse[1].' It is in this sense, he holds, that we can speak of a sameness or diversity of substance. Existence is itself here the *principium individuationis*, which has been the subject of so much

[1] II. 27. I.

controversy, inasmuch as every finite being which exists must exist at a particular place at a particular time, while in doing so it excludes all other beings of the same kind from that particular place at that particular time. The qualification 'of the same kind' is necessary, since Locke considers that a finite mind and a body may occupy the same place at the same time, while God is, as we know, regarded as in some way present in the whole of space. But 'though these three sorts of substances, as we term them, do not exclude one another out of the same place, yet we cannot conceive but that they must necessarily each of them exclude any of the same kind out of the same place; or else the notions and names of identity and diversity would be in vain, and there could be no distinctions of substances, or anything else, one from another[1].' Hence, when we can show continuity of existence of the same kind with that which existed at a particular place at a particular time in the past, we have shown real or individual identity of substance. Or, following our substance in thought to its first beginning, we may say that, that which 'had one beginning is the same thing, and that which had a different beginning in time and place from that, is not the same, but diverse[2].'

The above, Locke considers, would be a sufficient account of identity and the conditions in which it is realised, if the predication of numerical sameness were restricted to simple unchangeable substances, such as the atoms are supposed to be, or to mere collections or masses of these. This, however, is far from being the case. We speak of the same tree, or the same horse, but the identity which we thereby recognise is distinct from, and independent of, the identity of the particles of matter which compose them,

[1] II. 27. 2.

[2] II. 27. 1.

or of any collection of such particles. An oak, for instance, remains the same oak, although it has grown from a sapling to a vast tree, although its branches have been lopped from time to time, and although its material substance is the subject of constant change. 'It is not, therefore, unity of substance that comprehends all sorts of identity, or will determine it in every case; but to conceive and judge of it aright, we must consider what idea the word it is applied to stands for; it being one thing to be the same substance, another the same man, and a third the same person, if *person*, *man* and *substance* are three names standing for three different ideas; for such as is the idea belonging to that name, such must be the identity[1].'

In the above passage, Locke signalises the special form of identity with which he is most concerned. Before we proceed to consider his theory of personal identity we must, however, notice the important general principle which is here laid down. Identity, Locke insists, cannot be adequately understood as a mere abstract sameness of substance. Its meaning must depend upon, and vary with, the nature of the subject of which it is predicated. Moreover, as the phenomena of life imply, identity is not only consistent with, but may essentially involve substantial difference. The same considerations lead to the explicit recognition of the distinction between composition and organisation. This appears when we consider 'wherein an oak differs from a mass of matter....The one is only the cohesion of particles of matter anyhow united; the other, such a disposition of them as constitutes the parts of an oak, and such an organisation of those parts as is fit to receive and distribute nourishment, so as to continue and

[1] II. 27. 7. Sections 3 to 10 of this chapter are incorrectly numbered in Fraser's edition of the *Essay*.

frame the wood, bark and leaves, etc., of an oak, in which consists the vegetable life[1].'

Since, then, a plant consists of 'an organisation of parts in one coherent body, partaking of one common life[2],' its identity is to be found in the continuity of this organisation. The same principle holds good of an animal, though the manner of its organisation differs from that of a plant; while Locke holds that the identity of a man is similarly constituted by 'nothing but a participation of the same continued life by constantly fleeting particles of matter, in succession vitally united to the same organised body.' When, however, we come to enquire into the nature of personal identity, an entirely new set of conditions has to be taken into account.

§ 17. Since the nature of identity varies with that to which it refers, in order to understand what constitutes personal identity we must first consider the signification of the term 'person.' As we have seen, thinking is always accompanied, according to Locke, by what he calls consciousness, or by a reflex act by which we perceive or are aware of our thought as our own. 'When we see, hear, smell, taste, feel, meditate, or will anything, we know that we do so[3].' Now it is in virtue of this recognition of our thoughts as ours that 'everyone is to himself that which he calls *self*[4].' But while this consciousness, or reference to self, is invariably involved in my present perceptions and actions, it is not limited to these. It attaches as immediately to certain experiences and actions which I recognise as having belonged to myself in the past, as to the thoughts and actions of the present moment. Hence I own and impute to my 'self' past actions, 'just upon the same ground and for the same reason[5]' as present

[1] II. 27. 4. [2] *loc. cit.* [3] II. 27. 9. [4] *loc. cit.* [5] II. 27. 26.

ones. It is, then, upon this 'continued consciousness' that identity of self and identity of person depend. 'It is by the consciousness it has of its present thoughts and actions that it is *self* to itself now, and so will be the same self, as far as the same consciousness can extend to actions past or to come[1].' Where this consciousness is lacking, the identity of self does not extend, a truth which is embodied in the common expressions 'not himself' and 'beside himself,' as applied to one in whom there has been a notable breach in the continuity of consciousness. It will be observed that while Locke maintains that the identity of my self is dependent upon my awareness of self, he does not regard my self as limited in its range to my realisation of its contents at the present moment, but as extending as far as the immediate judgment of self-consciousness is capable of reaching. A proposition about my self, as well as a proposition about anything else, may be true, although I do not affirm it. If it be urged that, according to Locke's account of the matter, a proposition about my self must differ from all others in this respect, since my self is constituted by my thinking it, the objection betrays a misunderstanding. Like all thought which is true, the judgment of self-consciousness is determined for me and not by me. It is no arbitrary act of mine, by which I am a self to my self, or by which I recognise certain past actions as mine, whenever I think of them. In fact, like other forms of these relations, identity and diversity of self are 'relations and ways of comparing well-founded[2],' even though their foundation consists in nothing but my ability or inability to connect a past with a present perception by 'the same continued consciousness.'

§ 18. The immediacy which Locke attributes to the

[1] II. 27. 10.

[2] II. 27. 2.

'consciousness' of identity of self is not, then, a mere immediacy of feeling, although it involves this, but an immediacy of judgment, based upon an intellectual function of comparison. That personal identity can only exist where these higher mental functions are present is emphasised throughout. *Person*, we are told, stands for 'a thinking intelligent being, that has reason and reflection, and can consider itself as itself, the same thinking thing in different times and places[1].' It is a term which 'belongs only to intelligent agents capable of a law[2].' Personal identity is 'the sameness of a rational being[3].' This insistence upon the rational implications of personal identity suggests a question which Locke does not discuss, viz., the possibility of attributing it to the brutes. There can be no doubt that Locke holds that personal identity does not extend to the lower animals. The only identity which he would attribute to them is an identity of organism, in the sense which has been explained. At the same time, the brute is capable of perception, or of having ideas, and this, as we have seen, involves some kind of consciousness or awareness of self. We must, therefore, suppose that Locke would attribute to the brute an idea of self as involved in its present perceptions, but no ability to recognise an identity between the self of the present and the self of the past. This is, indeed, quite consistent with his general view that 'beasts compare not their ideas further than some sensible circumstances annexed to the objects themselves,' and are incapable of the higher form of comparison which presupposes abstraction and the capacity for general ideas[4].

§ 19. Assuming, then, the presence of this human form of consciousness, Locke treats 'self' and 'person' as

[1] II. 27. 9. [2] II. 27. 26. [3] II. 27. 9. [4] II. 11. 5.

having the same denotation. The only difference which he finds in their signification is a difference of point of view. This we might express by saying that, whereas a 'self' is a 'person' realised from within, a 'person' is a 'self' regarded from without. Or, in our author's own words, 'Wherever a man finds what he calls *himself*, there, I think, another may say is the same person[1].' The latter, he remarks, is 'a forensic term, appropriating actions and their merit[2],' and throughout the discussion he has in mind its practical application to the question of moral responsibility, and the justification of a system of rewards and punishments. Human justice, he recognises, cannot rely without reserve upon the principle that responsibility only extends as far as the consciousness of an identical self, because of its liability to be deceived in any attempt to apply this purely inward principle. Hence we punish a man for actions committed in a fit of drunkenness, of which he may have no consciousness in his restored state of sobriety. 'For though punishment be annexed to personality, and personality to consciousness, and the drunkard perhaps be not conscious of what he did, yet human judicatures justly punish him; because the fact is proved against him, but want of consciousness cannot be proved for him[3].' Nevertheless, the principle which identifies moral responsibility with the consciousness of identity of self remains the principle of ideal justice. 'In the great day, wherein the secrets of all hearts shall be laid open, it may be reasonable to think, no one shall be made to answer for what he knows nothing of; but shall receive his doom, his conscience accusing or excusing him[4].' It is embodied, too, in human laws, when, in the case of madness,

[1] II. 27. 26.
[2] *loc. cit.*
[3] II. 27. 22.
[4] *loc. cit.*

the breach of continuity in consciousness is capable of sufficient verification[1].

§ 20. On its metaphysical side Locke's theory is definitely set over against the current dogmatic view, which regarded the identity of self as consisting in an identity of spiritual substance. Those who take up this position are, he maintains, guilty of confusing two quite different conceptions—identity of substance and identity of person—the former of which 'concerns not personal identity at all[2].' For, on the one hand, an identity of substance, without the presence of the 'same continued consciousness,' would not suffice for the identity of a self or person. Thus, if, as the theory of pre-existence maintains, the immaterial substance or soul which now thinks in B, previously formed the mental substrate of another man A, whose life B has no ability to recall, this in no way destroys the separate personality of A and B, or constitutes them a single person. On the other hand, if we suppose that several different substances are successively the vehicle of 'the same continued consciousness,' there would in that case be only a single person. Whether either of these suppositions corresponds to fact, or whether identity of consciousness is only realised, or is even only capable of realisation, in conjunction with identity of substance, it is, Locke holds, impossible for us to say, in our complete ignorance of the ultimate nature of substance. Our very ignorance on this point, however, is a sufficient ground for asserting that the self, of whose existence and identity we have an immediate certainty, 'is not determined by identity or diversity of substance, which it cannot be sure of, but only of identity of consciousness[3].'

Locke's treatment of the question of the identity of

[1] II. 27. 20. [2] II. 27. 10. [3] II. 27. 23.

self is, in some respects, one of the most original and revolutionary of the positions developed in the *Essay*. It is even more fatal to the traditional realistic dogmatism, which is here attacked in its favourite stronghold, than his criticism of its use of the general conception of substance. Here, moreover, in the identity of self-consciousness, Locke has found a concrete unifying conception, in place of the empty thing-in-itself into which the idea of substance had finally resolved itself. That this conception, like that of a living organism, involves a genuine transcending of the mechanical view of nature and of mind, embodied in the composition theory, only adds to its significance. It must be observed, however, that even in this, the maturest product of his criticism, Locke does not succeed in entirely freeing himself from the old way of looking at things. Questions about the identity of an underlying spiritual substance are banished from the realm of our knowledge, but they are not declared to be intrinsically unintelligible. Locke still firmly believes that there is an unknown substrate to the mental life of the individual, and that the identity of consciousness must be realised either through the identity of one substance or in a number of such successively. Indeed, he even expresses the view that 'the more probable opinion is, that this consciousness is annexed to, and the affection of, one individual immaterial substance[1].' But a mental substance which is not only unknown, but has been shown to stand in no essential relation to the self of consciousness, can only be retained so long as it is not challenged. Nothing could show more conclusively than the mere statement of such a position, the entire uselessness of the traditional conception of substance for the interpretation of our self-conscious life.

[1] II. 27. 25.

CHAPTER VI

THE GENERAL NATURE OF KNOWLEDGE

§ 1. We have arrived at last at the main problem of the *Essay*, to the solution of which the whole content of the work is regarded by its author as subordinate and contributory. Having completed his survey of our ideas, and discussed their representation by words, and the misapprehensions to which this often gives rise, he considers himself to be in a position to attack the question of the nature and possible extent of the knowledge of which ideas are but the 'materials' or 'instruments.' In our exposition of his treatment of the subject, it will be convenient to consider, first, his view of the general characteristics of knowledge, and certain general distinctions which he makes in relation to it; leaving his account of the different kinds of knowledge, and of the limitations which he discovers in its extent, to be dealt with subsequently. Accordingly, in the present chapter, the questions with which we shall be concerned are (1) Locke's identification of knowledge with objective certainty, and the sharp line which he consequently draws between knowledge and everything of the nature of probable conjecture or opinion; (2) his account of what constitutes what he calls the 'reality' of knowledge, in virtue of which its validity transcends the ideas of the individual mind, with which it is immediately concerned; (3) the synthetic or instructive quality, which distinguishes what is valuable in knowledge from verbal trifling. We shall also touch upon his view of opinion, and upon his theory of the error which finds its *locus* within it.

§ 2. 'With me, to know and to be certain is the same thing. What I know, that I am certain of; and what I am certain of, that I know. What reaches to knowledge I think may be called certainty; and what comes short of certainty, I think cannot be called knowledge[1].' In these emphatic words Locke expresses his identification of knowledge with a form of cognition yielding certainty. As we have seen, the simplest element of knowledge is for Locke a judgment, or an act of thought by which an affirmation or denial is made. Judgments, however, are regarded by him as of two radically different kinds. The one comprises the absolutely certain judgments which constitute knowledge, in which we not only think that the connection affirmed or denied in the judgment holds good, but perceive that it does so; to the other belong the judgments which, failing to afford the complete intellectual satisfaction which characterises knowledge, constitute the region of opinion or probability. By an unfortunate ambiguity in his use of the term, 'judgment' is sometimes used by Locke to signify the special faculty by which the latter kind of affirmations and denials are made. In this narrower sense, instead of including knowledge as a species, 'judgment' is distinguished from and contrasted with it; knowledge and judgment being declared to be 'two faculties conversant about truth and falsity[2].' Having drawn attention to this ambiguity, we shall continue to employ the term in its more usual and wider signification, unless the contrary is expressly indicated.

[1] Second Letter to Stillingfleet, *Works*, vol. IV. p. 145. [2] IV. 14. 4.

The distinction between the two kinds of judgment, or between knowledge and opinion, is regarded by Locke as one of kind, and not of degree, as is indeed implied in the reference of them to different 'faculties.' Speaking of judgment in the narrower and more technical sense, he tells us that 'it never amounts to knowledge, no, not to that which is the lowest degree of it[1].' We shall have to consider, presently, in what sense Locke allows himself to speak of 'degrees' in a knowledge which he declares to be absolute; for the present we are only concerned in noticing the sharpness of the distinction which he draws between knowledge and opinion. Moreover, the difference between the two does not lie in their practical power of commanding our assent, or in an absoluteness of subjective conviction, which is present in the one case and wanting in the other. For, in the case of conclusions which rest merely on grounds of probability, as distinct from strict demonstration, we are told that 'sometimes the intermediate ideas tie the extremes so firmly together, and the probability is so clear and strong, that assent as necessarily follows it, as knowledge does demonstration[2].' Though only probable, the evidence 'naturally determines the judgment, and leaves us as little liberty to believe or disbelieve, as a demonstration does, whether we will know or be ignorant[3].' The point is more than once reverted to in the course of the controversy with Stillingfleet, in connection with Locke's view of the nature of religious 'faith.' Though there must always be uncertainty where the conditions of knowledge are not fully realised, this does not, he points out, necessarily involve the presence of subjective wavering or doubt. For 'the evidently strong probability may as steadily determine the man to assent

[1] IV. 17. 16. [2] IV. 17. 16. [3] IV. 16. 9.

to the truth, or make him take the proposition for true, and act accordingly, as knowledge makes him see or be certain that it is true[1].' The difference between the two, he declares, is that in bare belief, however strongly it may be held, our assent 'excludes not the possibility that it may be otherwise[2].' When we know, however, this possibility is excluded; and along with it not only the possibility of doubt, but of error. When knowledge has once been attained on any subject, we are in possession of something which no new facts or considerations can modify or annul. 'What we once know, we are certain is so; and we may be secure that there are no latent proofs undiscovered, which may overthrow our knowledge, or bring it in doubt[3].' No Rationalist could place the claims of knowledge higher, or insist more strongly upon the absoluteness and infallibility of our knowing power. When we find Locke dwelling upon the narrow range of human knowledge, we must be careful to bear in mind the rigorous nature of his requirements.

Knowledge, according to Locke's well-known definition, consists in 'the perception of the connection and agreement, or disagreement and repugnancy of any of our ideas[4].' The ability to perceive such agreements or disagreements is regarded by him as a fundamental power of our intellectual nature which, together with our powers of perceiving the ideas themselves in our minds, and of apprehending the signification of signs, constitutes the 'power of perception...which we call the Understanding[5].' It is in this special form of perception that he finds the certainty which constitutes knowledge. 'Where this perception is, there is knowledge; and where it is not, there,

[1] Third Letter to Stillingfleet, *Works*, vol. IV. p. 299. [2] *loc. cit.*
[3] IV. 16. 3. [4] IV. 1. 2. [5] II. 21. 5.

though we may fancy, guess or believe, yet we always come short of knowledge[1].' In the various forms of 'judgment,' as distinguished from knowledge, we are said to 'think,' 'take,' 'suppose' or 'presume,' our ideas to agree or disagree, but not to perceive their agreement or disagreement.

§ 3. This agreement or disagreement of ideas is in some cases immediately perceived by the mind, upon the mere consideration of the ideas in question; in others it is only mediately manifest, by the aid of other ideas. In the former we have intuitive knowledge, which is self-evident; in the latter, demonstrative knowledge, the evidence of which depends upon 'proofs' or 'intervening ideas,' which reveal an agreement or disagreement that cannot be directly perceived. The conception of intuition and the knowledge it affords play such an important part in Locke's theory that his account of it must be given in full.

'If we will reflect on our own ways of thinking, we shall find that sometimes the mind perceives the agreement or disagreement of two ideas immediately by themselves, without the intervention of any other; and this, I think, we may call *intuitive knowledge*. For in this the mind is at no pains of proving or examining, but perceives the truth, as the eye doth light, only by being directed towards it. Thus the mind perceives that white is not black, that a circle is not a triangle, that three are more than two and equal to one and two. Such kinds of truths the mind perceives at the first sight of the ideas together, by bare intuition, without the intervention of any other idea; and this kind of knowledge is the clearest and most certain that human frailty is capable of. This part of knowledge is irresistible, and like bright sunshine

[1] IV. I. 2.

forces itself immediately to be perceived, as soon as ever the mind turns its view that way; and leaves no room for hesitation, doubt or examination, but the mind is presently filled with the clear light of it....He that demands a greater certainty than this, demands he knows not what, and shows only that he has a mind to be a sceptic without being able to be so[1].'

Upon this fundamental power of intellectual intuition, moreover, demonstration is at every step dependent. The latter is in fact conceived as consisting of a connected series or chain of intuitions, in which the agreement or disagreement of each idea with the next in order is immediately perceived. In this way a connection is mediately established between the first and last terms of the series of ideas, which it would have been beyond our power to perceive directly. While possessing the same objective certainty as intuition, demonstration is subjectively more difficult and less clear. For since we are unable to survey all the intuitive connections involved at the same time, we are obliged to depend upon a remembrance of the earlier intuitions[2]. This dependence upon memory, however, opens the door to possibilities of mistake, which are not present in the simple intuitions themselves. It is in this subjective relation that Locke must be understood when he speaks of demonstration as an inferior 'degree' of knowledge to intuition, while at the same time maintaining that the certainty of knowledge as such is absolute. In so far as we can overcome the subjective hindrances to an adequate intellectual grasp of the more complicated subject-matter involved in a demonstration, we attain to the perfect clarity of insight possessed by intuition itself.

[1] IV. 2. I.

[2] IV. 17. 15.

§ 4. The definition of knowledge as consisting in a perception of agreement or disagreement among our ideas seems, at first sight, to commit us to an extreme subjectivism, which is certainly foreign to Locke's intention. In order to appreciate his position, we must remember, in the first place, that ideas are for him 'objects' present to the understanding, and that consequently the agreements and disagreements between ideas are agreements and disagreements between such 'objects.' Moreover, as long as we are dealing with ideas, and not with supposed independent substances, there is no suggestion that the relations in question must be foreign to the terms related, or are in any way arbitrarily imposed upon them. On the contrary, the most important relations of agreement and disagreement, the perception of which constitutes the most characteristic form of knowledge, are found to be involved in the very nature of the ideas themselves, as contents of thought. 'In some of our ideas there are certain relations, habitudes and connections, so visibly included in the nature of the ideas themselves, that we cannot conceive them separate from them by any power whatsoever....Thus, the idea of a right-lined triangle necessarily carries with it an equality of its angles to two right ones. Nor can we conceive this relation, this connection of these two ideas, to be possibly mutable, or to depend on any arbitrary power, which of choice made it thus, or could make it otherwise[1].'

These connections being involved in the intrinsic nature of the ideas in question, the perceptions which constitute knowledge of them are wholly determined by, and at the same time express the nature of, these objects of our thought. Not, of course, that the mind is to be conceived

[1] IV. 3. 29.

as determined to knowledge apart from any activity of its own. Just as we can decide for ourselves in what direction we will turn our eyes, and with what degree of care we will examine each object presented to our sight; so, both the objects of our consideration and the extent to which they occupy our thoughts are under the influence of our will. But given the ideas and the application of the mind to them, the matter passes from our control. Here, again, the analogy of vision holds good. Both the objects of vision and the agreements and disagreements which we discover among our ideas are in the last resort determined for us, and not by us[1]. Or, as Locke puts it elsewhere, 'Does not the agreement or disagreement depend upon the ideas themselves? Nay, so entirely depend upon the ideas themselves, that it is impossible for the mind, or reason, or argument, or anything else to alter it? All that reason or the mind does, in reasoning or arguing, is to find out and observe that agreement or disagreement: and all that argument does is by an intervening idea to show it, where an immediate putting the ideas together will not do it[2].'

So far, then, from being merely subjective or arbitrary, the perception which constitutes such knowledge must be said to possess an objective intellectual necessity. Not only is the judgment one which we cannot help making, the given ideas being before our mind, but since the agreement or disagreement in question is apprehended as involved in the intrinsic nature of the objects of our thought, the connection is itself perceived as necessary. The necessity of such knowledge is not that of blind determination, but of rational connection. We shall find, indeed, that there are judgments, based on actual experience,

[1] Cf. IV. 13. 1–3. [2] First Letter to Stillingfleet, *Works*, vol. IV. p. 62.

concerning the existence of particular things and the co-existence of their qualities, to which Locke is reluctant to deny the name of knowledge, although they fall short of this requirement, since they are not apprehended as involving a rational necessity. But, for this very reason, the position of these judgments remains ambiguous in his theory, and it is not in any case to them that we must look for our typical instances of what he understands by knowledge. His view of their nature, and the difficulties which they raise, will have to be considered later.

§ 5. Having seen what Locke understands by the certainty of knowledge, we must next consider what he calls its 'reality.' It might be objected that the certainty and objectivity, which we have so far claimed for knowledge, might apparently be possessed by 'the visions of an enthusiast,' as well as by 'the reasonings of a sober man.' Given the ideas of the former, certain agreements and disagreements may be seen to be necessarily involved in them. We have only to form the ideas of a harpy and a centaur to perceive intuitively that the one is not the other, or, again, that a centaur is an animal. Such propositions, however, do not afford us what Locke calls 'real' knowledge, since they are only concerned with fictions of our imagination. For real knowledge it is not only necessary that we should perceive an agreement or disagreement among our ideas, but that we should have a guarantee that the ideas in question 'agree with the reality of things.' We must, therefore, enquire in what sense this further agreement is to be understood, and the nature of the guarantees by which it can be assured.

It may be objected at once that if ideas are taken as objects, and the exclusive objects of the individual mind; and if things are regarded as transcendent entities which from the nature of the case cannot be present to it; it is *ipso facto* impossible for us to have an apprehension of a relation between them. But while Locke undoubtedly at times implies both these positions, the sharpness of their opposition is modified for his thought from both sides. For, on the one hand, ideas are regarded by him as essentially signs, which are from the first understood or intended by the mind to represent a world of reality. A tacit reference to such a world is involved even in purely imaginary ideas, such as that of a centaur; and it is only in virtue of this claim to represent something other than themselves that such ideas can be condemned as wanting in reality. And, on the other hand, it is always assumed that the world of real things, while distinct from our ideas, is yet presented in experience, however imperfect and superficial this presentation may be. Instead, therefore, of attempting to bridge the gulf, between a purely individual object of thought and a purely transcendent entity, Locke conceives that all that he has to do is to show that, in the case of certain kinds of ideas, the claim which they make, to represent some element or characteristic of the real world, can be seen to be valid from the nature of the idea and from the nature of its claim.

The justification of this claim, and the vindication of the 'reality' of our knowledge, must on no account be confused with establishment of a proposition affirming the real existence of something corresponding to an idea. Knowledge of real existence is of course real knowledge, but knowledge may be real without involving an affirmation of real existence. With the possible exception of our ideas of substances, concerning which Locke tends to waver[1], the reality of our knowledge is sufficiently

[1] See below, § 8.

guaranteed if the ideas which it contains can be known to be ideas of possible existents. Our propositions 'contain real truth' when their terms 'are joined as our ideas agree, and when our ideas are such as we know are capable of having an existence in nature[1].' For, when these conditions are fulfilled, with the possible exception just indicated, though nothing may really exist corresponding to them, our ideas are real in the sense of having a 'foundation in nature,' or of possessing that 'conformity' with the 'reality of things' which is 'intended' or 'supposed' by the mind, when it employs them in its endeavour after truth. We must, however, follow Locke in his detailed account of the claim to reality, as made by different kinds of ideas, and the conditions of its validity.

§ 6. The reality of all simple ideas is, according to Locke, guaranteed by their very simplicity. The impossibility of making such ideas for ourselves being taken to imply that they 'are not fictions of our fancies, but the natural and regular productions of things without us, really operating on us,' these ideas are held to 'carry with them all the conformity which is intended, or which our state requires[2].' We can, that is to say, be sure that each of these ideas corresponds to some element or characteristic of the real world. It should be observed that it is by no means essential to their reality that they should be copies or resemblances of an extra-mental entity, although some of them are held to stand in this relation. It may, however, be pointed out that the supposed resemblance between our ideas of primary qualities and an external reality constitutes the final point of connection between our ideas and the world of things. In respect of these ideas, the 'appearance' which is presented to our

[1] IV. 5. 8.

[2] IV. 4. 4.

mind is identical in content with the reality which appears.

§ 7. To establish the reality of our simple ideas, and of our knowledge in so far as it relates to them, carries us, however, but a little way. For, while we are thus furnished with a security that the elementary materials of our knowledge are something more than fictions of our imagination, we must look elsewhere for a guarantee of the reality of the complex ideas, of which they are merely the 'materials' or 'foundation.' Such a guarantee, Locke thinks, there is no difficulty in finding, in the case of all complex ideas except those of substances. Since our ideas of modes and relations are formed by the free activity of the mind, without reference to any external archetypes to which they are required to correspond, their reality cannot be dependent upon the fact of such correspondence. It is not, for instance, necessary to show that murder has ever been committed, in order to establish the reality of my idea of murder, or of the proposition that murder ought to be punished; nor is the geometer bound to convince us that the perfect circle, of which he treats, has ever had an actual existence, on pain of being condemned as dealing with mere fantasies. But what, in this case, it may be asked, does the claim to reality signify? Here, at least, Locke tells us, it is sufficient that our ideas are 'so framed that there be a possibility of existing conformable to them[1].' Thus, in the cases supposed, we must know that murder is an action capable of being performed, and that the circle, as the geometer describes it, is at least capable of existing. And such an assurance Locke finds in the case of these ideas in their mere consistency. Our ideas of modes and relations, he declares, cannot be

[1] II. 30. 4.

chimerical, 'unless one will jumble together in them inconsistent ideas[1].' For the reality of these ideas we may, Locke thinks, safely appeal to the rationalistic principle that the non-contradictory is possible or capable of real existence. For our recognition of the origin in experience, and consequent reality, of the simple ideas, which form their necessary basis, gives to these ideas indirectly a point of connection with experience and the real, the want of which is one of the principal defects of rationalism itself.

§ 8. When, however, Locke turns from our ideas of modes and relations to those of substances, and from the objects of the mathematical and moral to those of the natural sciences, he finds that the claim to reality cannot be made good by such an easy and *a priori* method. We are only justified, he maintains, in regarding our knowledge of substances as real, if our ideas of these substances have been derived from actual experience. We must be able to show that the combination of qualities, which constitutes the specific content of our idea, has been actually presented in experience. But while Locke invariably insists upon this fundamental distinction between the conditions of the reality of these two kinds of ideas, the grounds upon which he rests it are not always the same, nor are his explanations entirely consistent with each other.

In Books II and III, in which he is dealing with the reality of our ideas, as distinguished from that of the knowledge into which they enter, he seems to base the distinction upon an intrinsic difference between our ideas of substances and our other complex ideas. In accordance with the ontological view which finds in substances the ultimate constituents of reality, our ideas of substances are supposed to put forward a claim which no other idea

[1] *loc. cit.*

is capable of making. They claim to represent not merely a possible determination of reality but an integral constituent of it. Hence, every proposition about substances involves as such an affirmation of real existence. Substances being themselves self-subsistent beings, our ideas of substances, it is argued, must be intended to represent archetypes which have a real existence in nature. These ideas, therefore, 'carry with them the supposition of some real being, from which they are taken, and to which they are conformable[1].' Accordingly, they lack the reality intended, or are chimerical, if no such real being exists or has existed. Claiming to represent an actual constituent of reality, the reality of an idea of substance could not be made good by merely showing the possibility of an existence conformable to the idea. Hence, writing of such ideas as that of a centaur, Locke tells us that 'whether such substances as these can possibly exist or no, it is probable we do not know: but *be that as it will*, these ideas of substances, being made conformable to no pattern existing that we know, and consisting of such collections of ideas as no substance ever showed us united together, they ought to pass with us for barely imaginary[2].'

At other times, however, when dealing directly with the question of the reality of knowledge, rather than of the ideas upon which it depends, a different position is taken up. Locke no longer insists upon applying a different standard of reality in the case of substances from that which has been accepted as adequate for other complex ideas. Could we only be assured of the possible coexistence in the same being of the various qualities which are involved in an idea of substance, our knowledge, it is now held, would meet all the requirements needed to ensure its reality. The

[1] III. 5. 3.

[2] II. 30. 5 (italics mine).

difficulty which he now finds lies in the impossibility of determining this possibility *a priori* in the case of substances. Thus, in a passage a portion of which has already been quoted, we are told that propositions contain 'real' as distinguished from 'verbal' truth, when the terms are 'joined as our ideas agree, and when our ideas are such as we know are capable of having an existence in nature; which, in substances we cannot know but by knowing that they have existed[1].' And since it is only in experience that the existence of substances is revealed, our ideas of these must be derived from this source, and cannot be obtained by an *a priori* construction, as in the case of other complex ideas.

If it be asked, why an application of the principle of consistency or non-contradiction fails to guarantee the possibility of real existence corresponding to our ideas of substances, while it is held competent to secure this for our ideas of modes and relations, the final ground of difference must be found in the inadequacy of the former ideas as compared with the latter. For since an idea of a mode or a relation only professes to be concerned with an abstract feature of the real world, it is in its own limited way perfect and complete; whereas our ideas of substances always involve the recognition of an unknown remainder. In particular, every material substance possesses a 'real constitution,' which consists of the primary qualities of the minute particles of which it is composed, and upon this its secondary or sensible qualities depend. Now, we can neither know what this real constitution is, nor, were we to know it, or to suppose it, could we comprehend the dependence of the secondary qualities upon it. Hence

[1] IV. 5. 8. It seems here to be implied that the reality of our knowledge of substances would be sufficiently guaranteed could we be assured that our ideas represent possible existents. In this case, however, it is only real existence which can prove a possibility of existence.

it is impossible for us to tell, apart from experience, whether two such qualities are capable of coexisting in the same substance or not. The absence of overt contradiction is in this case no guarantee of real compatibility, since a knowledge of the unknown conditions upon which the sensible qualities depend might reveal a contradiction, although no inconsistency is apparent between these qualities considered in themselves. Accordingly, it is in this inevitable inadequacy of our ideas, when dealing with concrete being, that Locke finds the final hindrance to an *a priori* treatment of substances, similar to that which the mathematician applies to his subject-matter. 'Had we such ideas of substances as to know what real constitutions produce those sensible qualities we find in them, and how those qualities flow from thence, we could, by the specific ideas of their real essences in our own minds, more certainly find out their properties, and discover what qualities they had or had not, than we can now by our senses: and to know the properties of gold, it would be no more necessary that gold should exist, and that we should make experiments upon it, than it is necessary for the knowing the properties of a triangle that a triangle should exist in any matter; the idea in our minds would serve for the one as well as the other[1].'

§ 9. We have now seen wherein, according to Locke, the certainty and reality of our knowledge consists. But although the discovery 'wherein it is that certainty, real certainty, consists,' was signalised by him as one of the most important results of his enquiry, there is a further characteristic upon which he insists as essential, if our knowledge is to escape the charge of triviality. I refer, of course, to the distinction which he draws between

[1] IV. 6. 11.

'instructive' and 'trifling' propositions, in which he anticipates the Kantian classification of judgments as analytical and synthetical.

Under the head of trifling propositions Locke includes both the purely identical propositions, in which a term is predicated of itself, and those analytical propositions, the predicates of which signify some part, but not the whole, of the complex idea of which the subject is a name. Although such propositions are 'certainly true, yet they add no light to our understandings, bring no increase to our knowledge[1]'; the certainty, which they possess, is 'only a verbal certainty, but not instructive[2].' It is true that identical propositions are expressions of an intellectual function which Locke regards as of fundamental importance for knowledge. 'The foundation of all our knowledge,' he holds, 'lies in the faculty we have of perceiving the same idea to be the same, and of discerning it from those that are different[3].' But this is so far from justifying the use of identical propositions for the purpose of instruction, or of extending knowledge, that it is its explicit condemnation. For, such propositions teach nothing but what everyone, who is capable of discourse, knows without being told, viz. that the same term is the same term, and the same idea the same idea[4]. Analytical propositions, again, may serve a useful purpose in helping to explain the meaning of a name to one who is ignorant of it. But their function is confined to this verbal elucidation, and they effect nothing in the way of extending our real knowledge, or knowledge of things. For this purpose it is necessary that the predicate of our proposition should carry us beyond the idea for which its subject stands. While positive knowledge is found in the perception of an agreement between

[1] IV. 8. I [2] IV. 8. 8. [3] IV. 8. 3. [4] *loc. cit.*

ideas, the agreement perceived, in order to be instructive, must be something other than a relation between a whole of content and its part.

The synthetical character of all instructive propositions is asserted by Locke in the most emphatic manner. 'We can know,' he says, 'the truth of two sorts of propositions with perfect certainty. The one is of those trifling propositions which have a certainty in them, but it is only a verbal certainty, but not instructive. And secondly, we can know the truth, and so may be certain in propositions which affirm something of another, which is a necessary consequence of its precise complex idea, but not contained in it: as that the external angle of all triangles is bigger than either of the opposite internal angles; which relation of the outward angle to either of the opposite internal angles making no part of the complex idea signified by the name triangle, this is a real truth, and conveys with it instructive real knowledge[1].' Or, descending from the region of strict knowledge to propositions which, according to Locke, can only claim to be probable, the statements that all men have a notion of God, and that all men are sent to sleep by opium, are, he tells us, instructive propositions; for, 'neither having the notion of God, nor being cast into a sleep by opium, being contained in the idea signified by the word man, we are by such propositions taught something more than barely what the word man stands for[2].'

§ 10. We have now before us Locke's general conception of the nature of knowledge, though we have still to examine his attempt to work it out in detail, in relation to the different forms which knowledge assumes. Before entering upon this further task, however, something must be said of Locke's view of the nature and value of those

[1] IV. 8. 8. [2] IV. 8. 6.

judgments of opinion, which we have seen him contrasting with the judgments of knowledge; and since these judgments, unlike the judgments of knowledge, are capable of being erroneous, the treatment of this question will lead us to the consideration of his theory of error.

In the absence of the perfectly clear and distinct thought which for him constitutes knowledge, the mind is, according to Descartes, in a state of indifference. It still retains, indeed, its ability to affirm or deny, but such affirmation or denial is only effected by a purely arbitrary act of will, and can in no sense be regarded as even an imperfect substitute for knowledge So to judge is, in fact, necessarily to err, even though the judgment happen to be in accordance with fact; would we use our freedom aright, we must in all cases suspend our judgment until it can be determined by the full light of knowledge. 'It is a dictate of the natural light, that the knowledge of the understanding ought always to precede the determination of the will[1],' whether that determination take the form of theoretical judgment or of practical choice. With the theory of his predecessor, thus briefly indicated, Locke is at every point in disagreement.

In the first place, he denies the purely arbitrary character attributed to the judgments of opinion by Descartes. 'As knowledge is no more arbitrary than perception, so, I think, assent is no more in our power than knowledge[2].' The judgment of opinion is always grounded on certain features in the objects of our cognition, which serve as 'inducements' to the mind to accept the proposition as true, although they do not suffice to enable us to see that it is, and must be so. Locke does not, indeed, entirely overlook the presence of purely subjective factors in

[1] Meditation IV.

[2] IV. 20. 16.

determining our beliefs, but the rôle which he assigns to them is subordinate and indirect. Here, as in sense-perception and in knowledge, our will, interests and desires determine the employment or non-employment of our cognitive powers, and help to select the objects with which they are concerned; but our assent in a judgment of opinion, equally with the perceptions of agreement and disagreement which constitute knowledge, is in the last resort determined by the nature of the objects that are before the mind. The inferiority of belief or opinion to knowledge does not lie in the absence of objective determination, but in the fact that the connection asserted is not in this case seen, either immediately or mediately, to be involved in the intrinsic nature of the contents between which it is supposed to subsist. In the absence of intuitive evidence, upon which the possibility of demonstration depends, the mind makes use of 'proofs,' or intervening ideas, 'whose connection is not constant and immutable, or at least is not seen to be so[1].' These serve as 'inducements' to the mind to assent; but, failing to reveal a necessary connection, they yield opinion and not knowledge. 'Herein lies the difference between probability and certainty, faith and knowledge, that in all parts of knowledge there is intuition; each intermediate idea, each step has its visible and certain connection: in belief, not so. That which makes me believe is something extraneous to the thing I believe; something not evidently joined on both sides to, and so not manifestly showing the agreement or disagreement of, those ideas that are under consideration[2].' Thus Locke would say, that I do not strictly know, but only believe, that Julius Caesar invaded Britain, or that all crows are black. For in neither case do I apprehend the

[1] IV. 15. 1. [2] IV. 15. 3.

connection asserted as necessarily involved in the very nature of the objects of my thought. I cannot see that the act of invading Britain is necessarily involved in my idea of Julius Caesar, or that blackness is necessarily connected with the other characteristics by which I recognise a crow. The one statement I accept on the ground of historical testimony; the other I believe on the analogy of my own past experience. But these grounds are merely external supports, 'extraneous to the thing I believe,' which may determine and rightly determine my judgment, but cannot make good the want of inner connection.

In the account which Locke gives of these extraneous grounds of probability, he assumes in general a natural correspondence between their logical cogency and their psychological influence upon the mind. As the 'natural tendency' of the mind is 'towards knowledge,' so, in the dimmer region of conjecture, it is 'the nature of the understanding constantly to close with the more probable side[1].' It was, as has been pointed out, only in the fourth edition of the *Essay* that Locke was led to recognise the influence of 'chance or custom' in producing associations of ideas, and the irrational influence which might thus be exerted upon the judgment; and his account of the grounds of probability and degrees of assent was never revised in view of this new position.

§ 11. A general correspondence being thus supposed to exist between the psychological influence of the objective conditions of belief and their logical value, as indications of a 'likeliness to be true,' the problem of error is formulated by Locke in the form of the question, as to how it is possible for us to form a judgment which is contrary to probability.

[1] IV. 20. 12.

'If assent be grounded on likelihood, if the proper object and motive of our assent be probability...it will be demanded, how men come to give their assents contrary to probability[1].' In so far as the conditions of such wrong assent or error are merely negative, they present no particular difficulty from Locke's point of view. Thus, where there is ignorance of 'proofs' or relevant considerations, or want of skill, or want of will, to use them, the understanding may fall into error, although its assent is strictly in accordance with the logical value of the data upon which it works. He is forced, however, to recognise the existence of more positive causes of error, among which he enumerates the influence exerted upon the mind by preconceived opinions and hypotheses, deference to authority, and 'predominant passions.' These forms of bias lead the mind to check its enquiries and to refuse consideration to unwelcome evidence, in consequence of which the data present to the understanding in judging are artificially limited. That faculty, however, is not itself impaired in the performance of its function. Even in the case of 'predominant passions,' where the presence of a purely subjective factor is most conspicuous, our assent is in the last resort determined, not by us but for us, in accordance with the nature of the objects before the mind and their evidential value.

[1] IV. 20. 1.

CHAPTER VII

THE KINDS AND LIMITS OF KNOWLEDGE

§ 1. Locke's definition of knowledge as 'nothing but the perception of the connection and agreement, or disagreement and repugnancy of any of our ideas,' is at once followed by a classification of knowledge, based upon the different forms which may be assumed by the agreement or disagreement in question. 'To understand a little more distinctly wherein this agreement or disagreement consists, I think we may reduce it all to these four sorts: (1) Identity or diversity. (2) Relation. (3) Coexistence, or necessary connection. (4) Real existence[1].' That a formal objection may be taken to this division, on the ground that the species enumerated are not mutually exclusive, since identity and 'coexistence or necessary connection' are themselves relations, Locke is himself fully aware. These are, however, he maintains, 'so peculiar ways of agreement or disagreement,' and involve 'so different grounds of affirmation and denial' that they 'deserve well to be considered as distinct heads, and not under relation in general[2].' We shall find, indeed, that the above classification is little more than a preliminary survey of the ground, serving to set in relief the various topics to which Locke thinks it necessary to call special attention, but which does not adequately represent his final view of the different types of knowledge.

[1] IV. I. 3. [2] IV. I. 7.

§ 2. When 'identity or diversity' is spoken of by Locke as one of the four kinds of agreement or disagreement, it must be borne in mind that it is not the identity of a concrete individual, or even of an idea as a psychical occurrence, which is in question, but the identity of the content of an idea and its distinction from that of every other idea. Now a recognition of identity in this sense is, he holds, involved in the very meaning of an idea. 'It is the first act of the mind, when it has any sentiments or ideas at all, to perceive its ideas; and, so far as it perceives them, to know each what it is, and thereby also to perceive their difference, and that one is not another. This is so absolutely necessary that without it there could be no knowledge, no reasoning, no imagination, no distinct thoughts at all[1].' But although this ability to identify and discriminate the contents of our ideas is 'the foundation of all our knowledge[2],' it does not of itself afford us any 'positive knowledge' at all[3]. For the identical propositions which result from this identification of an idea with itself are, as we have seen, only examples of those 'trifling' propositions which are incapable of conveying or expressing any real knowledge. Hence, as Locke himself describes it, this first form of agreement or disagreement of ideas constitutes a necessary presupposition, rather than a kind, of knowledge. It may, in fact, be regarded as the point of transition, from the operation of the understanding which consists in the mere 'perception of ideas in our minds[4],' to the further form of perception which constitutes knowledge.

§ 3. Having insisted upon the abstract identity of the content of each idea, Locke is confronted with the necessity of explaining the possibility of predication in accordance with this view. For, if every idea is identical

[1] IV. I. 4. [2] IV. 8. 3. [3] IV. I. 5. [4] II. 21. 5.

with itself, and distinct from every other, how can one idea be affirmed of another? And yet, as we have seen, to affirm each of itself, and to deny its identity with any other, yields no positive knowledge at all. Locke's solution of the difficulty consists in pointing out that significant predication involves the assertion, not of bare identity or diversity, but of other and more determinate relations between the contents of our ideas. In confirmation of this, he points out that we cannot predicate one abstract noun of another which signifies a different abstract idea. 'All our affirmations, then, are only in concrete, which is the affirming, not one abstract idea to be another, but one abstract idea to be joined to another[1].' Had Locke developed further the significance of the reference to concrete being, which is here stated to be involved in all predication, he would greatly have strengthened his general position. Apart from this new and valuable suggestion, what is here stated is only an explicit recognition of the relational nature of knowledge which was already involved in Locke's definition of it. And since there are many ways in which ideas may be thus 'joined' or related to each other, the inevitable tendency of his logic is towards the recognition of a plurality of relational forms of propositions. So far from the subject-predicate relation being regarded by Locke as the fundamental type, to which all others must be reduced, it is itself regarded by him as secondary and derivative. Propositions in which a quality is predicated of a substance are, he holds, in so far as they express definite knowledge, assertions of relations of concomitance between contents. Thus, he tells us, that the proposition '*a man is white* signifies that the thing that has the essence of

[1] III. 8. I.

a man has also in it the essence of whiteness....*A man is rational* signifies that the same thing that hath the essence of a man hath also in it the essence of rationality[1].'

§ 4. We are thus driven on, from the consideration of the identity and diversity of our ideas to that of the specific relations which are apprehended between their contents, the perception of which constitutes Locke's second kind of agreement or disagreement of our ideas. Or, to put the matter in his own words: 'Since all distinct ideas must eternally be known not to be the same, and so be universally and constantly denied one of another, there could be no room for any positive knowledge at all, if we could not perceive any relation between our ideas, and find out the agreement or disagreement they have one with another in several ways the mind takes of comparing them[2].' The knowledge which Locke includes under the second of his four divisions is that which consists of a perception of relations between our abstract ideas, or between the content of one idea and that of another, when abstraction has been made of the spacial, temporal and other circumstances of sensible existence. It is assumed, and the assumption is fundamental for Locke's theory of scientific knowledge, that when abstraction has thus been made from the conditions of concrete existence, the contents thus conceived are not merely self-identical and isolated units, but are found to be definitely connected with each other by relations, which can be apprehended by our thought when it considers them. These relations are expressly distinguished from the relation of a whole of content to its parts, the statement of which would only yield analytical and consequently trifling propositions. These relations, moreover, being involved in the very

[1] *loc. cit.* [2] IV. I. 5.

nature of our abstract ideas, are perceived to be necessary. Thus this kind of knowledge complies in every respect with the requirements of Locke's general conception of knowledge, and constitutes its typical exemplification. Such knowledge, moreover, is universal, its universality being involved in the abstract character of its ground. For a relation which is seen to be involved in the very nature of certain abstract ideas must hold good in all cases in which these abstract contents receive embodiment in concrete being. Finally, the propositions which set forth these relations between abstract ideas may be designated as 'eternal verities.' Since the ideas in question have been expressly abstracted from all temporal conditions, their relations cannot be subject to temporal change. 'Names being supposed to stand perpetually for the same ideas, and the same ideas having immutably the same habitudes one to another, propositions concerning any abstract ideas that are once true must needs be eternal verities[1].' At the same time he insists that this time-transcending characteristic of abstract truth must be freed from the mystery and from the metaphysical implications which had been connected with it by the Cambridge Platonists and others. *Aeternae veritates* do not constitute a peculiar kind of universal propositions, distinguished from others by the special dignity and worth of their subject-matter; on the contrary, Locke declares 'all general truths are eternal verities[2].' Nor, again, does their eternal nature imply their innateness in the mind of man, or any special value as representative of a reality beyond the mind. 'Such propositions are, therefore, called *eternal truths*, not

[1] IV. II. 14.

[2] Letter to Molyneux of August 23rd, 1693, *Works*, vol. IX. p. 327. It should be noticed that Locke does not maintain that truth as such is independent of time, but only that universal truths are so.

because they are eternal propositions actually formed, and antecedent to the understanding that at any time makes them; nor because they are imprinted on the mind from any patterns that are anywhere out of the mind, and existed before; but because, being once made about abstract ideas so as to be true, they will, whenever they can be supposed to be made again at any time, past or to come, by a mind having those ideas, always actually be true[1].'

§ 5. Turning now from the general characteristics of this kind of knowledge to the truths by which in Locke's opinion it is exemplified, we find that his illustrations are almost invariably drawn from the propositions of arithmetic and geometry. It must not be supposed, indeed, that he considers such knowledge to be confined to the sphere of quantity. Thus, it is a perception of a relation of this kind between our abstract ideas which, in his view, constitutes the justification of the universal principles by which every mode is referred to a substance and every occurrence to a cause. For, although Locke thinks that he has shown that our ideas of substance and cause originate in experience, he holds that experience cannot constitute the logical justification of these or any other strictly universal principles. His view of the subject is most explicitly stated in the course of his controversy with Stillingfleet, but in a manner quite in accordance with the doctrine of the *Essay*. He there explains that '*Everything that has a beginning must have a cause*, is a true principle of reason, or a proposition certainly true; which we come to know by the same way, *i.e.* by contemplating our ideas, and perceiving that the idea of beginning to be is necessarily connected with the idea of some operation, and the idea of operation with the idea of something operating,

[1] IV. II. 14.

which we call a cause; and so, the beginning to be is perceived to agree with the idea of a cause, as is expressed in the proposition[1].' It is a similar necessity which compels us to refer the data of experience to a *substratum*, since we find ourselves unable to conceive them as self-subsisting, or as merely dependent upon one another.

§ 6. But single principles of this kind, however important they may be, do not of themselves constitute a body of scientific knowledge; whereas, the peculiar characteristics of relational knowledge show themselves in the most striking way in the systems of rationally connected truths which constitute demonstrative science. Demonstration itself, it is clear, is dependent upon our ability to perceive intuitively relations of necessary connection between the contents of our ideas, since we can only mediately perceive an agreement or disagreement between two ideas if each of these is seen to stand in some necessary relation to a third. Accordingly, in connection with the question of the extent of our relational knowledge, Locke discusses the possibility of applying the demonstrative method to different subject-matters.

In the mathematical sciences, and in these alone, was Locke able to find such a rationally systematised body of knowledge, already worked out. Accordingly, for him, as for most of his contemporaries, these sciences constituted the ideal, by reference to which other departments of knowledge were criticised and their short-comings revealed. But notwithstanding the predominant influence of mathematical conceptions and of the mathematical ideal, Locke does not follow Descartes in proclaiming *a priori* the universal applicability of the mathematical method. The possible extent of demonstrative science should, he holds,

[1] First Letter to Stillingfleet, *Works*, vol. IV. pp. 61–2.

be made the subject of a careful enquiry, which must seek to discover the reasons for the present unique position of mathematics, and to ascertain what other subject-matters, if any, are intrinsically capable of similar rational treatment.

It is fundamental for Locke's view of the mathematical sciences that they are not concerned directly with sensible or concrete existences but with ideal constructions. It is essential, indeed, as we have seen, for the 'reality' of these sciences, that we should know that these ideas are capable of embodiment in the real world; and this assurance Locke thinks we possess. But that the truth of a mathematical proposition is in any way dependent on the existence of objects conforming to its ideas, he emphatically denies. Its reference to real existence is purely hypothetical. The proposition implies that the relation which it expresses between our ideas will hold good of real things, if and in so far as real things exist corresponding to these ideas. 'The mathematician considers the truth and properties belonging to a rectangle or circle only as they are in idea in his own mind. For it is possible he never found either of them existing mathematically, *i.e.* precisely true, in his life. But yet the knowledge he has of any truths or properties belonging to a circle, or any other mathematical figure, are nevertheless true and certain, even of real things existing; because real things are no further concerned, nor intended to be meant by any such propositions, than as things really agree to those archetypes in his mind[1].' But this abstraction from the conditions of concrete existence, upon which the possibility of demonstrative science depends, seems at first sight capable of being made in reference to other modes and relations besides those of

[1] IV. 4. 6.

quantity. We must, therefore, enquire whether our spacial and numerical ideas possess any distinctive characteristics which render them alone, or in a pre-eminent degree, capable of demonstrative treatment. The question is one to which Locke recurs again and again.

§ 7. 'The reason why it (*i.e.* demonstration) has been generally sought for and supposed to be only in those (*i.e.* the mathematical sciences), I imagine has been, not only the general usefulness of those sciences, but because, in comparing their equality or excess, the modes of numbers have every the least difference very clear and perceivable: and though in extension every the least excess is not so perceptible, yet the mind has found out ways to examine, and discover demonstratively, the just equality of two angles, or extensions, or figures; and both these, *i.e.* numbers and figures, can be set down by visible and lasting marks, wherein the ideas under consideration are perfectly determined; which for the most part they are not, where they are marked only by names and words[1].' In this passage Locke summarises his view of the characteristics which render our mathematical ideas more readily capable of demonstrative treatment than others. Since a distinction is made between arithmetic and geometry in this respect, we must consider the two cases separately.

The demonstrative character of the science of number is made to rest primarily upon the perfect determination or precision of the ideas with which it is concerned, which in turn is dependent upon the discreteness of its subject-matter. As we are told elsewhere, the simple modes of number are 'of all other the most distinct; every the least variation, which is an unit, making each combination as clearly different from that which approacheth nearest to

[1] IV. 2. 10.

it, as the most remote; two being as distinct from one as two hundred, and the idea of two as distinct from the idea of three as the magnitude of the whole earth is from that of a mite. This is not so in other simple modes, in which it is not so easy, nor perhaps possible, for us to distinguish betwixt two approaching ideas, which yet are really different[1].' As a result of this perfect precision and definiteness of our ideas of numbers, the relations which subsist between them are at once laid bare to the mind's intuitive power. Simple arithmetical propositions, such as $3 = 2 + 1$, are declared to be apprehended by the irresistible light of intuition and are regarded as furnishing the foundation of the whole structure of the science. That such propositions are 'instructive' or synthetic is nowhere expressly stated, but to suppose that the science of arithmetic is built up by means of 'trifling' propositions would be to run counter to Locke's whole teaching on the subject.

Turning, now, to the case of geometry, we are told that it suffers under a disadvantage as compared with arithmetic, since 'in extension every the least excess is not so perceptible' as in numbers. The continuous nature of extension renders it impossible for us to distinguish with the same ease and certainty every difference in this kind of quantity. Since, however, geometry is not in Locke's view concerned with the sensible extensions of particular figures, except in so far as these may be employed to represent the universal ideas with which the science properly deals, the difference here insisted upon would appear to be one in the application of geometrical propositions to sensible existences rather than in their intrinsic nature. It is at all events not regarded by Locke as creating any real difficulty in the intuitive apprehension of relations

[1] II. 16. 3.

between these ideas, as the result of what he calls their 'juxtaposition' or 'immediate application' to each other. The point upon which he insists, as the peculiar glory of geometry, is the success with which the mind has 'found out ways to examine and discover demonstratively the just equality of two angles or extensions or figures,' by the use of intermediate ideas or 'proofs.' We must, I think, understand Locke to refer here primarily to the method of ideal superposition as employed in the geometry of Euclid, the only geometry in which he was really at home, though the recent application of algebra to the solution of geometrical problems was also in his mind, and appeared to him full of promise for other branches of knowledge as well[1].

The further advantage, which he assigns to arithmetic and geometry in common, is the use of 'visible and lasting marks, wherein the ideas under consideration are perfectly determined.' In the case of geometry, it is, of course, the employment of a sensible diagram which is referred to. Its value, in Locke's opinion, lies in its checking the tendency to variation in our ideas, by which one idea is unintentionally substituted for another, which constitutes so great and subtle a danger in our thinking. 'Diagrams drawn on paper are copies of the ideas in the mind, and not liable to the uncertainty that words carry in their signification. An angle, circle or square, drawn in lines, lies open to the view, and cannot be mistaken: it remains unchangeable, and may at leisure be considered and examined, and the demonstration be revised, and all the parts

[1] 'Who knows what methods to enlarge our knowledge in other branches of science may hereafter be invented, answering that of algebra in mathematics, which so readily finds out ideas of quantities to measure others by, whose equality or proportion we could otherwise very hardly or perhaps never come to know?' (IV. 12. 15).

of it may be gone over more than once, without any danger of the least change in the ideas[1].' It will be observed that the diagram itself is not the subject of the demonstration, but the 'ideas in the mind' of which it is a copy, its use to the geometer being, as he says elsewhere, 'steadily to suggest to his mind those several ideas he would make use of in that demonstration[2].' Moreover, as a common object of perception, it serves not only to guard against fluctuations in our own ideas, but to secure a common understanding with others.

A somewhat similar purpose is, Locke thinks, performed for arithmetic by the use of numerical symbols, although it cannot be claimed that these are 'copies' of our ideas of numbers themselves. That they do not fully perform the same functions as the geometrical diagram is implied in the remark that these symbols 'help not the mind at all to perceive the agreements of any two or more numbers, *that* the mind has only by intuition of its own ideas of the numbers themselves[3].' Their usefulness, accordingly, he declares, is limited to their aid to the memory in fixing in an unambiguous and lasting manner the results of our previous intuitions.

While the above characteristics account, in Locke's opinion, for the greater progress which has been made in the mathematical sciences, and explain the commonly received view that in these alone is demonstration possible, they do not, he considers, constitute an intrinsic superiority of the subject-matter of these sciences over all others in this respect, or justify the assumption that demonstration is necessarily confined to them. In so far as the advantages of arithmetic and geometry are conceived by him to consist in the use of artificial aids, by which the

[1] IV. 3. 19. [2] *Works*, vol. IV. p. 59. [3] IV. 3. 19.

requisite ideas are 'steadily suggested to the mind,' there seems no reason why similar aids should not be made use of with equal success in the investigation of other ideas; and Locke, as we have seen, is not without hope of what may be effected elsewhere by the aid of 'algebra or some thing of that kind.' For the rest, it is not anything in the intrinsic nature of our ideas of numbers or space upon which the demonstrative character of the sciences which deal with them depends; but in the one case the superior precision with which their content is determined, and in the other the fact that we have 'found ways' of indirectly establishing relations of equality. In one startling passage we are even told that, although our ideas of colours suffer from the disadvantage that we can neither 'perceive' nor 'find ways to measure' their 'degrees' with accuracy, yet, 'where the difference is so great as to produce in the mind clearly distinct ideas, whose differences can be perfectly retained, these ideas of colours, as we see in different kinds, as blue and red, are as capable of demonstration as ideas of number and extension. What I have here said of whiteness and colours, I think, holds true in all secondary qualities and their modes[1].' Although we must not take this to imply that these ideas of secondary qualities are as rich in intuitive connections, or as capable of systematic elaboration, the passage shows how strong was the tendency in Locke to assimilate our other ideas to those of quantity.

§ 8. It is perhaps not surprising that this inclination to minimise the peculiarities of the mathematical sciences should find its counterpart in a tendency to extend mathematical conceptions to the whole range of knowledge. Thus, we find Locke speaking of intuition in general, by

[1] IV. 2. 13.

which relations are apprehended between ideas, whatever the nature of these may be, as consisting in the 'juxtaposition' of ideas or in their 'immediate application' to one another. In a similar strain the employment of an intermediate idea or 'proof' in demonstration is compared to the use of a yard measure, for the purpose of comparing magnitudes which cannot be 'immediately applied' to one another or 'juxtaposed.' In fact, not only do the mathematical sciences furnish him with his most frequent illustrations of those necessary synthetic connections, the perception of which constitutes universal and instructive knowledge, but they colour his whole conception of knowledge. And while algebra may be spoken of, in a vague way, as a useful device for the advancement of knowledge, it is geometry, with its method of ideal superposition, which really furnishes the operative content of Locke's thought on the whole matter.

§ 9. It is in respect of ethics that Locke proclaims most definitely and with the greatest insistence the possibility of extending the application of the demonstrative method beyond the region of quantity, and we must now proceed to consider his conception of this science. In order to make clear his view of the subject it will be necessary to notice briefly his general view of ethics, which will be found to combine positions which have not often been held in conjunction. In the first place, while denying that the mind is always determined by the prospect of pleasure, or aversion to pain, he maintains that good and evil are 'nothing but pleasure or pain, or that which occasions or procures pleasure or pain to us[1].' Moral differs from natural good or evil simply by the fact that the pleasure or pain, to which it is relative, is such as is

[1] II. 28. 5.

attached by the maker of some law to its observance or non-observance, as distinguished from that which is 'the natural product and consequence of the action itself[1].' Without such 'sanctions,' to use the term of a later school of moralists, a moral law would, in Locke's opinion, be without force or obligation. Of laws he distinguishes three kinds. First, the civil law, with its definite rewards and punishments. Secondly, the law of opinion or reputation, with its less definite but not less real sanctions, of praise or blame, for actions which conform to or depart from the standards of conduct current in a particular society. Although this law of opinion is found to conform to the general rule that 'those actions are esteemed virtuous which are thought absolutely necessary to the preservation of society, and those that disturb or dissolve the bonds of community are everywhere esteemed ill and vicious[2]'; and although, consequently, 'as to the main,' virtue and vice are 'for the most part kept the same everywhere[3]'; such a standard is relative to some particular society, and could not be made the subject of a demonstrative science. A good deal of prejudice was created among Locke's contemporaries by his declaration that the law of opinion is 'the measure of virtue and vice,' which are consequently relative to conventional estimates of conduct. It is not, however, with these variable judgments of value that ethics, according to him, is properly concerned, but with the content of the divine law, which constitutes 'the unchangeable rule of right and wrong[4].' To this third and final kind of law the law of opinion ought to correspond, although it does not always do so. Finally, while he believed that the law imposed upon men by the

[1] II. 28. 6. [2] Paper 'Of Ethics in General,' Lord King, p. 309.
[3] II. 28. 11. [4] *loc. cit.*

divine will had been made the subject of revelation, he also maintained that its content could be ascertained by 'the light of nature.' It is the 'law of nature,' which expresses the divine will for man as such, and is capable of being learned by the proper use of our rational faculties, that Locke declares to be capable of demonstration. Thus in Locke's conception of ethics we find a denial of psychological hedonism combined with a strictly hedonistic theory of the nature of the good; while the insistence on the need of a theological basis, and of an appeal to sanctions, is united with a rational *a priori* method of determining what actions are right or wrong. It is, of course, with the nature of this method and the resulting judgments that we are here specially concerned.

§ 10. Locke's theory of demonstrative ethics is built upon the conception that ethics is, like mathematics, an abstract science, concerned with relations between the contents of certain abstract ideas, uncomplicated by the necessity of reference to the actual conditions of concrete existence. As in geometry we treat of the nature of the circle as such, without needing to consider whether this figure as defined has ever actually existed in the real world, so in ethics we deal with the abstract nature of certain actions, irrespective of their actual performance by men. Assuming, further, that the relations between the latter kind of ideas are as capable of intuitive apprehension and rational systematisation as those which belong to quantity, Locke held that universal propositions concerning certain kinds of actions could be demonstrated in the same manner, and with the same certainty, as mathematical conclusions. To constitute such knowledge 'real' the propositions in question must, indeed, be assumed to refer to actions which are known to be possible; and like the theorems of mathematics they involve a hypothetical reference to concrete real actions. But their combination of universality and certainty depends on the abstraction which has been made in their formulation from the circumstances of real existence. An important difference between ethics and mathematics would appear to result from the fact that, in Locke's view, the content of our abstract apprehension of moral relations possesses no genuine ethical significance until it has been shown to be an expression of the divine will. Thus, after all, ethics has its basis in an existential proposition asserting the real existence of God. This proposition, however, is one which is regarded by Locke as differing in kind from the propositions which merely assert existence on the ground of some particular experience. For, while these latter are always wanting in the apprehension of the intellectual necessity, which is essential to knowledge in the strict sense of the term, the existence of the Divine Being is held to be a matter of demonstration, and to possess a certainty which is only shared among existential propositions by the affirmation of my own existence. Hence, the necessity of a reference to it did not appear to Locke to detract from the demonstrative character of the science. 'The idea of a Supreme Being, infinite in power, goodness and wisdom, whose workmanship we are, and on whom we depend, and the idea of ourselves as understanding, rational creatures, being such as are clear in us, would, I suppose, if duly considered and pursued, afford such foundation of our duty and rules of action as might place morality amongst the sciences capable of demonstration; wherein, I doubt not, but from self-evident propositions, by necessary consequences, as incontestable as those in mathematics, the measures of right and wrong might be made out, to any one that will apply himself with the same indifferency and attention to the one as he does to the other of these sciences[1].'

Beyond the assertion of this general point of view, however, the *Essay* does not go. At the beginning of their correspondence, Molyneux expressed a wish that he would 'think of obliging the world with a treatise of morals, drawn up according to the hints you frequently give in the *Essay*, of being demonstrable, according to the mathematical method[2].' To this request, Locke replied that it is one thing to see that morality is capable of demonstrative treatment, and another thing to work out the demonstration; but promised, nevertheless, to turn his thoughts to the matter. Molyneux returned to the point again, and was not the only one who incited him to the attempt. In the end, though Locke was able to assure his correspondent that he had laid by some materials for the purpose, the intention was never carried out. The task, he was inclined to think, was too great for 'one in my age and health.' Besides, the gospel containing 'so perfect a body of ethics,' it seemed to him that 'reason may be excused from that enquiry, since she may find man's duty clearer and easier in revelation than in herself'; and that his own time and strength might be better spent 'in other researches,' in which he found himself 'more in the dark[3].' It is probable that Locke realised more fully the difficulties of the undertaking the more he thought about it. There seems, indeed, some indication of this in the changes of expression introduced in the fourth edition of the *Essay*, in which, while the demonstrability of ethics is still maintained, the position is put forward with somewhat greater reserve than in the earlier editions. If, in

[1] IV. 3. 18. [2] *Works*, vol. IX. p. 291.
[3] *Works*, vol. IX. p. 377.

conclusion, we consider the examples which Locke gives, in the *Essay*, of intuitive and demonstrative knowledge concerning moral ideas, we shall not find the outlook for the new science very promising. 'Property' being defined as 'a right to anything' and 'injustice' as 'the invasion or violation of that right,' it certainly follows that 'where there is no property, there is no injustice.' Or, to take his other illustration, 'the idea of government being the establishment of society upon certain rules or laws, which require conformity to them, and the idea of absolute liberty being for anyone to do whatever he pleases,' we may indeed declare with confidence that 'no government allows absolute liberty[1].' But it is not easy to see how either proposition could be defended against the charge of trifling. The fact that he compares the first of these examples to the demonstration that the internal angles of a triangle are equal to two right angles, only serves to show that, notwithstanding his insistence upon the necessity for synthesis for 'instructive' propositions, Locke here fails to maintain the distinction between the old view, that the sciences can be extracted by a process of analysis from definitions, and the more adequate theory which he seeks to put in its place.

§ 11. From the knowledge which consists in perceiving relations between our abstract ideas, Locke distinguishes, in his classification, a knowledge of 'coexistence or necessary connection.' What Locke has in mind is really a distinction between the relations which our thought discovers between the contents of our ideas, when abstraction is made from the conditions of actual existence, and the special relations which are involved in the fact of concrete existence itself. The conception of substance being regarded as the fundamental category for the interpretation of the real, these

[1] IV. 3. 18.

relations are conceived as primarily relations of coexistence or incompatibility of existence between determinations of the same substantial being.

It will be observed that in accordance with the requirements of Locke's general conception of knowledge, our knowledge of coexistence is spoken of as a knowledge of *necessary* connections. Where this necessity is wanting, not only are we 'utterly incapable of universal and certain knowledge[1],' but the general requirements of our ideal of knowledge are not themselves fully met. Thus, when Locke declares that our knowledge of this kind is 'very short, though in this consists the greatest and most material part of our knowledge concerning substances[2],' what he means is not that we can only make a small number of statements concerning coexistence, but that such propositions are mostly wanting in intellectual necessity. In some few cases, indeed, he thinks this is present. That 'figure necessarily supposes extension[3],' that 'receiving or communicating motion by impulse supposes solidity[4],' that 'two bodies cannot be in the same place[5],' and that the same subject cannot have more than one determination of the same primary quality or more than one sensible idea peculiar to each sense at the same time[6], are given as examples of propositions concerning coexistence which possess the same necessity and universality as our knowledge of relations between our abstract ideas. The difficulty is to defend them against the charge of 'trifling,' and to justify their separate classification. Apart, however, from a few propositions of this kind, Locke maintains that we can make no statements concerning coexistence which are at once certain and universal. We must notice the grounds of this contention.

[1] IV. 3. 28. [2] IV. 3. 9. [3] IV. 3. 14. [4] *loc. cit.* [5] IV. 7. 5. [6] IV. 3. 15.

§ 12. We have already seen that our thought is unable to determine, apart from a reference to experience, even the possibility of the coexistence of the sensible qualities, and of the powers of modifying the qualities of other bodies, which make up the chief part of our ideas of material substances. It is clearly still less capable of determining *a priori* a necessity of coexistence. Failing to discover intuitive connections between the abstract ideas of these qualities and powers, we must, perforce, resort to experience for our knowledge of coexistence. That our senses 'inform us' of the coexistence of various qualities in the same subject appears to Locke obvious. Such knowledge, however, he maintains, is confined to particular instances, which are incapable of furnishing the basis of a knowledge which is universal. For experience cannot yield the intellectual necessity by which we see that a connection cannot be otherwise, and without this there can be no strictly universal knowledge. The connection as given in experience is merely one of fact, and however frequent and uniform its occurrence may be, any extension to cases which have not been actually experienced is a matter of probability and not of knowledge. Thus, 'we cannot with certainty affirm that all men sleep at intervals, that no man can be nourished by wood or stones, that all men will be poisoned by hemlock, however highly probable these propositions may be[1].' In fine, 'coexistence can be no further known than it is perceived,' and where it cannot be perceived 'in general, by the necessary connection of the ideas themselves,' it can only be known 'in particular subjects by the observation of our senses[2].' Since science consists of certain and universal truths, this particularity of our

[1] IV. 6. 15.   [2] IV. 3. 14.

knowledge of coexistence has for Locke the important consequence of placing a science of physical nature beyond our reach. He is 'apt to doubt that, how far soever human industry may advance useful and experimental philosophy in physical things, scientifical will still be out of our reach[1],' and even declares that it would be 'lost labour' to seek after 'a perfect science of natural bodies[2].' It must be observed, however, that Locke regards this result as mainly due to the particular limitations of the human mind, rather than to any ultimate want of rational connection in the kind of reality in question. Though we can only refer the factual connections which experience reveals to the good pleasure of God, it does not follow that they are in themselves arbitrary. In the very passage in which he tells us that we cannot know that man is incapable of being nourished by wood or stones, he goes on to speak of the 'real constitution' of man, 'which is the root wherein all his inseparable qualities are united and from whence they flow[3].' Even when he seems to sound in anticipation the very note of the scepticism of Hume, he reaffirms the theory of real essences. It remains, in his view, 'past doubt there must be some real constitution, on which any collection of simple ideas coexisting must depend[4].'

This real constitution or essence being held to consist of the primary qualities of the insensible parts of body, Locke is led to speculate as to the possibility of a science of natural phenomena, upon the assumption of an improvement in our ideas of this minute structure. Could we obtain adequate ideas of the real essences of bodies, we would be able, he thinks, to determine *a priori*, in a demonstrative manner, the various modifications which take place as the result of their interactions. 'Did we know

[1] IV. 3. 26. [2] IV. 3. 29. [3] IV. 6. 15. [4] III. 3. 15.

the mechanical affections of the particles of rhubarb, hemlock, opium, and a man, as a watchmaker does those of a watch, whereby it performs its operations; and of a file, which, by rubbing on them, will alter the figure of any of the wheels; we should be able to tell beforehand that rhubarb will purge, hemlock kill, and opium make a man sleep: as well as a watchmaker can, that a little piece of paper laid on the balance will keep the wheels from going till it be removed; or that, some small part of it being rubbed by a file, the machine would quite lose its motion, and the watch go no more[1].'

Such a science as this presents itself to Locke as a possible extension of our present knowledge, since we are at least able to conceive necessary relations of interdependence among the mathematical and mechanical properties of matter, although those which experience reveals, such as the communication of motion by impulse, are not always thoroughly comprehensible. The chief bar to such knowledge lies, he thinks, in the inability of our senses to afford us ideas of the minute constitution of matter. But even if the possibility of such a science could be realised, the world of physical fact, as revealed in experience, would not be rendered completely intelligible. There would still remain 'another and more incurable part of ignorance[2].' For the objects of experience possess secondary or sensible qualities, and for their complete comprehension it would not only be necessary to discover the mathematical and mechanical determinations upon which these appearances depend, but to apprehend the manner in which they flow from them. But this we can never hope to do, since we are unable even to conceive in thought a necessary connection between factors so heterogeneous. 'We are

[1] IV. 3. 25. [2] IV. 3. 12.

so far from knowing what figure, size, or motion of parts produce a yellow colour, a sweet taste, or a sharp sound, that we can by no means conceive how any size, figure, or motion of any particles can possibly produce in us the idea of any colour, taste, or sound whatsoever; there is no conceivable connection between the one and the other[1].' Hence, even if we could discover the features of the real essence upon which these elements of sensible experience depend, our knowledge of this dependence would be barely factual or experiential, and as such wanting in perfect intelligibility.

It is in the immediacy of sensible experience, therefore, that Locke finds the final and insurmountable obstacle to a rational or scientific treatment of the physical world. And parallel to the impossibility of understanding the manner of production of the sensible appearances of things is the similar impossibility of conceiving how our minds can operate upon our bodies. From both sides the connection, which experience assures us exists, between our subjective consciousness and the spacial world, is found to be unintelligible. But even in this extreme case of discontinuity Locke does not doubt the reality of the relation of interdependence. Although, like the Occasionalists, he makes his final appeal to the will of God, this is not represented as producing an appearance of interaction where there is none in reality, but as endowing body and mind with powers of operating upon each other which are to us incomprehensible. The connection, he declares, is one which we can attribute 'to nothing else but the arbitrary determination of that all-wise Agent, who has made them to be, and to operate as they do, in a way wholly above our weak understandings to conceive[2].'

[1] IV. 3. 13. [2] IV. 3. 28.

The great majority, then, of our propositions concerning coexistence, are propositions which merely assert the coexistence of certain qualities in a particular subject or substance, on the ground of experience, and generalisations of such particular statements, which cannot claim to possess more than probability. But such propositions are in reality existential propositions, affirming the existence at some particular time of a substance possessing at once these particular qualities. As Locke puts it, 'all particular affirmations or negations that would not be certain if they were made general are only concerning existence; they declaring only the accidental union or separation of ideas in things existing, which in their abstract natures have no known necessary union or repugnancy[1].'

§ 13. No severer test can be applied to a general theory of knowledge than to ask how it works when it is applied to existential judgments; and it must be admitted that the question is one which causes Locke considerable embarrassment. His whole treatment of the subject is unfortunately very scanty, considering its importance, and is almost entirely concerned with the peculiarities of judgments concerning the existence of different kinds of objects, the questions of principle raised by existential judgments as such receiving only slight and incidental recognition. But it is just here that his theory has to meet a most formidable objection. For the recognition of a knowledge of real existence stands in formal contradiction to his general definition of knowledge, as consisting in 'nothing but the perception of the connection and agreement or disagreement and repugnancy of any of our ideas.' However much we may insist upon the objective character of Locke's ideas, the existential

[1] IV. 9. I.

judgment which declares that the content of my idea characterises something actually existing, cannot be represented as merely setting forth a connection of ideas. While the difficulty first meets us here in an acute form, it is one which has been waiting in the background all the time. For throughout his treatment of knowledge there has been involved an implicit reference to a real world distinct from our ideas. Indeed, the distinction between the four kinds of knowledge may be regarded, from one point of view, as a progressive correction of the abstraction of ideas from reality. It is only in our knowledge of the self-identity and abstract difference of our ideas that no reference at all is involved to a world of reality distinct from them; and such knowledge, we have seen, is unworthy of the name, being neither 'positive' nor 'instructive.' Our knowledge of relations between abstract ideas, although independent of the existence of anything corresponding to them, involves, in its claim to be 'real,' the recognition of a world of being in which these contents are capable of realisation. Our knowledge of coexistence, even in the cases in which it is intuitive and *a priori*, is a knowledge of the necessary existence together of certain determinations 'in the same subject,' by which Locke implies that the connection is one which actually holds good in the real world, as distinguished from mere relations between abstract ideas, which may or may not find realisation there. And in all but these few cases our knowledge of coexistences has been found to be nothing but a knowledge of the existence of particular concrete substances, in which experience has shown that the contents of the ideas in question are realised together. In proceeding to treat of our knowledge of real existence Locke is dealing, then, with something which has gradually asserted itself as an essential factor in all genuine knowledge, however inconsistent it may appear with his general definition of knowledge. While, therefore, on the one hand, it cannot be said that the claim to a knowledge of real existence is suddenly introduced as an *addendum* to an exposition of knowledge, which has hitherto moved solely among ideas; on the other hand, it must be admitted, that the difficulties which Locke's theory has to meet, in its attempt to deal with existential judgments, are difficulties which are also involved, although in a less striking manner, in his accounts of the other kinds of knowledge.

§ 14. The abstract opposition between the idea and real existence is stated by Locke in its most acute form. Not only are the two in general entirely distinct, but there is, he declares, no means by which a direct transition can be effected from the one to the other. For, 'the having the idea of anything in our mind no more proves the existence of that thing, than the picture of a man evidences his being in the world, or the visions of a dream make thereby a true history[1].' To the truth of this general contention a single exception had been alleged in the ontological argument for the existence of God, which had been recently revived and given an extended currency by Descartes. This argument maintained that the conception of God being that of the *ens realissimum*, or of a being possessing every positive quality or perfection; and existence being a perfection; the proposition, 'God exists,' could not be denied without contradiction. The existence of God was thus held to be established as a necessity of thought, without an appeal to anything but the idea of God itself. The validity of this proof was left undiscussed in the *Essay*, where Locke contented himself

[1] IV. II. I.

with entering a protest against the tendency, which he thought existed among the Cartesians, to belittle all other arguments in the interest of this favourite one[1]. It is, however, expressly rejected in his First Letter to Stillingfleet[2], and forms the subject of a paper, dated 1696, in the collection published by Lord King[3]. The objection which is there taken to the celebrated argument is based upon the principle already laid down in the *Essay*. 'By ideas in the mind we discover the agreement or disagreement of ideas that have a like ideal existence in our minds; but that reaches no further, proves no real existence; for the truth we so know is only of our ideas, and is applicable to things only as they are supposed to exist answering such ideas. But any idea, simple or complex, barely by being in our minds, is no evidence of the real existence of anything out of our minds answering that idea[4].' If it is said that we include the idea of necessary existence in our idea of God, he replies that this only amounts to 'supposing' his existence but does not prove it. 'Real existence,' he declares, 'can be proved only by real existence; and, therefore, the real existence of a God can only be proved by the real existence of other things[5].'

§ 15. It is clear that, if 'real existence can be proved only by real existence,' the possibility of such a proof must rest upon a direct apprehension of real existence, which does not itself stand in need of mediation. Such an immediate certainty of existence Locke, like Descartes, finds, and unlike him, finds only, in the existence of the conscious subject. As the point is one of such crucial importance, it will be necessary to quote the relevant passage at length. 'As for our own existence, we perceive

[1] Cf. IV. 10. 7. [2] *Works*, vol. IV. pp. 53–6. [3] Lord King, pp. 313–6.
[4] *loc. cit.* [5] *loc. cit.*

it so plainly and so certainly that it neither needs nor is capable of any proof. For nothing can be more evident to us than our own existence. I think, I reason, I feel pleasure and pain; can any of these be more evident to me than my own existence? If I doubt of all other things, that very doubt makes me perceive my own existence, and will not suffer me to doubt of that. For, if I know I feel pain, it is evident I have as certain perception of my own existence, as of the existence of the pain I feel: or, if I know I doubt, I have as certain perception of the existence of the thing doubting, as of that thought which I call "doubt." Experience then convinces us that we have an intuitive knowledge of our own existence, and an internal infallible perception that we are. In every act of sensation, reasoning or thinking, we are conscious to ourselves of our own being; and in this matter come not short of the highest degree of certainty[1].'

In designating the judgment by which the existence of self is affirmed as 'intuitive' knowledge, Locke claims for it a no less immediate and absolute certainty, than that which is possessed by our judgments concerning the relations which are immediately seen to be involved in the nature of our abstract ideas. The resemblance extends, however, no further; and the use of the single term 'intuition' must not be allowed to hide from us the unique character of the former judgment. For, as a judgment asserting existence, it possesses features which are quite unlike those of the abstract judgments of science. In their case the immediacy of the perception signifies that it is independent of the 'intervention of any other ideas'; in the special case we are concerned with, we have an apprehension of real existence which is immediate in the

[1] IV. 9. 3.

sense that the real existent is itself directly known, and does not stand in need of any idea, as a *tertium quid*, to connect it with the knowing mind. As the only judgment which thus asserts existence with immediate certainty, it is, indeed, *sui generis*. For all other existential judgments, except that asserting the existence of God, which depends upon it, are found to fall short of the perfect intellectual transparency of knowledge.

The unique nature of this judgment is due to the fact that, besides its ideas, the mind, and the mind alone, is 'present to the understanding.' Hence, in this one case, no idea is needed to serve as a sign or representation of the real being which is known[1]. Moreover, this 'presence' of the mind to itself can only signify that in some sense it is an object to itself. As it is impossible for ideas to be 'in the understanding' without being 'understood'; so, Locke holds, the mind cannot be present to itself without self-consciousness. In so far, at least, as it performs its 'proper action' of thinking, it is necessarily conscious of itself as doing so. Concerning the idea of self, as distinguished from that of personal identity, which implies it, Locke is completely silent. It is clear, however, that upon his view it is involved in every mental function. To think, as he says, is to be conscious that I think. The idea of self is, therefore, present in the total content of all our thoughts or mental functions, each of which affords us an immediate knowledge of our own existence. In this case, and in this case alone, reality and idea are so entirely at one, that any passage or transition from the one to the other is not only impossible but unnecessary. On the one hand, every activity of self carries with it self-knowledge; on the other hand, in our consciousness of

[1] Cf. IV. 21. 4.

self we are directly aware of real existence. That Locke does not enquire more fully into the nature and function of the idea of self, and the peculiar relation in which he supposes it to stand to reality, is one of the most serious omissions of the *Essay*; while, had he done so, he might have been led to revise his view of the general function of ideas in knowledge, and their relation to reality.

It is upon this one immediate certainty of existence that Locke bases his demonstration of the existence of God. Since, however, the chief interest of his argument lies in the light which it throws upon the influence which the current rationalistic dogmatism, based upon the principles and conceptions of Scholasticism, still exercised over his mind, notwithstanding the critical tendency of his thought, and his desire to keep in close contact with experienced fact, it hardly calls for consideration here. Attention will be called later on to some of its implications[1].

§ 16. We pass, therefore, to Locke's treatment of our knowledge of the existence of material things. As we have seen, he had never really placed himself at the point of view of subjective idealism, but had assumed from the start that ideas are essentially signs, which point beyond themselves to a realm of real being distinct from them. He had, moreover, taken it for granted, that the contents of our ideas of the primary qualities of matter are qualifications of a reality which exists beyond and independently of the mind. Even in his formal treatment of the subject no serious attempt is made to get behind these presuppositions, or to offer a formal justification for them. He was aware, indeed, that there were those who 'will question the existence of all things, or our knowledge

[1] Cf. ch. VIII. §§ 12, 13.

of anything,' on the ground that our waking life may be no better than a dream. But to so extreme a scepticism he does not particularly address himself. 'If all be a dream, then he doth but dream that he makes the question; and so it does not much matter that a waking man should answer him[1].' The result is that he tends to confuse the general problem of our knowledge of the existence of the material universe and its relation to the mind, with the more limited problem of determining the manner in which, and the extent to which, we can be assured of the existence of particular things within this universe, the reality and general nature of which are tacitly assumed.

Since such existence cannot be guaranteed by the content of our ideas of material things, or deduced from the existence of the thinking self, the justification of its assertion must be sought in the manner in which certain of these ideas, on certain occasions, are experienced by the mind which apprehends them. Such an assurance of real existence Locke considers is to be found in the peculiar characteristics of sense-perception. 'I ask anyone,' he writes, 'whether he is not invincibly conscious to himself of a different perception, when he looks on the sun by day, and thinks on it by night; when he actually tastes wormwood, or smells a rose, or only thinks on that savour or odour[2].' This difference, which he does not attempt to analyse, is, he maintains, as plain as that 'between any two distinct ideas.' Under the influence of the presuppositions to which attention has been called, the peculiar tang of reality, which is involved in the contents of sense-perception, is at once identified with a 'perception and consciousness' of 'the actual entrance of ideas' from 'particular external

[1] IV. 11. 8.

[2] IV. 2. 14.

objects[1]'; of the existence of which we are thus assured. But while this constitutes the primary ground of our justifiable confidence in the existence of material things, it does not stand alone, but receives confirmation from 'other concurrent reasons.' These ideas of actual sensation are found to possess a coerciveness of their own, which distinguishes them from the ideas of memory or imagination, and points to an external cause. 'If I turn my eyes at noon towards the sun, I cannot avoid the ideas which the light or sun then produces in me[2].' And even when their original production is due to an act of will, as in the formation of written letters, they exhibit a subsequent independence of this subjective initiation, which does not belong to the creatures of our imagination. The secondary position which is assigned to the coerciveness of sense impressions, as compared with what has been called their 'sensational intensity,' would appear to be due to the view, that while it suffices to assure us that there must be 'some exterior cause,' it does not yield of itself any unambiguous evidence of the nature of this cause. Finally, appeal is made to the dependence of ideas of a given kind upon the possession of the corresponding sense-organ, and to the mutual support of different senses.

Nevertheless, when all is said, Locke does not claim that the conviction of external existence which is thus obtained satisfies, to the full, the theoretical requirements of knowledge. Although it goes 'beyond bare probability[3],' and 'puts us past doubting[4],' it 'is not altogether so certain as our intuitive knowledge, or the deductions of our reason employed about the clear abstract ideas of our own minds[5].' For while we intuitively perceive that there can be no

[1] IV. 2. 14; cf. IV. 11. 1–2. [2] IV. 11. 5. [3] IV. 2. 14.
[4] *loc. cit.* [5] IV. 11. 3.

experience without an experiencing subject, the same necessity of thought does not attach to the connection between the content of sense-experience and the external thing, beyond and independent of experience, though similarly determined as regards the primary qualities, to which it is referred. From a theoretical point of view there is, therefore, a formal defect in our 'sensitive' knowledge of the existence of external things. Nevertheless, as carrying us beyond any real possibility of doubt, it is declared to be 'an assurance that deserves the name of knowledge[1].' And whatever its theoretical imperfections may be, Locke expresses himself as perfectly satisfied of its practical sufficiency. For, our pleasures and pains being bound up with our ideas of actual sensation, in a way in which they are not with any other ideas, the distinctive characteristics of these ideas give us all the certainty that we need as a guide to action. 'This certainty,' he declares, 'is as great as our happiness or misery, beyond which we have no concernment to know or to be[2].'

The assurance of real existence which Locke calls 'sensitive knowledge,' whatever its precise value, is regarded by him as from the nature of the case confined to the existence of particular things while they are actually objects of sense-perception, and to their existence in the past in so far as we remember having had such a perception. If we affirm the continued existence of an object which is no longer present to our sense-perception, we have definitely passed from the region of knowledge to that of probability. For we no longer have the indubitable assurance of 'sensitive' knowledge, while there is no necessary connection between the existence of a particular material thing at

[1] *loc. cit.*

[2] IV. 2. 14; cf. IV. 11. 8.

one moment and its continued existence at the next[1]. Whether this want of certainty extends to the existence of the very matter itself, in so far as it is unperceived, Locke does not definitely consider. It is probable that had the question been raised, he would have said its existence, too, is one of those things concerning which we cannot have that certainty which we strictly 'call knowledge'; such a view being in harmony with the contingent existence which, on other grounds, he ascribes to matter. Finally, he holds, that we cannot have knowledge, but only faith, as to the existence of other finite spirits[2]. This statement, it should be noticed, is intended to refer primarily, if not exclusively, to non-human beings. Like other philosophers of his age, Locke failed to give any special consideration to the question of our recognition of the presence of mind in our fellow men.

§ 17. Having completed our survey of Locke's treatment of our knowledge of real existence, we must briefly consider the relation in which it stands to his general theory of knowledge, and the final statement of his position in which it occupies a conspicuous place. That his theory of knowledge was primarily formed with reference to the universal truths which constitute the content of 'science,' in which, as he holds, abstraction is made from the conditions of actual existence, there can be no doubt. It is equally clear that he never fully realised the difficulty of bringing a knowledge of real existence into line with his general conception of knowledge. Even the formal contradiction, between the admission of a knowledge which transcends ideas and a definition which restricts knowledge to a perception of agreements or disagreements among ideas, receives no recognition; nor, as we have said, does

[1] IV. II. 9. [2] IV. II. 12.

he devote any separate consideration to the nature of the existential judgment as such. In the course, however, of his treatment of the various judgments in which existence is explicitly affirmed, the distinctive features of such judgments and the peculiar position which they occupy tend to become apparent.

With the exception of the judgment which affirms the existence of self, and that affirming the existence of God on the basis of the existence of self, all such judgments are found to be wanting in the intellectual transparency and necessity which his ideal of knowledge involves. Accordingly, over against the perfect certainty which completely satisfies our intellectual nature, he is compelled to place an assurance which falls short of this ideal, but to which, nevertheless, he cannot refuse the name of knowledge. Again, our knowledge of existence is found to stand in a different relation to experience from the knowledge which consists in the apprehension of intuitive connections between ideas. For while the latter kind of knowledge draws upon experience for the simple elements, out of which the ideas it employs are built up, the justification of the connections themselves is in no way dependent upon experience. But when we affirm existence, not only the 'materials' of our idea of that which we say exists, but the justification of the affirmation, must be derived from experience. This statement, too, however, is subject to some qualification. For even if we extend the conception of experience, as Locke would have us do, to cover the unique form of cognisance which arises from the mind's presence to itself, we are still left with the single exception of our knowledge of the existence of God. Connected, again, with the empirical nature of our knowledge of existence, is its limitation. Propositions which assert existence are all 'particular' or individual; and, with the single exception just mentioned, they are further restricted by a reference to the particular time at which we had experience of the thing in question. As soon as we seek to extend these empirically grounded judgments to other things, or to other moments of time, we have definitely left the region of knowledge for that of probability.

Distinguished from and opposed to this knowledge of real existence, which is obtained by actual contact with reality at particular points, and which can only give us an acquaintance with these, we have the universal knowledge of science. This is the knowledge which is due to the contemplation of our own abstract ideas, and is by its very nature debarred from asserting existence. Locke's theory, therefore, ends in the recognition of two ultimately distinct and exclusive types of knowledge, although the simplicity and consistency of his view are still impaired by the exceptional nature of the intuition which we have of our own existence, and the still more exceptional position which is assigned to the demonstration of the existence of God. The distinction between these two radically different kinds of knowledge is not only the final outcome of the enquiry instituted in the *Essay*, but is frequently made use of throughout its progress. We find, even in the earlier books, an implied contrast between a knowledge which is merely 'experimental' or 'historical,' concerned with 'matters of fact,' and a knowledge which is 'scientific,' concerned with matters of 'speculation,' and based upon a perception of necessary connections among ideas.

To this duality of type the fourfold classification of knowledge made at the beginning of the Fourth Book must be regarded as subordinate. It constitutes an initial plan for the survey of the field, rather than a final delimitation of its parts. The judgments which merely affirm the identity of an idea with itself, or its difference from another idea, are we have seen set aside as furnishing no 'positive' or 'instructional' knowledge. The vast majority of our judgments concerning coexistence, possessing validity as knowledge only so far as they are guaranteed by experience in particular instances, are reduced by Locke to existential judgments .There remain only the small number of judgments which Locke regarded as certain and universal, although concerned with coexistence. These, in his final classification, must find their place under the head of universal abstract knowledge, unless they are set aside as uninstructive.

§ 18. Such, then is the conclusion to which Locke is led, as the result of his survey of human knowledge. That neither of the two irreducible types, to which our knowledge is found to conform, is beyond the reach of criticism, he is himself aware. But their defects, he thinks, are inherent in our present capacity for knowledge, while they may be held to point to the existence of a higher. On the one hand, the particular propositions concerning existence are wanting in the primary requisite of intellectual clarity. Throughout his account of our knowledge of coexistence there is implied the conception of a possible knowledge of substances which is not merely empirical, but penetrates to their 'real essences,' from which their various determinations would then be seen to follow with rational necessity. And although such knowledge cannot be attained by us, we may suppose it to be possessed by rational beings of greater perfection than ourselves. It is not to be doubted, he tells us, that 'spirits of a higher rank than those immersed in flesh may have as clear ideas of the radical constitution of substances as we have of a triangle, and so perceive how all their properties and operations flow from thence[1].' And such knowledge the Divine Being, at least, must possess[2].

In our rational knowledge, too, he discovers defects. While intuitive knowledge is 'the highest of all human certainty,' it is narrow in extent, and requires to be supplemented by a discursive process of thought, making use of intermediate ideas. But although the discovery of these 'proofs' may be 'the hardest task' of our reason, it is not therefore 'its highest perfection[3].' Locke, accordingly, hazards the surmise that 'angels have now, and the spirits of just men made perfect shall have in a future state,' an enormous increase in the range of the knowledge in which there is 'no use of the discursive faculty, no need of reasoning[4].' A still more radical imperfection of the knowledge which constitutes our science is elsewhere indicated. Such knowledge, we have seen, is concerning the relations between the contents of our abstract general ideas. But there is 'reason to suspect' that general ideas are themselves 'marks of our imperfection[5].' Although an essential instrument of our knowledge, the general idea is 'something imperfect, which cannot exist[6].' And this imperfection is inherent in its abstract nature, in virtue of which it only gives us a partial and mutilated representation of concrete reality. These different lines of reflection, upon the imperfections of our present intellectual state, converge upon the conception of a form of knowledge in which justice is at once done to the fullness of concrete reality and to the demand

[1] III. II. 23. [2] III. 6. 3. [3] IV. 17. 6.
[4] IV. 17. 14; cf. IV. 3. 6. [5] IV. 7. 9. [6] *loc. cit.*

that the object of knowledge shall be perfectly transparent to intelligence; and in which, consequently, the distinction between the two types of our present knowledge is transcended. While pointing us to this conception of what perfect knowledge would require to be, Locke holds that not only is it unattainable by us, but that we cannot even definitely conceive the conditions of its possibility.

CHAPTER VIII

LOCKE AND SCHOLASTICISM

§ 1. The question of the historical setting of the *Essay* is admittedly in an unsatisfactory position, and for this more than one circumstance must be held responsible. The fact that it constitutes the starting-point of the classical development of philosophy in England has led to a concentration of attention upon its influence, to the comparative neglect of the sources from which it is derived. Nor, it must be admitted, does Locke himself, in the course of that work, give much assistance to the enquirer into the historical antecedents and relations of its doctrine. So little store does he set upon a knowledge of other men's opinions, on matters concerning which reason should be the judge, that it is only on the rarest occasions that he refers to the views of other writers in a manner sufficiently definite to enable them to be identified. When he would cite a supposed matter of fact, such as the virtues which were cultivated by the people of Peru, the capacity of a parrot for rational conversation, or the non-existence of the idea of God among the Carribee Islanders, he is ready with his references, including chapter and page. But in matters of speculation, where the appeal is made to the reader's own intelligence, he prefers to set forth his view of what he conceives to be the truth, contrasting it when necessary with opposing principles, but without encumbering it with references and quotations. Hence, as we have found, even the bearing of the directly controversial parts of the

Essay is not always immediately apparent. A further difficulty, which has stood in the way of the attempt to reconstruct the intellectual environment of his work, lies in the fact that many of the influences which affected it were by no means of the first order, and consequently can claim no permanent place for their own sake in the history of thought.

Along with Locke's contempt for the cumbrous learning which so often took the place of individual thought, there went a keen appreciation of the value of the stimulus to be derived from intellectual intercourse with others. He had a habit of organising small circles of congenial spirits for the discussion of questions which interested him. Indeed, as we know, it was in a gathering of this kind that the problem of the *Essay* first suggested itself. Hence, though he was a constant reader, it is not improbable that in the formation of his own views he owed as much, or even more to personal intercourse than to his study of books. Before proceeding to consider the internal evidence of the *Essay* itself as to its sources, it may, therefore, be well to indicate briefly the light which the known facts of his life throw upon the nature of the intellectual forces with which he was brought into the closest contact.

§ 2. At Oxford he had found a weakened form of Scholasticism still holding undisputed sway in philosophy. In later life he complained that he had 'lost a great deal of time at the commencement of his studies, because the only philosophy then known at Oxford was the Peripatetic, perplexed with obscure terms and useless questions[1].' Little as such studies might be to his taste, he nevertheless

[1] Le Clerc, *Éloge de M. Locke.* Quoted in Fox Bourne's *Life of Locke*, vol. I. p. 48.

went through the regular course in the Aristotelian Logic, Metaphysics, Physics and Ethics; and even for a time gave instruction in the last-named subject, upon his appointment in 1664 to the position of Censor of Moral Philosophy. The awakening in himself of a genuine philosophical interest he always attributed to his introduction to the writings of Descartes, which seems to have taken place before the close of his residence at Oxford. During the prolonged periods of his travels and sojourns on the continent, he was brought into contact with members of the Cartesian School, both in France and in Holland. Among others, he appears to have met Malebranche, for whom, he wrote to Molyneux, he entertained a personal kindness[1]. In all his wanderings, however, he remained a typical representative, not only of his age, but of his country, in close touch with the liberal and progressive movement in England, whether in politics, philosophy, theology or science. In our attempt to indicate the influences which helped to mould his thought, we shall, then, have to consider his relation (1) to the traditional scholastic doctrine which he unwillingly imbibed at Oxford, (2) to Cartesianism, (3) to contemporary thought in England. To each of these we shall find the doctrine of the *Essay* is intimately related, though their influences are shown in markedly different ways. To Cartesianism he owed his original philosophical awakening, and it was in close relation to Cartesianism that he developed his most characteristic positions. Although his attitude towards Scholasticism is one of marked and avowed hostility, we shall find that it was from this despised source that he and Descartes alike derived the metaphysical scheme by which they envisaged reality. While these

[1] *Works*, vol. IX. p. 357.

constitute the two most important, because the most profound and far reaching influences which helped to determine his thought, his work stands in intimate relation to the many-sided progressive movement in England. In its general outlook on life, as well as in its bearing on ethics, politics and religion, the *Essay* is by far the most characteristic product of the English liberalism of his age. And when we pass from such general agreement to the consideration of particulars, we shall find that on many points of detail the doctrine of the *Essay* is closely connected with that of his English contemporaries, to whose thought there are occasionally direct though not always obvious references.

§ 3. Although Locke's conscious attitude to the doctrine of the Schools was in general one of contemptuous antagonism, he always speaks in terms of respect of Aristotle himself. He regarded him, he tells us, as 'one of the greatest men among the ancients, whose large views, acuteness and penetration of thought, and strength of judgment few have equalled[1].' In particular, he expresses his sense of the great service rendered by him in his account of the forms of argument[2], and even expresses the opinion that, had the Stagirite carried his analysis a step further, he would have been in complete agreement with Locke's own position, which places certainty in the mind's perception of agreement or disagreement between its ideas[3]. The mistake made by his followers, which has had such disastrous consequences, consisted not in recognising his greatness, but in raising him to the position of a 'dictator in the commonwealth of letters.' In doing this, however, his admirers have been unfaithful to his spirit and example,

[1] IV. 27. 4. [2] *loc. cit.*

[3] Third Letter to Stillingfleet, *Works*, vol. IV. p. 383.

since his admitted pre-eminence was the result of his 'not keeping precisely to the beaten tracks.' Of the doctrines which had been elaborated on the basis of his thought, and for which his authority was claimed, there are two in respect of which Locke develops at length his opposition. These are (1) the theory of the nature and method of knowledge, and (2) the doctrine of substantial forms in its bearing upon the process of classification. With the former of these we shall begin our account of Locke's relation to Scholasticism.

§ 4. The theory of knowledge which Locke attributed to 'scholastic men' has already been briefly indicated, in the course of our discussion of his polemic against innate principles. According to it the method of science consists of syllogistic deductions from certain 'maxims,' 'axioms' or 'principles,' which, as the indispensable starting-points of the deductive processes, must themselves be accepted upon authority or declared innate. These principles were either special to a particular science, or such as are presupposed in all rational knowledge whatsoever. Thus, we are told, 'the masters of mathematics' were accustomed to place 'at the entrance to their systems' such maxims as that 'the whole is equal to all its parts,' or 'the whole is bigger than a part[1],' and to regard all other mathematical propositions as deductions from this first principle of the science. And the Laws of Identity and Contradiction being the principles upon which the validity of the syllogistic process itself was held to depend, they were regarded as 'the foundations' upon which, not one particular science, but knowledge in general was 'built.' Without going again into the question of innateness, we must consider Locke's

[1] IV. 7. 11; cf. I. 4. 6, and IV. 12. 3.

criticism of the position assigned to such principles, and of the view which regarded the syllogism as the sole method of demonstration.

§ 5. 'The rules established in the Schools, that all reasonings are *ex præcognitis et præconcessis*, seem to lay the foundation of all knowledge in these maxims[1], and to suppose them to be *præcognita*. Whereby, I think, are meant these two things: first, that these axioms are those truths that are first known to the mind; and, secondly, that upon them the other parts of our knowledge depend[2].' Taking 'first known' to imply a temporal priority, Locke has no difficulty in reducing the former of these positions to absurdity. 'Who perceives not that a child certainly knows that a stranger is not its mother, that its sucking-bottle is not the rod, long before he knows that it is impossible for the same thing to be and not to be? And how many truths there are about numbers, which it is obvious to observe that the mind is perfectly acquainted with, and fully convinced of, before it ever thought on these general maxims to which mathematicians in their arguings do sometimes refer them[3]?' Moreover, these more particular propositions are themselves every whit as certain and self-evident, as the principles upon which they are said to depend. Nor are they any better or more certainly known, when we do come to recognise the so-called 'axioms[4].' To state this, indeed, is equivalent to a tautology, since knowledge and certainty do not admit of degrees. In answer to the claim of the Laws of Identity and Contradiction to constitute the foundation of all knowledge, Locke points out that these famous principles are 'only about identical predications, and influence, if

[1] *I.e.* the Laws of Identity and Contradiction.

[2] IV. 7. 8. [3] IV. 7. 9. [4] IV. 7. 10.

any at all, none but such[1].' And if we turn to the 'other less general maxims,' we find again that 'many of them are no more than bare verbal propositions, and teach us nothing but the respect and import of names one to another. "The whole is equal to all its parts"; what real truth, I beseech you, does it teach us? What more is contained in that maxim than what the signification of the word *totum*, or "the whole" does of itself import?' The synthetic and necessary propositions, which alone constitute 'instructive real knowledge,' cannot therefore even be regarded as particular examples of the general relations expressed in such axioms as these, but require an entirely different justification.

§ 6. Turning from the maxims themselves to the method by which the edifice of knowledge was supposed to be reared upon them, we find Locke denying that the syllogism is 'the proper instrument of reason,' or 'the only proper instrument and means of knowledge,' as is 'generally thought[2].' So far is this from being the case that the syllogism is of no help in the performance of the initial step in the process of reasoning, viz. the discovery of 'proofs' or intermediate ideas. 'When we find out an idea, by whose intervention we discover the connection of two others, this is a revelation from God to us by the voice of reason. For we then come to know a truth that we did not know before[3].' But to this revelation the syllogism contributes nothing. 'This way of reasoning discovers no new proofs, but is the art of marshalling and ranging the old ones we have already[4].' Hence it is but 'the art of fencing with the little knowledge we have, without making any addition to it[5].' As regards its fitness for the performance of the subordinate functions here ascribed to it,

[1] IV. 7. 11. [2] IV. 17. 4. [3] IV. 7. 11. [4] IV. 17. 6. [5] *loc. cit.*

Locke is willing to admit that 'all right reasoning may be reduced to' syllogistic form[1]. Accordingly we find him, on more than one occasion in the course of his controversy with Stillingfleet, challenging his opponent to put his argument, if he has one, in the form of a syllogism[2]. He denies, however, that the syllogism furnishes the only valid way of exhibiting the process of reasoning, or that it constitutes the best method that can be adopted for the assistance of the candid seeker after truth. Indeed, its use 'very often confounds the connection[3]' of ideas, which would be more readily grasped by an order of exposition which reproduced more closely the order of thought. 'To show it in a very plain and easy example: let *animal* be the intermediate idea, or *medius terminus*, that the mind makes use of to show the connection of *homo* and *vivens*; I ask, whether the mind does not more readily and plainly see that connection in the simple and proper position of the connecting idea in the middle, thus:

Homo—Animal—Vivens,

than in this perplexed one,

Animal—Vivens—Homo—Animal,

which is the position these ideas have in a syllogism[4]?' Even for the purpose of exposing fallacies and detecting incoherences of thought, for which Locke tells us he at one time regarded the syllogistic form as necessary, he now claims a superiority for what he considers the more natural order[5].

§ 7. Having seen how Locke developed his antagonism to Scholasticism upon the question of the nature and method of knowledge, it might be expected that we should now turn to the other point on which we find him

[1] IV. 17. 4. [2] *Works*, vol. IV. pp. 268 and 362. [3] IV. 17. 4.
[4] *loc. cit.* [5] *loc. cit.*

maintaining a prolonged polemic against the doctrine of the Schools. But since this controversy turns primarily upon the meaning to be ascribed to 'essences of sorts of things,' it must be postponed until we have dealt with the conception of essence itself and the general system of thought to which it belonged.

It has been remarked more than once that while insisting that an enquiry into knowledge must precede the attempt to determine the nature of reality, Locke never succeeded in freeing himself from certain presuppositions as to the general nature of that which possesses real being. At the outset, in the very endeavour to abstract from considerations of a metaphysical character, he takes for granted the validity of the categories which were fundamental for the thought of his age, and their adequacy for the interpretation of reality. And these categories were, in truth, a direct inheritance from Scholasticism. In the course of his enquiry, difficulties and perplexities arose in the endeavour to reconcile these metaphysical conceptions with the new point of view of the experiential theory of knowledge. But even when he finds himself compelled to recognise their uselessness for the purposes of our knowledge, he does not question their ultimate validity. They are still regarded as representing the genuine nature of reality, though this is now declared to be beyond our comprehension. They are thus preserved from the destructive force of his criticism by being relegated to the region of the unknown, and to us unknowable. To the consideration of the traditional ontological scheme, and of the reaction of Locke's thought upon it, we must now turn.

§ 8. In this scheme the paramount position was occupied by the conception of substance. Everything that is real, it was held, is either a substance or a modification, quality or attribute, of a substance. These latter are dependent aspects of reality, incapable of existing on their own account, which consequently imply a more ultimate form of being, viz., the substance to which they belong. This substance is at once self-existent and the necessary basis or support of qualities. Further, the existence of a plurality of real beings having been accepted as a dictate of common sense, reality was conceived as consisting of a number of such entities, each complete in itself and independent of the rest.

Locke accordingly begins by assuming as axiomatic that reality can consist of nothing but substances and their modifications. For him, as for the Schoolmen, the idea of substance is 'the foundation of all the rest[1].' It is, he declares, the idea which, of all others, we should expect to be innate[2]. The accusation of Stillingfleet, that he had 'almost discarded substance out of the reasonable part of the world,' appeared to him an inexcusable misunderstanding. 'As long as there is any such thing as body or spirit in the world, I have done nothing towards discarding substance out of the reasonable part of the world. Nay, as long as there is any simple idea or sensible quality left, according to my way of arguing, substance cannot be discarded; because all simple ideas, all sensible qualities, carry with them a supposition of a *substratum* to exist in, and of a substance wherein they inhere[3].' The existence of substance is as certain to him, he declares, as his own being. 'Having everywhere affirmed and built upon it that man is a substance, I cannot be supposed to question or doubt of the being of substance, till I can question or doubt of my own being[4].'

[1] IV. 3. 23. [2] I. 4. 18.

[3] First Letter to Stillingfleet, *Works*, vol. IV. p. 7.

[4] *Ibid.* *Works*, vol. IV. p. 18.

But, although he could not doubt the being of substance, Locke found, as we know, that we can form no satisfactory idea of what substance is in itself. The only idea we can form of this supposed absolute turns out to be merely relative; that which is above all positive and concrete is for our thought destitute of all definite content. In view of this startling discrepancy between his presuppositions and the result of his reflection, Locke is led at times to question 'the very great clearness there is in the doctrine of substance and accidents,' and asks to be shown 'of what use they are in deciding of questions of philosophy[1].' In particular, he refuses to abandon the view to which he has been led concerning the reality of space, when met with the customary challenge to declare 'whether this space void of body be substance or accident[2]'; although he does not go so far as to say, as Gassendi had already done, that it is a third kind of being, which is neither the one nor the other. Again, as we have seen, he traces the difficulty of understanding how the mind thinks, and explaining its relation to its ideas, to the current determination of the soul as a simple substance; while the complementary supposition that our ideas are modifications of this substance is declared to be irreconcilable with the obvious fact of experience that we perceive different and inconsistent ideas at the same time[3].

But, although in these different ways the truth is forced home upon him that the traditional conceptions of 'substance and accident are of little use in philosophy,' he never pronounced these conceptions either invalid or inadequate for the determination of reality. The emptiness which he finds in *our* idea of substance is in the end to him only an indication that 'the ideas we can attain to by our faculties

[1] II. 13. 20. [2] II. 13. 17. [3] Cf. above, ch. I. § 13, pp. 27–8.

are very disproportionate to things themselves[1].' But superior intelligences may be supposed to possess a 'positive, clear, distinct' idea of substance, although this is 'concealed from us.' So, notwithstanding the difficulties and apparent contradictions to which the conception is seen to lead, he continues to think of reality as composed of a number of independent substances, and of the mind itself as one among these.

§ 9. An important consequence of Locke's acceptance of the traditional ontological scheme must now be noticed. Reality being conceived as exhaustively comprehended under the categories of substance and quality, no place can be found in it for relations, which are *prima facie* neither the one nor the other. Moreover, the admission that relations to one another entered into the being of substances would have been fatal to the self-contained and independent existence which these were thought to possess. Accordingly, when relations forced themselves upon the notice of philosophers, they were conceived as purely accidental and 'external,' having no basis in the nature of their terms; while, in the last resort, the attempt was made to preserve the purity of the doctrine of substance by declaring them to be merely ideal, and to have no place at all in the reality of things. While Locke's denial of the reality of relations is too prominent to be overlooked, the grounds on which he maintained this position have been generally misunderstood. It is not, as Green supposed, because they cannot be given as units of merely sensible experience, that Locke declares that relations do not belong to the reality of things; but because their admission would be inconsistent with his strictly ontological presuppositions. They are unreal, because they do not

[1] IV. 3. 23.

belong to 'things as they are in themselves[1].' They are 'not contained in the real existence of things' but are 'something extraneous and superinduced[2].' And by this latter expression Locke does not mean that they are an addition made by the mind to the simple data of Sensation and Reflection, but that they are 'superinduced to the substance[3].' In explaining this position, he tells us that whereas a positive name, such as 'man' or 'white' signifies something which really exists in the things of which the name can be predicated, a name which connotes a relation does not do so. It is merely, in the scholastic phraseology which he adopts, an 'external denomination.'

Moreover, in support of the traditional position, Locke argues in the traditional manner. 'The nature, therefore, of relation consists in the referring or comparing two things one to another; from which comparison one or both come to be denominated. And if either of those things be removed, or cease to be, the relation ceases, and the denomination consequent to it, though the other receive in itself no alteration at all; *e.g.* Caius, whom I consider to-day as a father, ceases to be so to-morrow, only by the death of his son, without any alteration made in himself. Nay, barely by the mind's changing the object to which it compares anything, the same thing is capable of having contrary denominations at the same time: *e.g.*, Caius, compared to several persons, may truly be said to be older and younger, stronger and weaker, etc.[4]' But that which can come and go 'without any alteration made in himself,' cannot belong to the being which Caius possesses as a substance; nor can contrary predicates belong together to his real being. Under the influence of the traditional metaphysics even the relation of father and

[1] II. 25. 1. [2] II. 25. 8. [3] II. 25. 4. [4] II. 25. 5.

son is regarded as an extrinsical one, which makes no real difference to its terms.

But here again, as in the case of substance itself, the living force of Locke's own thought runs counter to his inherited metaphysics. While he is content to adopt the old positions, and repeat the old arguments, concerning a reality which he does not profess to investigate; as soon as he approaches the question from the point of view of knowledge and the ideas which enter into it, the importance of relations forces itself upon him. Although no place can be found for relations in the real world as conceived by the current dogmatism, our ideas of relation are held to constitute a distinct class of ideas, co-ordinate with those of substances and modes. Not only so, but it turns out that all our ideas, 'when attentively considered,' include some kind of relation; while knowledge itself is nothing but a perception of relations among our ideas. Relations, then, are recognised as everywhere intimately involved in the ideas and knowledge with which the *Essay* is directly concerned, notwithstanding the alleged aloofness from relations of the substances, whose existence in the realm of transcendent reality is simply taken for granted. But since knowledge itself is for Locke a representation of reality, it was inevitable that the relations which are essential to knowledge should at times be transferred to real things themselves. 'Things,' we are told, 'agree or disagree as they really are; but we observe it only by our ideas.' And all our ideas of relation have a 'foundation' in the things compared, in reference to which they cannot, therefore, be entirely unreal. There is thus more than a discrepancy between reality, as it is attempted to be conceived in the metaphysics which Locke accepts, and the reality to which our ideas refer, and with which our knowledge is found to be concerned.

§ 10. The influence upon Locke of the traditional scheme of thought extends beyond his general acceptance of the current view concerning the nature and value of the conception of substance, and the doctrine of the unreality of relations, which this entails. As soon as he passes from the consideration of the idea of substance in general, and begins to treat of our ideas of particular substances and their kinds, it becomes clear that he is still largely under the influence of the scholastic doctrine of essence. Although he has come to hold that we can know nothing of the nature of substance in itself, he accepts without hesitation a theory as to the internal organisation of its qualities which is based upon the presuppositions of scholastic rationalism. Every substance, he thinks, must have a real essence, from which, could we only know it, we could deduce its other and more superficial characteristics. This essence signifies 'the very being of anything, whereby it is what it is' and consists of 'the real internal... constitution of things, whereon their discoverable qualities depend[1].' In accordance with the isolating implications of the conception of substance, this constitution is declared to be something 'which everything has within itself, without any relation to anything without it[2].' Had we only ideas of these real essences, which substances possess in themselves, the 'properties' and even the 'operations' of substances would be seen to flow from them, as the properties of a triangle follow from its definition. In that case, indeed, the gulf which according to the *Essay* separates the natural from the mathematical sciences would be crossed, since the former would be enabled to assume

[1] III. 3. 15. [2] III. 6. 6.

the deductive form of geometry. 'Had we such ideas of substances as to know what real constitutions produce those sensible qualities we find in them, and how those qualities flowed from thence, we could, by the specific ideas of their real essences in our own minds, more certainly find out their properties, and discover what qualities they had or had not, than we can now by our senses: and to know the properties of gold it would be no more necessary that gold should exist, and that we should make experiments upon it, than it is necessary for the knowing the properties of a triangle, that a triangle should exist in any matter[1].' And among the substances possessing essences, it must be remembered Locke included minds, which have 'their proper natures, constitutions and operations, as well as bodies[2].' In controverting the Cartesian view that thought constitutes this essence, we even find him appealing for confirmation to the scholastic principle that essences do not admit of degree[3].

Nor is such knowledge for Locke merely an ideal, with which we may contrast the poverty of our intellectual possessions. Although it is beyond our reach, it may, as we have seen, be attained by other finite minds, and must be ascribed to the Supreme Being. Thus, 'had we such a knowledge of that constitution of man, from which his faculties of moving, sensation and reasoning, and other powers flow, and on which his so regular shape depends, as it is possible angels have, and it is certain his Maker has, we should have a quite other idea of his essence than what now is contained in our definition of that species, be it what it will: and our idea of any individual man would be as far different from what it is now, as is his who knows all the springs and wheels and other contrivances within

[1] IV. 6. 11. [2] IV. 21. 2. [3] II. 19. 4.

of the famous clock at Strasburg, from that which a gazing countryman has of it, who barely sees the motion of the hand, and hears the clock strike, and observes only some of the outward appearances[1].'

This conception of essence, like that of substance, and like the denial of the reality of relations, is clearly a presupposition which Locke has never thought of calling in question. He knew 'nobody that ever denied the certainty of such real essences[2],' and he did not think of doing so himself. But here, again, the new knowledge could not be contained within the old bottles. In a lengthy section he develops and illustrates the modern conception of the interdependence of all physical things, which is the negation of the supposition that the properties of each thing flow from an internal constitution which it 'has in itself without any relation to anything without it.' With the actual facts in mind, he declares that 'we are then quite out of the way, when we think that things contain within themselves the qualities that appear to us in them; and we in vain search for that constitution within the body of a fly or an elephant, upon which depend those qualities and powers we observe in them....This is certain: things, however absolute and entire they seem in themselves, are but retainers to other parts of nature, for that which they are most taken notice of by us. Their observable qualities, actions and powers are owing to something without them; and there is not so complete and perfect a part that we know of nature, which does not owe the being it has, and the excellencies of it, to its neighbours; and we must not confine our thoughts within the surface of any body, but look a great deal further, to

[1] III. 6. 3.

[2] First Letter to Stillingfleet, *Works*, vol. IV. p. 82.

comprehend perfectly those qualities that are in it[1].' Such reflections clearly require the rejection of the conception of material things as self-contained substances, each with an essence from which all its properties and operations flow, and from a knowledge of which they could be deduced. But Locke refrains from drawing so revolutionary a conclusion. As has been pointed out[2], he only uses the above considerations to reinforce his view of the hopelessness of our getting to know the real essences, which substances are still supposed to possess. The conception of essence, like that of substance, finds a shelter in the unknown.

§ 11. Having seen Locke's acceptance of the general conception of essence, we are now in a position to consider his criticism of the form and application of the doctrine to which he takes exception. Running through the greater part of the Third Book of the *Essay*, we find a polemic directed against the theory of substantial forms, and its supposed bearing upon the processes of classification and naming. Holding, for himself, that in the 'proper original signification of the word,' essences are to be attributed to individual substances[3], Locke recognises that 'essence, in the ordinary use of the word, relates to sorts[4].' Nor has he any quarrel with this conception of essences of sorts of things. He holds, at least, that 'it is past doubt there must be some real constitution on which any collection of simple ideas coexisting must depend[5]'; and such a collection of ideas, considered in reference to the particular instances in which it may exist, is what we mean by a sort. The question at issue is, therefore, that of

[1] IV. 6. 11.

[2] Norman Smith, *Studies in the Cartesian Philosophy*, p. 204, note.

[3] III. 3. 15. [4] III. 6. 4. [5] III. 3. 15.

the nature of these essences of sorts of substances and their relation to the process of classification.

The doctrine which Locke opposes assumed that substances, and more particularly those possessing life, have been fashioned in accordance with a limited number of objective types or patterns. These constituted the so-called substantial forms. Fixed lines of division were, therefore, conceived as running throughout nature, by which the individual substances which possessed the same form constituted a species or sort. Moreover, to these fixed lines of division language was supposed to furnish a clue, a general name being primarily the name of one of these 'general natures,' in accordance with which particular things have been formed.

The Schoolmen's 'substantial forms,' Locke regards as 'wholly unintelligible,' since 'we have scarce so much as any obscure or confused conception in general' as to the meaning of the term. Real essences, whether of individual substances or of 'sorts,' can only be understood as consisting in the primary qualities of the insensible particles of which bodies are composed. In this sense we have at least a clear 'conception in general' of their nature, although their constitution in detail is hidden from us. Against the assumption that Nature always works according to fixed types, corresponding to the classes represented in our familiar terminology, Locke cites the occurrence of monsters and changelings[1]. Whether there are or not in nature 'prefixed bounds' of species, he is not prepared to say. But if there be, he is confident that '*our* boundaries of species are not exactly conformable to those in Nature[2].' If 'precise and immovable boundaries' of species are 'made by Nature,' they have not at all events been 'established

[1] III. 3. 17. [2] III. 6. 30.

by her amongst men[1].' It is, then, against the assumption that our classification of substances can be made with reference to this purely objective standard that the brunt of his criticism is directed. For the purpose of 'ranking' things into 'sorts,' real essences cannot be employed by us, for the simple reason that we do not know them. 'Patterns' of some sort classification does indeed involve; but these can be nothing but our own abstract ideas. The question as to whether a certain substance belongs to a certain species, only becomes intelligible and capable of being answered when it is understood as an enquiry as to whether it corresponds to one of our general ideas, and is consequently entitled to be called by a certain general name.

Classification, therefore, must be carried out by reference to 'nominal essences' or the abstract ideas for which our general or 'sortal' names stand; and these are 'made by the mind and not by Nature[2].' Instead of being once for all fixed and rigid, our classes are relative to the degree of insight which we have obtained into the phenomena of nature, and must adapt themselves to our growing knowledge. While a perfect system of classification of substances would be made according to 'those qualities which would best show us their most material differences and agreements,' our immediate needs necessitate a more superficial and provisional division, according to their 'obvious appearances[3].' The subjective and arbitrary element which classification involves is, however, limited by the proviso, that in forming ideas of substances we may only unite qualities which have been actually experienced together, since only so can we be assured of the reality of these ideas.

[1] III. 6. 27. [2] III. 6. 26. [3] III. 6. 30.

While Locke's criticism is directed against what he regarded as an implication of scholastic Realism, it must be observed that his own position cannot be identified with that of extreme Nominalism. So far from maintaining that universality attaches exclusively to names, he holds that 'words become general by being made the signs of general ideas[1].' These general ideas, it is true, are all declared to be 'particular in their existence,' their generality consisting in their capacity for representing an indefinite number of possible existents. And this is a 'capacity they are put into by the understanding[2].' Accordingly, 'general and universal belong not to the real existence of things, but are inventions and creatures of the understanding, made by it for its own use[3].' Generality, however, though it is 'something imperfect, which cannot exist,' has its foundation in experience and in reality. For, we find, that 'many particular substances are so made by Nature, that they have agreement and likeness one with another, and so afford a foundation of being ranked into sorts[4].' Hence, the general idea, that product of the mind's own workmanship, does not falsify the reality presented to us in experience, but furnishes an indispensable instrument for our comprehension of it. This is so, although, like all instruments, it suffers from defect, and would have no place in that ideal form of knowledge, at once concrete and rational, which we cannot possess and can only dimly divine.

§ 12. As long as the ideal of 'physical' knowledge, in Locke's wide use of that term, consists in the deduction of the 'properties and operations' of a thing from an essence which belongs to it in itself, it is clear that only a very

[1] III. 3. 6. [2] III. 3. 11. [3] *loc. cit.* [4] III. 6. 30.

subordinate place can be assigned to the conception of causation. Nor could this conception itself remain unaffected by the dominant mode of thought. In accordance with the presuppositions of conceptional rationalism, it had been regarded as axiomatic among the Schoolmen, that a cause can give rise to no positive qualifications in its effect which it does not itself possess. The whole reality of the effect must, it was held, somehow be contained in its cause. The relation of God to the material world seemed, indeed, to present a serious difficulty on this assumption. For God was conceived as at once immaterial and the first cause of the universe. In order to reconcile the axiom of causation with their theological views, the Schoolmen were consequently forced to make a distinction. The perfection or reality which characterises the material world does not, they said, exist in God *formaliter*, or in the same way as it exists in the effect; it is, however, present *eminenter*, or in a superior manner, in the purely spiritual being who is the world's cause.

Now, both this general doctrine, and the distinction to which it gave rise, meet us in the *Essay*. There is, Locke considers, a sense in which a thing may be said to be 'in its cause[1].' It is upon this ground that he argues that the Being which we must conceive as existing from eternity must possess the characteristic of thinking, and consequently cannot be matter. And in the development of the argument, the scholastic position is presented in its fully developed form. 'Since, therefore, whatsoever is the first eternal being must necessarily be cogitative; and whatsoever is first of all things must necessarily contain in it, and actually have, at least, all the perfections that can ever after exist; nor can it ever give to another any

[1] II. 23. 9.

perfection that it hath not, either actually in itself' (*i.e. formaliter*), 'or at least in a higher degree' (*i.e. eminenter*), 'it necessarily follows, that the first eternal being cannot be matter[1].'

§ 13. Finally, if we turn to the idea of God itself, the same scholastic influence is again easily discernible. The divine attributes, he tells us, 'do without doubt contain in them all possible perfection[2],' although we can only conceive their infinity in a negative and quantitative manner. Once more he falls back upon the disproportion between the ideas which we are capable of forming, and the strictly incomprehensible reality, which we seek to determine by means of them. From the same point of view, he rejects the scholastic conception of eternity as a *punctum stans*[3], and the attempt to distinguish different kinds of 'ubiety[4],' in order to explain the way in which the soul is present in the body, as 'unintelligible ways of speaking,' by which we merely conceal from ourselves our want of ideas concerning a reality which transcends our powers of knowledge.

[1] IV. 10. 10. [2] II. 17. 1. [3] II. 17. 16. [4] II. 23. 21.

CHAPTER IX

LOCKE AND DESCARTES

§ 1. We may take as the starting point of our discussion of the relation of the *Essay* to the work of Descartes, Locke's own account of what he owed to the great Frenchman. This is contained in his First Letter to Stillingfleet, who had insinuated a want of originality in the *Essay*, and an undue dependence upon Descartes. 'Though I must always acknowledge to that justly admired gentleman, the great obligation of my first deliverance from the unintelligible way of talking of the philosophy in use in the Schools in his time, yet I am so far from entitling his writings to any of the errors or imperfections which are to be found in my *Essay*, as deriving their original from him, that I must own to your lordship they were spun barely out of my own thoughts, reflecting as well as I could on my own mind, and the ideas I had there; and were not, that I know, derived from any other original[1].' In complete agreement with this is the account which Lady Masham gives, as the result of their conversations. 'The first books, as Mr Locke himself has told me, which gave him a relish of philosophical things, were those of Descartes. He was rejoiced in reading these, because, though he very often differed in opinion from this writer, he yet found that what he said was very intelligible; from whence he was

[1] *Works*, vol. IV. pp. 48–9.

encouraged to think that his not having understood others had possibly not proceeded from a defect in his understanding[1].' It is thus clear that Locke himself definitely attributed his own philosophical awakening to the influence of Descartes. But while freely recognising his indebtedness for his emancipation from 'the unintelligible way of talking of the philosophy in use in the Schools,' and the general value of the stimulus which he had received from the Cartesian writings, he did not regard himself as sharing any considerable body of doctrine in common with his intellectual deliverer. On the contrary, he was much more frequently conscious of differences than of agreements, between the results of his own thought and the system of his predecessor. What he conceived himself to owe to Descartes was not a set of principles, but the inspiration and example of an 'intelligible' way of dealing with philosophical questions, standing in sharp contrast with the traditional scholastic methods, which had already aroused his disgust.

§ 2. A writer's estimate of his own relation to another can, of course, never be accepted as final. It often happens that where the connection is most close and intimate, it most easily escapes his notice, just because the thought of the other has become so completely a living part of the structure of his own mind. In the present instance, it cannot, I think, be doubted that Locke has indicated quite correctly at least the primary aspect of his indebtedness to Descartes. He learned from him, in the first place, that it was possible to deal with philosophical questions in a manner which made throughout a direct appeal to the individual's intelligence; and he acquired from him

[1] Lady Masham to Le Clerc, 12th Jan., 1705–6. Quoted in Fox Bourne's *Life of John Locke*, vol. I. pp. 61–2.

the conception of a form of knowledge which was completely satisfying, by virtue of its perfect clarity and intellectual necessity, while at the same time capable of advancing to new truths with the force of demonstration.

The passage we have quoted from the controversy with Stillingfleet indicates, however, a further relation, even in its very repudiation of a more specific dependence. For though Descartes could not be held responsible for anything that Locke might 'spin out of his own thoughts,' as the result of his 'reflection upon his own mind and the ideas he found there,' it can hardly be doubted that the whole conception of 'ideas' as the proper objects of knowledge is Cartesian in origin. In fact, the general point of view from which the enquiry of the *Essay* is carried on, and many of its special doctrines, must be regarded as having their historical basis in the Cartesian treatment of self-consciousness. Without the influence of the Cartesian view of knowledge and the Cartesian conception of self-consciousness, it is not too much to say that the *Essay*, as we know it, would never have been written. At the same time, we shall find that the way in which Locke develops the view of knowledge which he found in Descartes, and the very different use to which he puts the conception of self-consciousness, suffice to negative at once the suggestion of any want of originality in his fundamental positions. So freely, indeed, does he transform the Cartesian principles, that the existence of any positive relation of dependence upon them has frequently been ignored by the historian of philosophy, and the positions of Descartes and Locke have been set in antithetical opposition to each other.

§ 3. Whatever similarity we may find in certain respects between Locke's conception of knowledge and that of Descartes, there was at all events a profound difference in the point of view and purpose with which they approached its consideration; a difference, moreover, which affected their whole treatment of the subject. Descartes was above all a system-builder, to whose temper the critical attitude of Locke was entirely foreign. Important as is the place which is occupied by the theory of knowledge in his philosophy, its treatment is only preliminary and subordinate to the actual construction of the system. While insisting that the foundation of well-grounded certainty is only to be reached by the attempt to render doubt universal, he held that doubt had served its purpose when it had laid bare the fundamental truth of the existence of self. The process of doubting, as he says, is one which we have to go through 'once in our life[1].' Having obtained his indubitable starting-point, what he sought above all in his consideration of knowledge was to discover the true method by means of which a connected system of knowledge might be reared upon it. Assuming that the unity of the knowing mind must be reflected in the structure of knowledge, there must, he thought, be some one method by the use of which knowledge may be extended in new directions, whatever its subject-matter may be. And this method, by following which the path of discovery will become easy and smooth, he was convinced he had found. Henceforth the enquirer may proceed in perfect confidence, and without further reflections on the instrument, to construct the system of knowledge. Nothing could have been further from his thought than the necessity or even the possibility of a criticism of categories. No difficulties or obscurities lurked for him in such conceptions as substance or causality, which were accepted as deliverances

[1] *Principles of Philosophy*, Part I. § I. Cf. beginning of Meditation I.

of the 'natural light,' the validity and adequacy of which for the determination of the real no doubt could assail.

Very different, we know, was Locke's conception of his problem. The attempt to furnish a new method of knowledge he expressly repudiates. His aim, he declares, was 'not to teach the world a new way of certainty...but to endeavour to show wherein the old and only way of certainty consists[1].' And hence the relation of his undertaking to the actual extension of scientific knowledge is much more modestly conceived. He has no thought of instructing 'a Boyle or a Sydenham,' 'the great Huygenius,' or 'the incomparable Mr Newton,' as to the method they should employ in their investigations, but holds that 'it is ambition enough to be employed as an under-labourer in clearing the ground a little, and removing some of the rubbish that lies in the way to knowledge[2].' Leaving to others the attempt to extend the actual bounds of knowledge, he would seek by a process of systematic reflection to ascertain its nature and possible extent. Instead of seeking a method which, once discovered, will enable us to proceed dogmatically, he proclaims the need of criticism.

There is, indeed, one passage in the *Regulae* in which Descartes seems almost verbally to anticipate Locke's formulation of his problem. Though attention has been called to it by Kuno Fischer and others, it will be well to quote it at length. 'Now there does not arise here any problem the solution of which is of greater importance than that of determining the nature of human knowledge and how far it extends; two points which we combine into one and the same enquiry, which it is necessary first of

[1] Third Letter to Stillingfleet, *Works*, vol. IV. p. 459.

[2] *Essay*, The Epistle to the Reader.

all to consider in accordance with the rules given above. This is a question which one must face once in one's life, if one has ever so slight a love of truth, since it embraces the whole of method, and as it were the true instruments of knowledge. Nothing seems to me to be more absurd than to discuss with boldness the mysteries of nature, the influence of the stars, and the secrets of the future, without having once asked whether the human mind is competent to such enquiries[1].' But even in this passage which so closely adumbrates Locke's statement of his problem, there is a striking difference of spirit from that in which the *Essay* was composed. The question which is here recommended to each man for consideration 'once in his life' became for Locke the subject of a lifelong study, a satisfactory comprehension of which could only be hoped for as the result of a laborious and detailed investigation. The difference cannot be better illustrated than by comparing the extract just given from Descartes with the following passage written by Locke in 1677, some six years after the inception of the *Essay*. 'It would be of great service to us to know how far our faculties can reach, that so we might not go about to fathom where our line is too short; to know what things are the proper objects of our enquiries and understanding, and where it is we ought to stop and launch out no further, for fear of losing ourselves or our labour. This, perhaps, is an enquiry of as much difficulty as any we shall find in our way of knowledge, and fit to be resolved by a man when he is come to the end of his study, and not to be proposed to one at his setting out; it being properly the result to be expected after a long and diligent research, to determine what is knowable and what not; and

[1] *Regulae ad directionem ingenii*, VIII.

not a question to be resolved by the guesses of one who has scarce yet acquainted himself with obvious truths. I shall, therefore, at present suspend the thoughts I have had upon this subject, which ought maturely to be considered of[1].'

§ 4. But, opposed in spirit and intention as is Locke's investigation of knowledge to that of Descartes, his account of what constitutes knowledge takes as its starting point the Cartesian view of its nature. It was, indeed, inevitable that a thinker at all in touch with the contemporary progress in science should find his ideal of knowledge in the rational systems of truth of which the mathematical sciences were the most perfect, if not the only examples; but Descartes was at all events the first to attempt to develop a general theory of knowledge from this point of view. And not only so, but the accounts which they give of this intellectually satisfying rational knowledge are in many respects similar. The difficulty of determining how far Locke's views on this subject were formed under the direct influence of Descartes is increased by the fact that the closest resemblances between the two appear when we compare Locke's position with the exposition of Descartes' views contained in the *Regulae ad directionem ingenii*, an unfinished fragment, which was only published in 1701, fifty-one years after the death of Descartes, and eleven years after the first appearance of the *Essay concerning Human Understanding*. The exposition which is there given of the Cartesian conception of knowledge, and of the proper method of pursuing it, is indeed on the whole only a more detailed and complete account of the view which finds expression in the better known and earlier published works of its author. It is, however, not impossible that during

[1] From a paper entitled 'Study during a Journey,' Lord King, p. 106.

Locke's prolonged residence on the continent, with its opportunities for intercourse with members of the Cartesian School, he may have been indirectly influenced by the more elaborate but unpublished account of the views of its founder.

However this may be, we find Descartes, in the work in question, applying the term 'intuition' to the mental function by which we apprehend the perfectly clear and distinct conceptions and self-evident principles of reason, which constitute for him the simple constituents of our knowledge; a use of the term which he notices as novel. Again, the 'deduction' of the *Regulae* is indistinguishable from the 'demonstration' of the *Essay*, each being conceived as consisting of a connected chain of intuitions. Not only is the way the same in which the relation of the two forms of knowledge to each other is described by the two writers, but we find in Descartes the same inconsistency as regards the absolute certainty of deduction which we have already noticed in Locke. At one time he writes of both intuition and deduction as incapable of error; while elsewhere an inferior degree of certitude is assigned to the latter, in view of its complex character and its dependence upon memory.

§ 5. But if, as we seem forced to recognise, Locke's view of the general nature of scientific knowledge, including his conception of intuition as the sole source of certainty and of its relation to demonstration, is due directly or indirectly to the influence of Descartes; it must be added that he did not merely receive, but rendered more definite, and modified and developed in new directions, the Cartesian doctrine. In the first place, there is an almost studied carelessness in the terms used by Descartes to designate the general nature of the contents of intuition, which are spoken of indifferently as 'simple natures,' 'conceptions' or 'notions,' 'propositions' or 'principles.' This vagueness in their designation may perhaps be regarded as connected with the peculiar Cartesian view which attributed the affirmation or denial which constitutes judgment to the will, the understanding being restricted to the apprehension of the ideal contents involved in the judgment. For, while the understanding is defined as the faculty by which we apprehend ideas, without making any affirmation or denial, its function is regarded as extending beyond that of the contemplation of single ideas. It 'proposes' connections to the will, and 'inclines' that faculty to the affirmation or denial which it is itself unable to make. Nay, 'the minds of all have been so impressed by nature as spontaneously to assent to whatever is clearly perceived by the understanding[1].' Thus, the full function of the understanding exceeds the formation of isolated concepts, while falling short of judgment. With Locke, on the other hand, the rôle assigned to intuition is definitely that of grasping necessary connections between the contents of different ideas, while the act of judgment is itself conceived as a function of understanding. The fact that Descartes at times speaks of ideas as 'true,' though recognising that in themselves they are incapable of falsity, signifies that he had not definitely abandoned the theory which finds the primary form of knowledge in the concept for the view advanced by Locke, according to which it is only to be found in the judgment. It is not, therefore, surprising that Locke should have regarded his own definition of knowledge as something novel, which even the writer to whom his general conception of knowledge admittedly owed most had failed to anticipate. 'Nobody that I ever

[1] *Principles of Philosophy*, Part I. § 43.

met with,' he tells us, 'had in their writings particularly set down wherein the act of knowing precisely consisted[1].' And of Descartes he specifically declares that he did not 'place certainty in the perception of the agreement or disagreement of ideas[2].'

§ 6. The hesitation in Descartes between the view which accepts concepts as the primary data of knowledge, and that which maintains that the very simplest item of knowledge involves a judgment, has a distinctly prejudicial effect upon the actual working of his method. Its results are seen in the tendency to accept mere conceivability as the criterion of truth, in place of the apprehension of necessary connection, to which Descartes inclined in his better moments, and upon which Locke insisted. Thus, according to Descartes, it is 'sufficient to assure us that two substances are really mutually distinct, if only we are able clearly and distinctly to conceive the one of them without the other[3].' Since he can 'in thought exclude from himself every other substance, whether thinking or extended,' it is to him 'certain that each of us thus considered is really distinct from every other thinking and corporeal substance[4].' Equally loose and unsatisfactory, in Locke's view, was the complementary tendency to regard an inability to conceive the nature and manner of existence of anything as a sufficient ground for denying its actuality or possibility. To all such easy roads to truth, Locke's attitude is expressed in the words applied by him to a particular instance of this procedure. 'This, I am afraid, is to be sure without proofs, and to know without perceiving[5].'

[1] Second Letter to Stillingfleet, *Works*, vol. IV. p. 143.
[2] Third Letter to Stillingfleet, *Works*, vol. IV. p. 362.
[3] *Principles of Philosophy*, Part I. § 60. [4] *loc. cit.*
[5] II. I. 18.

§ 7. The advance made in Locke's general conception of knowledge becomes more marked when we notice his insistence on the distinction between the synthetic connections, which constitute the content of 'instructive' propositions, and the merely analytic relations, which are set forth in those which are 'trifling.' For, although Descartes, in contrasting his own conception of deduction with the syllogism, objects to the latter that its function is limited to the exposition of what we know already, and that it is consequently incapable of yielding any new truth, he never really grasped the distinction between an analytic and a synthetic procedure of thought. That 'a triangle is bounded by three sides' was to him as valuable a revelation of intuition as any in mathematics, and he was always best pleased when he thought he had exhibited a fundamental axiom in a form the denial of which would involve a contradiction in terms. Thus Descartes, and to a still greater extent his followers, constantly gave expression to the view that knowledge is to be obtained by an analytical manipulation of concepts.

§ 8. We have seen, so far, that Locke's account of scientific knowledge differed from that of Descartes in its clearer recognition of the judgment as the unit of knowledge, and in its rejection of merely analytic judgments as 'trifling.' We reach a still more profound difference in Locke's view of the limitation of rational or scientific knowledge. Regarding it as axiomatic that all knowledge must conform to a single type, Descartes had identified knowledge with the content of clear and distinct thought, and had sought to eliminate from its final form all reference to the dim and obscure region of sense-experience. Against this theory of the purely rational constitution of knowledge, Locke sets his theory of a duality of type in our knowledge, which we cannot transcend. So far from laying bare to our gaze the innermost nature of being, rational or scientific knowledge is, he maintains, restricted to the contemplation of the relations of our abstract ideas, and is incapable of giving us a knowledge of real existence. For that we must appeal to the experience which Descartes had despised, even though in doing so we may be obliged to sacrifice the form of intellectually transparent cognition, and in the end find ourselves only in superficial contact with reality at particular points.

§ 9. Having noticed the general relation of Locke's conception of what constitutes knowledge to that of Descartes, we may illustrate the difference of view by an examination of the passages in Locke's writings which are expressly directed against some of the leading positions in the Cartesian system. We shall find that his criticism is primarily based upon his view of the inadequacy and vicious nature of the Cartesian logic. However 'intelligible' he might find the writings of Descartes, the Cartesian method seemed to him to show only a partial escape from the toils of Scholasticism. It implied that the nature of real being could be determined by a purely abstract process of thought. Seeking to decide questions of matter of fact without reference to experience, its 'demonstrations' are found to consist of analyses of presupposed conceptions or definitions, in which the question at issue is simply begged.

These objections of method are clearly implied in Locke's criticism of Descartes' use of the ontological argument, to which attention has already been called[1]. Existence, he urges, is only 'supposed' and not 'proved'

[1] Cf. above, ch. VII. § 14.

in that argument. Nor, he proceeds, can it be proved by any amount of consideration of our ideas. 'Real existence can be proved only by real existence'; and our knowledge of existence, upon which alone a proof of existence can be based, must be derived from experience of some kind. The same objections will be found to underlie Locke's criticism of the two fundamental Cartesian positions to which exception is taken in the *Essay*; viz. (1) that thought is the essence of mind; (2) that extension is the essence of body or material substance.

§ 10. Having secured the starting-point of his Metaphysics by means of the *Cogito ergo sum*, Descartes at once applied to the thinker, whose existence he found to be indubitable, the current conceptions of substance and essence. What the act of thought revealed to us was, he declared, the existence of a substance of which thought was the essence or fundamental quality. And since a substance could not exist without its essence, this carried with it the conclusion that the mind is always thinking. 'Thought,' too, it must be remembered, meant for Descartes, thought which was conscious of itself. The difficulties in which Descartes and his followers inevitably became entangled, when they attempted to explain the familiar experience of sleep, or the hypothetical soul-life of the unborn infant, in accordance with this *a priori* position, offered an easy target for Locke's criticism and ridicule. With this, however, we are not here concerned, but with the way in which Locke brings his conception of the nature and conditions of knowledge to bear upon the question. To him, the contention that the mind always thinks, was not only unfounded, but was of the very kind which his theory had shown to be intrinsically incapable of justification, viz., a universal statement concerning matter of fact. As such it could obtain a warrant neither from experience nor from the consideration of our abstract ideas. Let us take first the evidence of experience. 'We know certainly, by experience, that we sometimes think; and thence draw this infallible consequence, that there is something in us that has a power to think. But whether that substance perpetually thinks or no, we can be no further assured than experience informs us[1].' The deliverance of experience being thus limited, let us see what can be effected when the appeal is made to abstract thought. The statement that the soul always thinks is not, Locke declares, a self-evident proposition[2]. And when he examines the Cartesian attempt to exhibit it as a content of clear and distinct thought, he finds that this consists in the question-begging derivation of the proposition from a presupposed conception, or definition of the soul's nature. 'To say that actual thinking is essential to the soul and inseparable from it, is to beg what is in question, and not to prove it by reason[3].' Or, as he elsewhere contemptuously exclaims, with reference to the Cartesian position, 'it is but defining the soul to be "a substance that always thinks" and the business is done[4].' We may indeed, he allows, frame hypotheses concerning matters of fact which lie beyond the range of actual experience, although such hypotheses are from the nature of the case incapable of demonstration and can at best only possess a certain degree of probability. But such hypotheses, he maintains, must be based on the results of observation, and framed on the analogy of our experience. The Cartesians, he complains, instead of doing this, seek to determine matters of fact by their abstract conceptions, though these are in truth but ungrounded hypotheses or

[1] II. I. 10. [2] *loc. cit.* [3] *loc. cit.* [4] II. I. 19.

suppositions. 'It is doubted whether I thought all last night or no. The question being about a matter of fact, it is begging it to bring, as a proof for it, an hypothesis which is the very thing in dispute; by which way one may prove anything; and it is but supposing that all watches, whilst the balance beats, think, and it is sufficiently proved and past doubt that my watch thought all last night. But he that would not deceive himself ought to build his hypothesis on matter of fact, and make it out by sensible experience, and not presume on matter of fact, because of his hypothesis, that is, because he supposes it to be so[1].' The same objection to the Cartesian procedure is expressed again when he declares that 'he that will suffer himself to be informed by observation and experience, and not make his own hypothesis the rule of nature, will find few signs of a soul accustomed to much thinking in a new-born child[2].'

§ 11. Similar objections of method are urged against the Cartesian contention that extension is the essence of body or material substance, and that consequently a vacuum is impossible. Here again he finds the Cartesians offering a mere analysis of conceptions or definitions, as a means of determining a question of fact. 'He that, with Descartes, shall frame in his mind an idea of what he calls "body" to be nothing but extension, may easily demonstrate that there is no vacuum, *i.e.*, no space void of body, by this maxim, "What is, is." For, the idea to which he annexes the name "body" being bare extension, his knowledge that space cannot be without body is certain[3].' But, as he goes on to point out, the futility of such procedure becomes apparent when we consider that the contradictory proposition can just as easily and as well

[1] II. I. 10. [2] II. I. 21. [3] IV. 7. 12.

be 'demonstrated' by this method. 'If another should come and make to himself another idea, different from Descartes', of the thing, which yet with Descartes he calls by the same name, "body," and make his idea, which he expresses by the name "body," to be of a thing that hath both extension and solidity together; he will as easily demonstrate that there may be a vacuum, or space without body, as Descartes demonstrated the contrary[1].' In the denial of the possibility of a vacuum, as in the assertion that the soul always thinks, Locke finds an attempt to determine matters of fact in an altogether illegitimate way, by means of abstract thought; the Cartesian contention, in the last resort, resolving itself into the mere assumption that space is always filled space, 'a supposed matter of fact, which experiment can never make out[2].'

Locke is not satisfied, however, with pointing out the fallacious nature of the Cartesian procedure, but proceeds to adduce arguments in favour of a different view of the relation of extension to body. In addition to extension, body, he maintains, involves solidity, by which it fills or occupies space, and absolutely resists the entrance of any other body into the portion of space which it occupies. Moreover, he urges, the parts of 'pure space' are inseparable, even in thought, and incapable of movement; by which characteristics our idea of space is further distinguished from that of body.

Having thus brought out the difference between the two ideas, Locke proceeds to argue against the Cartesian contention, that since extension is merely an attribute of material substance, empty space is an impossibility. He appeals, in the first place, to the assumed finiteness of the material universe, beyond which space must be conceived

[1] IV. 7. 13. [2] II. 13. 22.

as stretching to infinity. The Cartesians are accordingly presented with the dilemma, that they 'must either own that they think body infinite, though they are loth to speak it out, or else affirm that space is not body[1].' But the former alternative is one which 'no one will affirm[2],' the supposition of an 'abyss of infinite matter' being, indeed, 'the most absurd and most incomprehensible of all others[3].' Another argument is drawn from the abstract possibility of the annihilation of a portion of matter, while surrounding bodies remain at rest. The argument, however, to which Locke attaches most importance is that which infers the existence of empty space as a necessary condition of the possibility of movement.

In so far as Locke assumes that the Cartesian position involves a complete identification of our ideas of body and space, it must be confessed that he does his opponents less than justice, for, while denying any real difference between body and space, Descartes and the more careful of his followers had allowed that there is a difference in our manner of conceiving them. For, as they observed, we regard the same portion of space as successively occupied by different bodies[4]. This difference, indeed, they could only conceive, in accordance with their rationalistic bias, as that between a class and its members. The unity of space was, therefore, declared to be generic.

Nor does any particular importance or originality attach to Locke's arguments in favour of the reality of empty space. Two at least of them were commonplaces in the discussion of the subject; while Locke's favourite argument, that without empty space movement would be impossible, involves a *petitio principii*, when urged

[1] II. 13. 21. [2] *loc. cit.* [3] II. 23. 27.

[4] Cf. Descartes, *Principles of Philosophy*, Part II. §§ 10–12.

against the Cartesian view. For it derives its whole force from the tacit assumption that matter ultimately consists of discrete and absolutely solid parts; whereas Descartes had regarded matter as possessing the continuity which characterises its essential attribute, extension.

§ 12. We must now turn from the consideration and illustration of the relation of Locke's general conception of knowledge to that of Descartes, to an examination of the influence exerted upon his position by the Cartesian conception of self-consciousness. We have already seen that he follows Descartes in declaring that the certainty of the existence of self is involved in every act of thought, and that the knowledge of existence thus obtained is intuitive. Indeed the uniqueness of this implication of being in thought is of even greater importance for Locke than for Descartes. For to the latter the ontological argument afforded a second direct point of connection between thought and being, which we have seen Locke expressly rejected.

Again, we are certainly justified in seeing the influence of Descartes in the presupposition which Locke accepts as axiomatic, needing neither discussion nor defence, that apart from the unique presence of the mind to itself, and the cognisance of self which results therefrom, the only immediate objects of the understanding are 'ideas'; while these ideas are apprehended by the mind to which they are present as signs or representations of a world of things beyond it. For while the dualism of mind and external reality underlying this conception, and the theory of representative perception which it involves, are both older than Descartes, the form in which they appear in Locke bears the unmistakeable stamp of that master.

§ 13. But while in the ways just indicated the Cartesian conception of self-consciousness helped to determine two of the fundamental positions of Locke's theory of knowledge, a still more important influence remains to be indicated. It was by a transformation of the Cartesian conception of self-consciousness that Locke reached what is most peculiar and distinctive in his own method. In the *Cogito ergo sum* a priority had been assigned to our knowledge of the conscious subject as compared with that of the objective universe. To Descartes, however, this priority had been little more than an incidental device of method. With the interpretation of thought as the essence of a mental substance the point of view shifts to that of dogmatic realism, for which self-consciousness is merely the leading characteristic of a particular kind of real being. That Locke's own theory of consciousness is not free from elements of a similar realism we have already recognised. While refusing to follow Descartes in regarding thought as the essence of mind, he admits the necessity of referring it as an activity to a substance beyond experience. It remains true, nevertheless, that in the *Essay* the attempt was made for the first time to work out a theory of knowledge from the standpoint of conscious experience. Instead of adopting the point of view of the conscious subject as a temporary expedient, destined to be superseded as soon as the foundations of his system had been laid, Locke sought to make it the permanent centre from which his survey of the whole contents of knowledge should be taken. And profound as is the difference between Descartes' dogmatic interpretation of self-consciousness and Locke's employment of it as the vantage-ground for a critical examination of knowledge, its treatment by Locke has its roots in the work of his predecessor. The very conception of the 'historical' plain method, which seeks to investigate the functions of mind in knowledge, without troubling itself to examine 'wherein its essence consists,' or to consider the relation of mental to physical facts, would have been impossible had not Descartes once for all shown that consciousness possesses positive features of its own, which enable it to be conceived without confusion with the characteristics of physical reality, and which, indeed, absolutely preclude the ascription to it of those spacial determinations which necessarily pertain to physical existence.

§ 14. Taking then his stand upon the ground of conscious experience, which Descartes had indicated but had not sought permanently to occupy, Locke finds himself in a position from which the dogmatic pretensions of the system of his predecessor are still further discredited. Not only are we unable to determine the essence of material and mental substances by a process of abstract thought, but a knowledge of the real essences of substances is found to be an ideal which is for ever beyond our grasp. Our ideas of matter and mind turn out from this new point of view to be alike 'superficial'; our idea of body being only that of 'an extended solid substance, capable of communicating motion by impulse,' while that of spirit is the idea of 'a substance that thinks and has a power of exciting motion in body by will or thought[1].' These 'primary qualities or properties' of body and of spirit experience reveals to us, but of the inner nature and manner of operation of each we are entirely in the dark. In place of two substances from whose clearly defined essences the whole of their further determinations are conceived as deducible, body

[1] II. 23. 22.

and mind are only knowable as objects of a partial and therefore imperfect experience. Further, as we have also seen, since the idea of substance is in both cases alike merely that of 'a supposed I-know-not-what' to which the attributes revealed in experience are referred, we cannot set aside the possibility that one and the same *substratum* or substantial basis may be involved, both in that which we experience as solid and extended and in our own conscious life. There is, he maintains, 'no contradiction in it that the first eternal thinking Being should, if he pleased, give to certain systems of created senseless matter, put together as he thinks fit, some degrees of sense, perception and thought[1].' Whether he has done so or not is a matter which we cannot settle 'by the contemplation of our own ideas,' and concerning which we may never be able to attain to knowledge.

That in opposing the dogmatic determination of the soul as an immaterial substance, on the ground that 'it becomes the modesty of philosophy not to pronounce magisterially, where we want that evidence that can produce knowledge[2],' Locke had the procedure of Descartes specially in view, is evident from a passage in his Third Letter to Stillingfleet. He there declares that he knows 'nobody before Descartes that ever pretended to show that there was any contradiction[3]' in the supposition that the power of thinking may be bestowed upon a material substance. To the Cartesian hypothesis, according to which a mental and a material substance have been in some unexplained manner united in the individual human being, an incidental reference is also made. It is, he remarks, 'in respect of our notions, not much more remote from our comprehension to conceive that God

[1] IV. 3. 6. [2] *loc. cit.* [3] *Works*, vol. IV. p. 469.

can, if he pleases, superadd to matter a faculty of thinking, than that he should superadd to it another substance with the faculty of thinking[1].'

If then Locke failed to find in his new point of view a positive solution of the difficulties concerning the relation of the mental and the material, it at least sufficed to destroy the pretensions of opposing dogmatisms. So, too, although Locke, like Descartes, begins by taking for granted the current categories for the interpretation of the real, they have not for him the same fixity and rigidity as for his predecessor, but inevitably, as we have seen, tend to be disintegrated or transformed when regarded from the point of view of conscious experience.

§ 15. The difference between Locke's and Descartes' use of the principle of self-consciousness shows itself, in another way, when we compare the accounts which they give of the nature of conscious process. Here, as elsewhere, there is an initial community of doctrine of a kind which shows the dependence of Locke upon his predecessor. For him, as for Descartes, consciousness necessarily involves self-consciousness, though neither thinker is able to maintain this position with perfect consistency. Descartes is obliged to forget it, in the interest of his metaphysical positions; at times Locke tends to ignore it, in the pursuit of some piece of psychological analysis. Again, for both thinkers this principle carries with it the identification of mental activity with volition, and as a consequence of this, the passivity of the understanding in relation to ideas which it does not consciously fashion for itself. Locke, too, follows Descartes in his ultimate classification of mental functions under the two heads of

[1] IV. 3. 6.

'perception' and 'willing,' the operations respectively of 'understanding' and 'will[1].'

When, however, we come to the treatment in detail of the contents of the mind, the differences between the two interpretations of self-consciousness show themselves in a marked way. Having attributed self-consciousness as its essence to an immaterial substance, Descartes is led, in the first instance, to limit the operations of the mind to the function of pure thought, as distinguished from sense-perception and imagination. For the latter depend upon physical conditions and cannot, therefore, belong to the essence of an immaterial being. Pure thought, on the other hand, must be conceived as exercised apart from the influence of anything in our bodily state. As the result of this abstract limitation of the sphere of self-consciousness, the fullness of the content of concrete experience is excluded from the Cartesian conception of mind. The very existence of sense-perceptions, appetites and emotions, becomes an inexplicable anomaly; belonging, as they do, neither to the mind nor to extended substance, but arising from a union of the two which, upon Cartesian principles, is theoretically impossible. It is not, however, to the contradictions involved in the Cartesian position that we would here draw attention, but to the obstacles which it placed in the way of the rise of an empirical psychology, which should take the processes of conscious experience as such for its field of investigation. The function of 'pure' thought did not easily lend itself to psychological description or analysis; while, with reference to the obscure phenomena which arose from the union of mind and body, attention was naturally concentrated mainly upon the psycho-physical problem. Accordingly, the explanations

[1] II. 6. 2; cf. Descartes' *Principles of Philosophy*, Part I. § 32.

which Descartes has to offer of the facts of sense-perception, imagination and memory, consist of elaborate hypotheses concerning the physical processes involved in them, supplemented by a reference to the mysterious operation by which the mind 'turned itself towards' the final member of the physical series. By this act the contents of sense-perception and imagination are supposed to be taken up into self-consciousness, though they inevitably remain a foreign element, which it cannot completely assimilate. While, then, the *Cogito ergo sum* placed in a strong light the reality of the mental life, the metaphysical interpretation of self-consciousness prevented this from being made the subject of serious study. Though designed for another purpose, the prosecution of the 'historical plain method' at once made it possible to do justice to the concrete fullness of experience and laid the foundations of modern psychology.

§ 16. The difference between Descartes' view of mind and that of Locke finds its final and most famous expression in the opposition between the Cartesian theory of innate ideas and Locke's theory of the origin of ideas in experience. This conflict of opinion, however, is not, as is often supposed, a primary and ultimate divergence of view, but is itself a further consequence of their different ways of regarding and treating the self-consciousness which is for both the starting-point of philosophy. Not only so, but the theory of innate ideas occurs in Descartes in two distinct forms, one of which is the outcome of his abstract theory of self-consciousness as identical with pure thought, while the other results from the more concrete view of its nature, towards which he was driven by the facts of sense-experience. The theory in both its forms rests upon the view that thought is the essence of mind. In its first and more familiar form the theory of innate ideas meets us in the *Meditations*, where ideas are divided into three classes with reference to their origin. These are (1) 'innate' ideas, which have their origin in the very constitution of the mind itself, or of our faculty of thought: (2) 'adventitious' ideas, which are produced in the mind by the operation of external things; and (3) 'factitious' ideas, due to the mind's own voluntary activity. The important point, of course, is the ground of distinction between (1) and (2). To the class of innate ideas are referred all those clear and distinct ideas which are the objects of pure thought. For, the faculty of pure thought constituting the essence of the mind, its ideas cannot be received from without. More particularly Descartes argues, and upon this argument he lays great stress, that these ideas being universal cannot be due to corporeal motions, since these are always particular. Experience, indeed, may be needed to serve as the occasion on which the mind brings forth from itself these riches, which it previously contained only virtually, but they can be in no sense produced by experience.

But, as we have seen, Descartes found it impossible to adhere consistently to his wholly abstract view of self-consciousness. Room had to be found within the mind somewhere, and at whatever sacrifice, for the data of sense-experience; and with their inclusion in the mind the theory of innate ideas had also to extend its bounds. In however equivocal a form, the mental nature of the data of sensation had in the last resort to be admitted, and as mental they could not really be produced by anything that took place in a second and inferior substance, the body. Accordingly, Descartes is in the end somewhat reluctantly brought to the view, that even the ideas of sense must be 'natural' to the mind, or 'innate'; the bodily condition only serving to determine the time at which ideas shall be formed, while their intrinsic nature depends entirely on our faculty of thought, in which they must have been virtually present all along. Upon this second view, therefore, instead of innate ideas forming a special class of ideas, innateness is a characteristic which belongs to all ideas as such.

§ 17. In an earlier chapter the view has been put forward that the argument of the First Book of the *Essay* was primarily directed against the adherents of the scholastic method, who found in a theory of innate principles the basis they needed for their employment of the syllogism. At the same time, it was suggested that the Cartesian doctrine was also regarded by Locke as within the range of his criticism. We must now consider in more detail the justification for this view, in so far as it refers to Descartes.

That the polemic had not the Cartesian position primarily in view appears from the fact that it is with 'innate principles,' and not innate 'ideas,' that the argument as a whole is concerned. Locke even tells us that if the upholders of the theory had realised that without innate ideas there can be no innate principles, 'they would not, perhaps, have been so forward to believe' in the existence of the latter[1]. This remark, by itself, is sufficient to refute the supposition that the polemic is primarily directed against the Cartesians. Again, the theory as it appears in Descartes is not bound up with the crude appeal to 'universal consent,' with which it is directly connected by Locke. On the other hand, the distinction between 'ideas' and 'principles' was not, as we have seen, clearly drawn by Descartes, and

[1] I. 4. I.

the denial of innate ideas is itself an essential part of Locke's argument. Moreover, as has already been pointed out, the contrast which we find in the *Essay* between innate and 'adventitious' ideas seems to be directly drawn from the first form of the Cartesian theory. It is, of course, in this form that the theory is directly exposed to Locke's attack, and there is no evidence that he was aware that when pushed Descartes had been obliged to admit that for him all ideas must be innate. On the contrary, when Locke argues that 'if the capacity of knowing be the natural impression contended for, all the truths a man ever comes to know will by this account be everyone of them innate[1],' this conclusion is put forward as an inference of his own from the alleged premises, and not as a position which he regarded as having been actually held. Against both forms of the theory, as held by Descartes, the principle that 'to be in the understanding is to be understood' applied with overwhelming effect, since it cannot be evaded by one who accepts the Cartesian view that the essence of mind consists in self-conscious thought. Others might have difficulty in explaining what they meant by the existence in the mind of ideas of which there was no consciousness. By Descartes and his followers, such a supposition should have been rejected as a contradiction in terms.

§ 18. Moreover, as we have seen, though it was from Descartes that Locke had first learned the possibility of a better method of knowledge than the scholastic, by an appeal to the mind's own faculty of intuition, he was of opinion that his predecessor had made only an imperfect use of this principle. In the attempt to determine fundamental questions of fact in an *a priori* manner, apart from

[1] I. 2. 5.

any reference to experience, and in the tendency to offer an exposition of conceptions in place of a synthetic demonstration, there was evidence that after all Descartes had not completely emancipated himself from the toils of the scholastic logic. And since these features were precisely those which a theory of innateness was designed to support, the defects of method and the presence of the offending theory could hardly fail to be connected in Locke's mind. And if there were good grounds for suspecting the theory of innate ideas as it occurred in the master, the use which was made of it by many of his followers was still more open to objection. On this point it will be sufficient to quote the testimony of Leibniz who, while strenuously opposing Locke's position, admits that he was justified on methodological grounds in opposing the use to which innate principles and ideas were put both by the 'vulgar philosophers,' or representatives of the current scholastic tradition, and by the Cartesians. 'He has doubtless had good reasons for opposing himself on this point to ordinary prejudices, for the name of ideas and principles is greatly abused. The vulgar philosophers manufacture for themselves principles according to their fancy; and the Cartesians, who profess greater accuracy, do not cease to entrench themselves behind pretended "ideas" of extension, of matter, and of the soul, desiring to avoid thereby the necessity of proving what they advance, on the pretext that those who meditate on these ideas will discover in them the same thing as they; that is to say, that those who will accustom themselves to their manner of thought will have the same prepossessions, which is very true[1].'

[1] Leibniz, *Reflexions sur l'essai de l'entendement humain de M. Locke.*

CHAPTER X

LOCKE AND CONTEMPORARY ENGLISH PHILOSOPHY

§ 1. In an enquiry into the influence upon Locke's philosophy of the thought of his own countrymen, the names of the two greatest of his English predecessors naturally occur to us first. Of the work of Bacon there is not the slightest trace in the *Essay*. The undoubted references to Hobbes are invariably hostile, and are not of such a character as to imply a close study of his writings. In one passage, the answer which 'an Hobbist' would give to the question as to why men should keep their contracts is contrasted with those of a Christian and of the 'old heathen philosophers[1].' Nor can it be doubted that Locke's insistence upon the demonstrability of morality is mainly directed against the theory of the dependence of the moral law upon the civil power, which was thought to be implied in the doctrine of the *Leviathan*. Again, in his defence of the idea of spiritual substance, and in his elaborate argumentation[2] for the immateriality and mental nature of the Eternal Being, Locke has clearly in view the positions of Hobbes; while his reference, in the course of this argument, to 'people whose thoughts are immersed in matter[3],' or to 'men devoted to matter[4],' indicates his view as to the relation between the moral and intellectual aspects of Hobbism. His relative ethics and his materialism were, however, the two points in Hobbes' teaching which had been universally seized upon, and against which refutation after refutation teemed from the press.

[1] I. 3. 5. [2] IV. 10. 9–19. [3] II. 23. 22. [4] IV. 10. 13.

Nor can I find any justification for the view of Fox Bourne, that before commencing the *Essay* Locke had been 'a diligent and wise student of Hobbes[1],' and had learnt quite as much from his *Treatise of human nature* and his *Leviathan*, as from the *Discours de la méthode* and the *Meditationes* of Descartes; but subsequently 'repudiated with some unconscious injustice his debt to the first English teacher of the philosophy of experience[2].' This judgment is apparently based upon a supposed similarity between the first rough draft of Locke's thoughts on the subject of the *Essay*, contained in his commonplace book, and the positions of Hobbes. A careful reading of this interesting document fails, however, to discover any traces of the alleged dependence. The entry in Locke's commonplace book is as follows: 'Sic cogitavit de intellectu humano Johannes Locke, anno 1671. Intellectus humanus cum cognitionis certitudine et assensus firmitate. I imagine that all knowledge is founded on, and ultimately derives itself from, sense or something analogous to it, and may be called sensation; which is done by our senses conversant about particular objects, which give us the simple ideas or images of things, and thus we come to have ideas of heat and light, hard and soft, which are nothing but the reviving again in our minds these imaginations which those objects, when they affected our senses, caused in us, whether by motion or otherwise it matters not here to consider; and thus we do when we conceive heat or light, yellow or blue, sweet or bitter. And therefore I think that those things which we call sensible qualities are the simplest ideas we have, and the first object of our understanding[3].' Now there is no need to assume an influence by Hobbes to

[1] *Life of John Locke*, vol. II. p. 89. [2] *loc cit.* p. 94.

[3] Lord King, *Life and Letters of John Locke*, p. 6.

account for the general theory of the dependence of all our ideas, and hence of all our knowledge, upon the contents of sense-experience, a doctrine which was indeed regarded at the time as a part of orthodox Aristotelianism. And when we consider the peculiar form in which the doctrine is here expressed, we find that, although more crudely stated, it contains already the main characteristics which distinguish the theory of the *Essay* from the position of Hobbes. The 'physical' enquiry as to whether our ideas are produced 'by motion or otherwise' is already set aside, as irrelevant to the investigation of knowledge, whereas Hobbes' constant endeavour is to show that mind and its knowledge can be understood, and can only be understood, by being included in the material system. The whole conception of Locke's criticism is, in fact, radically opposed to the metaphysics of Hobbes. We have, again, in the statement that 'sense or something analogous to it' is the ultimate source of our knowledge, an anticipation of the recognition of Reflection as a distinct source of ideas, upon which Locke's vindication of our idea of mental substance depends. Finally, 'a diligent and wise student of Hobbes' would hardly have used the term 'imaginations' to cover the sense-experiences from which Hobbes had formally distinguished them; while to speak of ideal reproductions as 'revivings' of previous experiences is to ignore the peculiar features of his doctrine of imagination as 'decaying sense.' If any further confirmation of our view is required, it may be found in Locke's treatment of Association, to which a position of such fundamental importance had been assigned in Hobbes' psychology. As has already been pointed out[1], the chapter on the subject was only added as an afterthought, in the

[1] Ch. I. § 11.

fourth edition of the *Essay*. The use which is then made of Association, as merely a principle by which we can explain some part of the oddness and extravagance of men's opinions and actions, certainly does not suggest a close study of the contents of the *Leviathan*.

§ 2. If Locke owed little or nothing, in the way of positive inspiration, to the greatest of his English predecessors, his work stands in the closest relation to the contemporary movements of thought in his own country, whether in religion, ethics, politics, or science. It was an age, moreover, in which those whose interests lay primarily in these special fields generally regarded it as incumbent upon them to connect their views with more general philosophical positions. The speculations of Hobbes had led to a widespread and vigorous attempt to find a rational basis for the moral and religious consciousness, while the natural sciences had not yet cut themselves adrift from enquiries of a more fundamental character. For an influence of the deepest kind we cannot, indeed, look to this source, since those who were most fully conscious of the philosophical significance of the questions at issue were not independent thinkers of the first order. We shall find, however, that if Locke owed to Descartes his original philosophical impulse, and many of his most characteristic positions; and if the scheme in which he envisaged reality was an unwitting inheritance from Scholasticism; yet both in the general spirit of his work, and in the detailed working out and application of his thought, he is most constantly in touch with the English writers of his day.

Foremost amongst these stands the group of thinkers who have come to be known as the Cambridge Platonists.

With their outlook in theology and ecclesiastical politics Locke was in complete sympathy. Like them, he dreaded equally the arrogant claims of authority and the warm fancies of 'enthusiasm'; like them, he sought in reason the basis of a simplified theology, the acceptance of which would lead to toleration in non-essentials. With at least some of the minor members of the school, he was intimately acquainted. The enquiry is inevitably suggested as to how far the agreement extends to more definitely philosophical positions, and whether any direct influence of the school can be traced in the doctrine of the *Essay*.

That clear indications of such an influence exist can hardly, I think, be doubted. Its importance, however, seems to me to be exaggerated in the elaborate work of Dr von Hertling[1]. Distinguishing sharply between an empirical and a rationalistic tendency in Locke's thought, he attributes the latter exclusively to the influence of the Cambridge school. Such a view ignores entirely Locke's relation to Descartes, about the reality of which there can be no doubt whatever. It must be remembered, too, that in the sense in which Locke accepted the Cartesian theory of ideas, which certainly formed the starting point of his own original reflections, the rational and empirical tendencies were united from the first; although it is clear that the rationalistic aspect of his theory came to be more definitely conceived, and more sharply emphasised, as his reflection proceeded. There is, then, no justification for the supposition that he first approached philosophy from a purely empirical point of view, and that a different and opposite direction was subsequently given to his thought from an external source.

[1] *John Locke und die Schule von Cambridge.*

It must be observed, too, that on at least two points of fundamental importance there was a profound divergence between Locke and the members of the Cambridge school. In the first place, nothing could have been further from the minds of the Cambridge thinkers than the conception of an examination of the nature and extent of knowledge, apart from any assumptions or inferences concerning the nature of reality. For, while the question of knowledge receives frequent treatment at their hands, its consideration is entirely subordinated to ontological, theological and ethical interests. Thus, the elaborate discussion of our faculty of knowledge which is contained in Cudworth's *Intellectual System*, occurs in the course of a polemic directed against Materialism and Atheism. More's reflections upon knowledge, again, form an ingredient of his *Antidote against Atheism*, or occur as links in an argument for the immortality of the soul. And what is true of Cudworth and More is true of the less celebrated members of the school. Further, an essential part of the support, which the consideration of the nature of knowledge was thought by these writers to yield, for the refutation of the metaphysics of Hobbes, lay in the establishment of the theory of innate ideas, with its variously interpreted spiritualistic implications. Indeed, nothing, Cudworth declared, could more directly promote atheism than the Aristotelian maxim, 'Nihil est in intellectu quod non fit prius in sensu.'

§ 3. If, however, we turn to the account which the Cambridge men give of the nature of science, or rational knowledge, as distinguished from its metaphysical implications, we shall find a striking similarity to the position of Locke, both in their views and in the terms in which they are expressed. The objects of knowledge, they insist, are not the particular mutable things of sense, but universal, intelligible ideas or essences, which are insusceptible of change. Although these ideas 'exist nowhere but in minds[1]'; and although it depends upon our will whether we shall contemplate them or not; when contemplated they are found to possess 'certain determinate and immutable natures of their own, which are independent upon the mind[2].' Their nature is 'such that the mind of man cannot possibly deny but that they are such and such distinct ideas, and that such and such affections belong to them[3].' Descartes, indeed, had similarly dwelt upon the objectivity and necessity which belong to the content of our innate ideas. He had not, however, explicitly insisted on the relational character of knowledge, as an apprehension of a connection between ideas. The Cambridge writers, on the other hand, are ever calling attention to the 'natural dependencies and correspondencies[4]' of our innate ideas; to their 'necessary' relations[5]; to their 'mutual respects one to another, congruities and incongruities, dependencies and independencies[6]'; to 'the necessary mutual respects and relations of things to one another[7].' These relations, they point out, are dependent solely on the nature of the ideas themselves, and are consequently as immutable and as independent of our subjective activity as their contents. Thus, by the apprehension of these relations the mind is supplied with a cognition of eternal truths, which they maintain, in opposition to Descartes, are independent even of the divine will.

[1] Cudworth, *A Treatise concerning eternal and immutable morality*, bk IV. ch. 5, § 3. [2] *op. cit.* p. 245.

[3] More, *An Antidote against Atheism*, Appendix, ch. II. § 2.

[4] More, *op. cit.* bk I. ch. 8, § 7.

[5] Cudworth, *Intellectual System*, edition of 1845, vol. III. p. 401.

[6] More, *Conjectura cabbalistica*, Preface, § 3.

[7] Rust, *A Discourse of Truth*, § 1.

Their agreement with Locke's position is not confined to their general conception of the nature of rational knowledge, but extends to their view of the subjects in respect of which such knowledge can be obtained. Their favourite illustrations of these intelligible ideas, and of the knowledge which results from the apprehension of their relations, are drawn from the mathematical sciences, more especially from geometry. The members of the school delight to point out that the objects with which this science deals are incapable of existing in the material universe or of being perceived by sense[1]. On the other hand, they are capable of *a priori* determination, and the truths which are obtained from their consideration are universal and necessary. While mathematics thus furnished the readiest example of a system of 'eternal' truths, independent of the existence of anything in the sensible world, one of the chief aims of the school was to exhibit a similar objectivity, immutability and certainty, in the principles of conduct. The supposed parallel between mathematics and ethics constituted, in fact, the basis of their defence of an 'eternal and immutable morality,' against the relativism which they attributed to Hobbes.

In their insistence upon the apprehension of necessary relations between ideas, in their conception of mathematics as an ideal science dealing with these relations without the assumption of any corresponding sensible existence, and in the analogy which they seek to establish between mathematics and ethics, these writers clearly anticipated the positions of the *Essay*. But, as has already been pointed out, their theory of knowledge is itself part and parcel of a metaphysical doctrine. From the nature of these

[1] John Smith, *A discourse demonstrating the immortality of the soul*, ch. 6; Cudworth, *Treatise*, bk. IV. ch. 3, § 17; More, *Antidote*, bk. I. ch. 6, § 1.

intelligible ideas they considered that important ontological consequences could be directly drawn. Their 'eternal' validity is at once identified with a permanence of existence. From the eternal nature of the ideas, and the fact that they are not always present to our finite minds, Cudworth infers the existence of an eternal mind, in which their constant and eternal being is realised. The soul's capacity for an intuition of eternal truth is to Smith a demonstrative argument for the permanent existence of its essence. The inability of matter to furnish exact instances of the notions of geometry is similarly valued chiefly for the ontological consequences which it is thought can be drawn from it. Thus, to Smith our apprehension of such perfect notions is an argument for the immaterial nature of the soul; while to More it is only explicable on the assumption of prenatal knowledge in the soul, derived from a previous and purer state of existence. Against the point of view implied in these inferences, Locke's whole procedure is a protest. In particular, as we have seen, he is careful to guard himself against the ontological consequences which were drawn from the doctrine of 'eternal' truths[1].

§ 4. Both in his general philosophical position, and in the working out of his account of our mathematical and ethical knowledge, Cumberland stands nearer to Locke than do the Cambridge Platonists. His views on these questions receive, indeed, no systematic development, but are incidentally expressed in his exposition of 'the laws of Nature.' Refusing to build upon the hypothesis of innate ideas, he puts forward a theory of the derivation of our ideas from experience, which bears a close resemblance to the much more fully developed doctrine of the

[1] Cf. above, ch. VII. § 4.

Essay. The 'simple apprehensions' which constitute the primary data of our cognition are referred by him to two sources, which are spoken of as internal and external sensation. They are obtained, 'first, by the immediate presence and operation of the object upon the mind; in which manner the mind is conscious of its own actions, and also of the motions of the imagination, or of the phantasms which appear to it; secondly, by means of our external senses, nerves, and membranes[1].' Among the higher faculties by which the mind operates upon the data thus obtained, he includes a power of forming universal notions by omitting the distinguishing accidents of things. Like Locke he holds that upon this faculty of abstracting and generalising depends the possibility of scientific knowledge, and of the formulation of moral laws which are unchangeable, and therefore 'in a sense' eternal.

It is in his treatment of our mathematical and ethical knowledge that Cumberland approaches most nearly the position of Locke. The notions which form the subject matter of these sciences have, he tells us, the peculiarity that they arise from the free constructional activity of the mind. In mathematics we are thus concerned with ideal or mental objects, to which no existing thing may actually correspond in the real world. At the same time these objects are by no means arbitrary or fictitious, since when once the constructions in question are made they are found to possess a logical necessity. 'We freely add, subtract, etc., and yet whoever performs these operations, according to the rules prescribed, necessarily finds out the sum, which is equal to all the parts added....And in general, in every question whose solution is possible from

[1] *De Legibus Naturae*, ch. 1, § 5.

what is given, the answer is necessarily found from the operations duly performed[1].' We are thus supplied with a sphere of universal judgments, the truth of which is guaranteed by the coherence of their notions, without reference to the actual existence of anything corresponding to them. At this point, however, a difficulty confronts both Cumberland and Locke, which had no existence for the Cambridge Platonists. According to the latter writers, the intelligible ideas which form the objects of knowledge possess in themselves a reality superior to that of the world of sensible things. For Cumberland and Locke, on the other hand, the notions and ideas with which the mathematician and the moralist are concerned are the creations of our own minds, while some kind of conformity to a reality beyond our ideas is admittedly involved in the conception of truth. To this difficulty Cumberland gives the answer which was subsequently adopted and developed by Locke. Mathematics and ethics afford us what Locke calls 'real' and Cumberland 'useful' knowledge, because, though primarily concerned with ideal creations, and only carrying a hypothetical reference to external things corresponding to them, we know that the existence *in rerum natura* of something at least closely approximating to them is possible.

'There are mathematical propositions, and others of like kind might be found by reflection, which may be called true, though there exists nothing to which they are conformable. For such conditional propositions, because they pronounce nothing concerning things without the mind, are not to be compared with them; for their truth consists only in an agreement among the terms of which they are composed. But propositions of this kind are of no use in

[1] *op. cit.* ch. 1, § 7.

human life unless we find something effected, or unless something is effected by us, which differs in nothing considerable from our notions. If their subject, or something extremely like it, cannot exist, the propositions are trifling (*nugatoriae*) and are only equivocally called true. For the truth of propositions which consists only in the agreement of terms, if the terms themselves cannot exist, is not of the same nature as that which affirms the agreement of terms possible at least, if not existing in the present or future. The former kind of truth is perfectly useless[1].' How we can determine the possibility *a priori* Cumberland does not explain, though he assumes that in mathematics and ethics this can be done.

Not only have we in Cumberland a striking though less developed statement of Locke's theory of mathematical and ethical knowledge, but there is internal evidence that Locke wrote with his predecessor's work in view. For, after all, Cumberland holds, there is one respect in which ethics is inevitably inferior to mathematics. 'I confess, however,' he writes, 'that those things which in morality are taken for granted, or assumed as known, viz., God and man, their actions and mutual relations, are not so exactly known as those things which in a determinate measure or quantity are regarded as data in mathematics; and that, therefore, the conclusions thence drawn must labour under some want of exactness[2].' There seems no doubt that Locke had this passage in mind, when he noticed and gave his answer to the objection it contains. 'Nor let any one object, that the names of substances are often to be made use of in morality, as well as those of modes, from which will arise obscurity. For as to substances, when concerned in moral

[1] *op. cit.* ch. 2, § 6. [2] *op. cit.* ch. 4, § 4.

discourses, their divers natures are not so much enquired into as supposed; *e.g.*, when we say that man is subject to law, we mean nothing by man but a corporeal, rational creature; what the real essence or other qualities of that creature are, in this case, is no way considered[1].' In fact, this 'moral man' is all that we are concerned with in ethics, and of him we have 'a clear settled idea.'

§ 5. Before proceeding to compare Locke's theory of our knowledge of nature with the views which were current among his contemporaries in England, it is necessary to consider some of the presuppositions of the physical sciences, as regards which Locke's thought developed in the closest relation to that of his countrymen. The Cartesian theory that extension is the essence of material substance was universally rejected by English thinkers: who were consequently bound to explain, on the one hand, the kind of reality which belongs to space as distinguished from body; and on the other hand, what in addition to extension is required to constitute body. To the different ways in which they dealt with the first of these problems we now turn.

As against Descartes and his followers, Hobbes maintained the necessity of distinguishing space from the extension of bodies. Space is not that which is filled by body, but that which is capable of being so filled; moreover, the same space is successively occupied by different bodies. While, therefore, the extension or magnitude of a body is an accident of it, the space which it occupies and in which it moves cannot be so conceived. But if, as Hobbes assumes, bodies and their accidents are the only real beings, what account can we give of the nature of

[1] III. II. 16.

this space, which is neither the one nor the other? It can only be, he replies, a 'phantasm' or object of our imagination; as such, it is, in fact, an accident of our minds. This conclusion Hobbes supports by the consideration that if we feign the world to be annihilated, with the exception of one man, this man would still retain his consciousness of space, which would appear to him as something external and as 'not at all depending upon any power of the mind[1].' How to reconcile the positions, that body presupposes space, and that space is an accident of the mind, while yet body is the only substance, Hobbes does not of course explain.

The necessity of distinguishing space from the extension of matter formed one of the few points of agreement between the Cambridge Platonists and their arch adversary, although their way of conceiving its nature was very different from his. The point was raised by More in his first letter to Descartes, and is one which he never tired of pressing and elaborating throughout his later works; while it passed from him to other members of the school. Instead of extension being, as Descartes held, the essence of one kind of substance, it is for More a characteristic of all substances whatsoever. Not only bodies, but minds, even including the Divine Being himself, are extended; unextendedness being equivalent to nonentity. Moreover, beyond the limits of the material universe space must be regarded as stretching out to infinity, forming the eternal and immovable background of movable matter. Now the space which is thus not only logically distinguishable but really distinct from body, can be no merely imaginary being, as Hobbes had supposed. In what, then, can its reality consist? In accordance with the accepted metaphysical

[1] *De corpore*, ch. 7, § 1.

categories it must either be a substance or a qualification of a substance. Since it is neither a substance nor a qualification of a material substance, it must have as its subject an immaterial substance or spirit. Moreover, from the unity, eternity, infinity, etc., of space, it follows that this spirit can be none other than God. Space and its attributes thus furnish us with a confused and abstract conception of the Divine Being. To the Cartesian challenge to declare what could keep apart the sides of a vase from which all matter had been removed, More replied boldly that the divine extension would continue to separate them.

It is not to be supposed that Cudworth would neglect so easy and triumphant a method of turning against 'the Democratic and Epicurean Atheists' their own hypothesis of a real empty space. We accordingly find the proof of an incorporeal deity from the nature of space among the many arguments of the *Intellectual System*[1]; while the view that spirits as well as bodies are extended was generally adopted by members of the school. More's view appears, moreover, to have carried weight with the greatest of his Cambridge contemporaries. The reality of 'absolute space' which, 'in its own nature, without regard to anything external, remains always similar and immovable,' forms one of the fundamental presuppositions of the Newtonian physics[2]. Nor did Newton hesitate to follow More into the theological side of his doctrine. His agreement with this is implied in the well-known reference in the *Optics* to space as the 'boundless, uniform sensorium' of God. As the soul of man is immediately present to the 'species' of things which find an entry into its limited 'place of sensation'; so God, who is 'in all places,' is 'everywhere present to the things themselves, and perceives them by

[1] Edition of 1845, vol. III. p. 232.

[2] *Principia*, Def. 8, Scholium 2.

his immediate presence without the need of organs.' It is, however, most clearly stated in the concluding pages, added in the second edition, of the *Principia*. The omnipresence of God, he there maintains, must not be understood, as Aquinas had taught, with reference only to his power. God is, on the contrary, substantially present in every portion of space. 'He endures for ever, and is everywhere present; and by existing always and everywhere he constitutes duration and space[1].'

§ 6. The metaphysics of space had occupied Locke's thought in the years 1676–8, and forms the subject of three short papers written in those years. In the first and shortest of these he definitely takes up the position that space is an affection of body, and can have no real existence where there is no matter. 'Imaginary space,' *i.e.*, the space which we think of as extending beyond the bounds of the material universe, 'seems to me to be no more anything than an imaginary world; for if a man and his soul remained, and the whole world were annihilated, there is left him the power of imagining either the world, or the extension it had, which is all one with the space it filled; but it proves not that the imaginary space is anything real or positive. For space or extension, separated in our thoughts from matter or body, seems to have no more real existence than number has (*sine* enumeration) without anything to be numbered; and one may as well say the number of the sea-sand does really exist, and is something, the world being annihilated, as that the space or extension of the sea does exist, or is anything, after such annihilation. These are only affections of real existences; the one, of any being whatsoever; the other, only of material beings[2].'

[1] *Principia*, Bk. III. Prop. 42, General Scholium. [2] Lord King, p. 66.

It is probable that in writing this p[illegible]ssage Locke had Hobbes directly in view. For Hobbes, [illegible]e have seen in his exposition of the subject, had ad[illegible] of 'feigning the world to be annihilated,' wit[illegible] of one man, and asking what would remai[illegible] think about. By sweeping on one side the [illegible] position of space in Hobbes' theory, as on the [illegible]d an accident of the mind, and as on the other the presupposition of material existence, in favour of the view that it is merely an affection of matter, Locke shows that he as yet fails to realise the ideal priority of space to body, which Hobbes, however imperfectly, had sought to account for. A different position is taken up by him in the papers written in the two following years. In them Locke is seen more and more definitely to incline to a purely relational theory of space, based upon the view that space is at bottom nothing but distance. 'When we speak of space (as we ordinarily do) as the abstract of distance, it seems to me to be a pure relation'; and the 'extension' which we regard as 'a positive inherent property' of body is, he declares, 'nothing but the relation of the distance of the extremities[1].' Now an actual relation presupposes real existents as its terms. It is true, indeed, Locke now argues, that we can and must conceive space without body. But when so conceived, it is not to be regarded as 'any real thing,' but merely as 'a bare possibility of body to exist[2].' Hence, 'space, as antecedent to body, or some determinate being, is in effect nothing[3],' and its supposed infinity, though something we are 'apt to conceive,' is not a property of any real being.

While this is the doctrine which Locke at this time accepted as most satisfactory, he seems to have felt that

[1] *op. cit.* pp. 338–40. [2] *loc. cit.* [3] *loc. cit.*

it was not free from difficulties, and suggested as a possible alternative the theory of More. 'If it be possible,' he wrote in the paper of 1677, 'to suppose nothing, or in our thoughts to remove all manner of being from any place, then this imaginary space is just nothing, and signifies no more but a bare possibility that body may exist where now there is none. If it be impossible to suppose pure nothing, or to extend our thoughts where there is, or we can suppose, no being, this space void of body must be something belonging to the being of the Deity....If it be a necessity to suppose a being there, it must be God, whose being we thus make, *i.e.* suppose extended, but not impenetrable[1].'

§ 7. Between 1678 and the publication of the *Essay* in 1690, Locke's views on the whole subject underwent a further change. Instead of regarding 'space in itself' as the abstraction of a relation from the real terms between which it subsists, he now conceives it as something 'uniform and boundless,' within which, by means of sensible marks, we determine the position of finite beings in relation to each other[2]. And having abandoned the relational theory of space, Locke now gives his adherence to the view of More and Newton, concerning the connection of the real space in which he had come to believe with the Deity. The two theories are, indeed, mentioned in one passage as alternatives, between which it is not necessary to choose, in order to make good the distinction between space and body[3]. But his own preference is now clear and unambiguous, although his expressions are less dogmatic than those of either of the other writers. 'Nor let any one say, that beyond the bounds of body there is nothing at all, unless he will confine God within the limits

[1] *op. cit.* pp. 337–8. [2] II. 15. 5. [3] II. 13. 27.

of matter....God every one easily allows fills eternity; and it is hard to find a reason why any one should doubt that he likewise fills immensity. His infinite being is certainly as boundless one way as another; and methinks it ascribes a little too much to matter to say, "Where there is no body there is nothing[1]."'

Since the distinction between 'space in itself,' as something 'uniform and boundless,' and the extension of body which is presented to us in sense-perception, can hardly be regarded as the direct product of Locke's own principles, it is natural to look for some external influence to account for the doctrine of the *Essay*. Now we know that Locke was a diligent student of the less mathematical portions of Newton's *Principia*[2], which was published in 1686, four years before the *Essay*. We can hardly, it would seem, be wrong in connecting Locke's recently acquired views about 'space in itself' with Newton's exposition of 'absolute space,' which, 'in its own nature, without reference to anything external, remains always similar and immovable[3].'

Still more clearly does Locke's distinction between 'duration itself,' which goes on 'in one constant, equal, uniform, course,' and 'time,' as duration set out and measured by sensible occurrences, depend upon the contrast which Newton draws between 'absolute, true and

[1] II. 15. 2–3.

[2] 'The celebrated Locke, who was incapable of understanding the *Principia*, from his want of geometrical knowledge, inquired of Huygens if all the mathematical propositions in that work were true. When he was assured that he might depend upon their certainty, he took them for granted, and carefully examined the reasonings and corollaries deduced from them. In this manner he acquired a knowledge of the physical truths in the *Principia*, and became a firm believer in the discoveries it contained. In the same manner he studied the treatise on "Optics," and made himself master of every part of it which was not mathematical.' Brewster (*Memoirs of Sir Isaac Newton*, vol. I. p. 339) quotes this from Desagulier, who says he was told the story several times by Sir Isaac himself.

[3] *Principia*, Def. 8, Scholium 2.

mathematical time,' which, 'by another name is called duration,' and 'relative, apparent or common time.' Not only is the doctrine the same, but there is a notable similarity in the terms used to express it; while Locke follows Newton in pointing out the impossibility of ensuring the perfect accuracy of our measures of time, and in the further remark that such imperfections in no way detract from the even course of duration itself[1].

The new light which had come to Locke from his study of the *Principia* clearly involved the abandonment of the view that space is nothing but a relation. Instead of considering the relation of distance as the one fundamental constituent of all our spacial ideas, Locke in the *Essay* includes space among our simple ideas. That is to say, while admitting that like all other ideas, our ideas of space, 'when attentively considered,' are seen to include 'some kind of relation,' he now recognises in them a positive constituent which cannot be resolved into relations. Distance itself is the space presented to sight or touch, 'considered barely in length between any two beings,' and 'each different distance' is declared to be, not a different relation, but 'a different modification of space[2].' The 'uniform, infinite ocean' of space is now held to have

[1] *Principia*, Def. 8, Scholium 1. *Essay*, II. 14. 21. It may be pointed out that the obligation was not all on one side. When, for instance, in the Scholium of 1713, Newton writes that 'every particle of space is always, and every indivisible moment of duration is everywhere,' we can hardly fail to find the origin of the remark in that 'combination of two distinct ideas' to which Locke had drawn special attention, whereby 'expansion and duration do mutually embrace and comprehend each other; every part of space being in every part of duration, and every part of duration in every part of expansion' (II. 15. 12). Compare, too, Newton's remarks in the same *scholium* about our inability to know 'what the real substance of anything is'; this 'inward substance' of bodies, as distinguished from their sensible appearances, being declared incapable of being known, 'either of our senses, or by any reflex act of our minds.'

[2] II. 13. 3.

positive characteristics and a reality of its own, distinct from and prior to the bodies which exist and move within it. As to the kind of reality which it possessed, Locke not unnaturally fell back upon the theory of More, which he had previously mentioned as a possible alternative to the theory he had then held. The 'boundless invariable oceans of duration and expansion, which comprehend in them all finite beings,' he now declares, can, 'in their full extent belong only to the Deity[1].'

From his theory of the reality of absolute space, Newton himself, as we have seen, drew the same theological consequences. But as these were only hinted at in the *Optics* and were not fully developed until the second edition of the *Principia*, published more than twenty years after the *Essay*, we cannot attribute to him a direct influence upon Locke as regards this point. While, therefore, the teaching of Newton seems to have been of decisive importance for Locke's final conception of space, we must look to More for the common source of Newton's and Locke's views of its theological implications.

That More's writings exerted an influence upon Locke on this and other points hardly admits of doubt. When Locke remarks that the Cartesians 'must either own that they think body infinite, though they are loth to speak it out, or else affirm that space is not body[2],' he is only repeating More's insinuation that Descartes' view that the world is 'indefinite' in extent is merely a device to evade the legitimate conclusion of his theory[3]. With More's doctrine that all substances, including spirits, are extended, we may compare Locke's view that 'it is near as hard to conceive any existence, or to have an idea of any real being, with a perfect negation of all manner of expansion, as it is to

[1] II. 15. 8. [2] II. 13. 21. [3] First Letter to Descartes.

have the idea of any real existence with a perfect negation of all manner of duration[1].' If Locke held that after all 'extension' is most properly limited to bodies, though 'expansion' has a wider signification, More had been obliged to distinguish between the extension of body, as implying a juxtaposition of parts, and the sense in which a spirit, being without parts, can be said to be extended. While More had taught that spirits are essentially penetrable, Locke remarks that whereas one moment of time is common to many things, it is beyond his comprehension whether angels and spirits 'have any analogy to this in respect of expansion[2].' Finally, in what he calls his 'extravagant conjecture,' that spirits may possess the advantage over ourselves of being able 'to frame and shape to themselves organs of sensation or perception, as to suit them to their present design and the circumstances of the object they would consider[3],' we seem to have an echo of the remarkable powers of self-dilation and self-contraction which More attributed to them.

§ 8. Having endeavoured to trace the historical antecedents of Locke's theory of space, we must now turn to the consideration of the views which were prevalent in England at the time concerning the nature of matter. To Hobbes, who held that space by itself is a subjective 'phantasm,' it seemed that body could be sufficiently distinguished from it by reference to its independent objective reality. Body was accordingly defined by him as 'that which having no dependence upon our thought, is coincident or coextended with some part of space[4].' Those who, differing from Hobbes, held that space in itself

[1] II. 15. 11. [2] *loc. cit.* [3] II. 23. 13.
[4] *De Corpore*, ch. 8, § 1.

is objectively real, were, however, bound to point to some further characteristic of body which would distinguish it from space. This characteristic they found, with one accord, in its impenetrability. Thus, More defines body as 'a substance impenetrable and discerptible,' whereas spirit is 'a substance penetrable and indiscerptible[1]'; Boyle defines matter as 'a substance extended, divisible and impenetrable[2]'; and Newton regards impenetrability as 'an universal property of all bodies whatsoever[3].' While Locke prefers to designate the characteristic indicated as 'solidity,' on the ground that 'impenetrability' is a negative term, and denotes 'perhaps more a consequence of solidity than solidity itself,' he agrees that this characteristic is 'the idea most intimately connected with and essential to body, so as nowhere else to be found or imagined, but only in matter.' The mind, moreover, finds it 'inseparably inherent in body, wherever or however modified[4].' It is this conception of solidity, as at least involved in the essence of body, which leads him, while professing to find the origin of the idea in sensation, to attribute to it an absoluteness which is obviously foreign to sensible experience. Solidity, as distinguished from hardness, which he regards as relative to the organism, is declared to consist in 'repletion, and so an utter exclusion of other bodies out of the space it occupies[5],' the body offering a resistance 'so great that no force, however great, can surmount it[6].'

To proceed to a further point. Whereas the Cartesian theory of extension as the essence of body implied that matter is continuous and indefinitely divisible, the English writers of whom we are speaking, including Locke, agreed in holding that matter consists of a number of discrete

[1] *Immortality*, bk. I. ch. 3, § I. [2] *The Origin of Forms and Qualities*, p. 2.
[3] *Principia*. [4] II. 4. I. [5] II. 4. 4. [6] II. 4. 3.

parts, which, although extended, are not capable of actual division. That such a theory, if regarded as ultimate, involves difficulties and apparent contradictions, they were well aware. These, however, they unanimously regarded not as indications of weakness in their theory, but as imperfections from which it is impossible to free our conceptions of matter. They point to them, again and again, in support of the contention that our ideas of spiritual substance are as clear and as intelligible as those of matter, and as illustrations of the danger of denying on *a priori* grounds the reality of that which we cannot adequately conceive. Of the puzzles and apparent contradictions which they most frequently used for this purpose, one sprang directly from the atomic theory, while the other seemed to them common to all theories of matter. In the first place, the assumption that matter consists of a number of discrete atoms rendered acute the problem as to how these separate and independent beings come to unite or cohere, so as to form the complex and more or less 'hard' bodies of experience. And secondly, however successfully the atom might resist actual division, as extended it must be admitted to contain distinguishable parts. We have, therefore, on our hands all the well-worn puzzles concerning the infinite divisibility of a real finite extended being.

The difficulty of understanding the union of the parts of matter on purely mechanical principles is one to which More frequently reverts. Rejecting all the current hypotheses, he urges that this union is as 'unimaginable' as that of soul and body, but is yet an undeniable fact of experience[1]. Concerning 'the entanglements which extension brings with it,' he declares that 'extended matter

[1] *Antidote*, Appendix, ch. III. § 7; cf. *Immortality*, bk. I. ch. 7, § 5.

consists either of indivisible points or of particles divisible *ad infinitum*. Take which of these you will (and you can find no third), you will be wound into the most notorious absurdities that may be.' From this consideration he draws the conclusion that 'if the difficulties of framing a conception of a thing must take away the existence of the thing itself, there will be no such thing as body left in the world; and then all will be spirit or nothing[1].' In much the same way, Boyle instances the difficulties *de compositione continui*, in support of his contention that our physical conceptions and principles do not possess all the clearness and certainty that are often claimed for them, and in respect of which the physical sciences are commonly considered superior to theology[2]. Finally, Glanville brings into juxtaposition the questions of the union of the parts of the matter and its infinite divisibility, and cites them as insoluble problems which undermine the certainty of our boasted science[3].

Now these are precisely the difficulties which Locke finds in our ideas of body, and which he brings forward in support of the thesis that there is no greater obscurity in our idea of the soul as an immaterial substance than in that of matter. We can, he maintains, no more understand 'how the solid parts of body are united or cohere to make extension' than how an immaterial spirit performs the function of thinking, or initiates movement. In each case, indeed, 'the matter of fact is clear'; but 'when we would a little nearer look into it, and consider how it is done, there, I think, we are at a loss, both in the one and the other; and can as little understand how the parts of

[1] *Antidote*, bk. I. ch. 4, § 2.
[2] *The excellency of Theology*, § 3, *Works*, vol. III. pp. 432–3.
[3] *Scepsis Scientifica*, ch. 7, §§ 3–4.

body cohere, as how we ourselves perceive or move[1].' Having contended that the manner of the communications of motion by impulse is no more intelligible than its initiation by thought, he finally calls attention to the difficulties which cluster round the problem of the infinite divisibility of matter. 'I would fain have instanced anything in our notion of spirit more perplexed, or nearer a contradiction, than the very notion of body includes in it; the divisibility *ad infinitum* of any finite extension involving us, whether we grant or deny it, in consequences impossible to be explicated or made in our apprehension consistent; consequences that carry greater difficulty, and more apparent absurdity, than anything that can follow from the notion of an immaterial knowing substance[2].'

§ 9. In passing from the consideration of our idea of matter to the question of the nature and extent of our knowledge concerning physical phenomena, we must part company with the Cambridge men. Having vindicated the conception of spiritual substance against the materialism of Hobbes, their further interest in physical science lies entirely in their opposition to the purely mechanical theory of Nature, which was held in common by Hobbes and Descartes, and their insistence on the need of teleological conceptions for the comprehension of natural phenomena. Their views on this subject have clearly little relation to the doctrine of the *Essay*. There are, however, two contemporary English writers who in certain respects anticipated the positions of Locke, concerning the inevitable imperfections and limitations of our physical knowledge.

The first of these, Joseph Glanville, was connected, on the one hand, with the Cambridge men, by his support of their theological position; and on the other, with the

[1] II. 23. 25. [2] II. 23. 31.

upholders of experimental methods in natural science, with whom he was associated in the newly formed Royal Society. There is, however, no evidence of any personal intercourse between him and Locke; and whether Locke read any of his books is a matter of conjecture, which cannot be determined with anything approaching certainty. Nor can we look to Glanville for any systematic treatment of the subject. In his various works, which largely cover the same ground, he confines himself to a desultory and purely negative criticism of the various dogmatic systems, which were then in vogue, without always being careful to preserve his own consistency. There are, nevertheless, certain points of resemblance between him and Locke on the question before us which deserve notice.

In one respect his conception of the problem of the physical sciences may be regarded as an advance upon that of Locke, since he states it in terms of causation in place of substance. We have, he argues, no intuitive knowledge of the connections between causes and their effects, which must consequently be learned from experience. But causality is itself insensible. All that sense perception can yield is a 'continual accompanying' of one sensible phenomenon by another. Nor can we safely infer causality from such concomitancy[1]. Indeed, the true causes are not sensible phenomena at all, but have to be sought in the minute particles of which matter is composed, and the changes which take place among them. One might, therefore, as well expect to be able to make a watch from a view of its exterior, without any knowledge of its wheels and their movements, as hope to trace the working of natural operations from their sensible appearances[2]. Moreover, like Locke, he finds in the interdependence

[1] *Vanity of Dogmatising*, pp. 189–90. [2] *op. cit.* p. 180; cf. *Essay*, III. 6. 9.

of all natural phenomena a still further bar to the possibility of a science of nature. For, 'to the knowledge of the most contemptible effect in nature it is necessary to know the whole syntax of causes, and their particular circumstances and modes of action[1].' Thus 'we cannot know anything' in such matters 'without knowing all[2].' In our attempts to understand the processes of nature, we must, therefore, be content with an inductive investigation of sensible particulars, without claiming to attain to certainty of principles. We must, in fact, remember, that 'the best principles, excepting divine and mathematical, are but hypotheses[3],' and can only yield a hypothetical certainty.

As to what it is that constitutes the superior certainty which is here claimed for theology and mathematics, Glanville has little to tell us. In explanation of the peculiar position of mathematics, he is sometimes content to say after Bacon, that progress in this subject has been due to the absence of undue reverence for authority in relation to it[4]; or, after Hobbes, that it is to be accounted for by the circumstance that in mathematics alone have names a fixed signification[5]. He approaches more nearly to the position of Locke when he remarks, that 'the knowledge we have of the mathematics hath no reason to elate us; since by them we know but numbers and figures, creatures of our own, and are yet ignorant of our Maker's[6].' The remark remains, however, a mere *obiter dictum*, which no attempt is made to develop or explain.

§ 10. While it must remain a matter of uncertainty whether the scepticism of Glanville exerted any influence at all upon Locke, no such doubt can be felt in the

[1] *op. cit.* p. 217.
[2] *op. cit.* p. 213; cf. *Essay*, IV. 6. 11.
[3] *op. cit.* p. 195.
[4] *op. cit.* p. 208.
[5] *op. cit.* p. 160.
[6] *op. cit.* pp. 209–10.

case of Boyle, who was no light free-lance, but one of those 'master-builders' of the sciences, to serve whom as an 'under-labourer, in clearing the ground a little, and removing some of the rubbish that lies in the way to knowledge[1],' was the declared ambition of the author of the *Essay*. Between these two there had, moreover, been long and intimate personal relations. Their intercourse, beginning in Locke's Oxford days, continued until the death of the great chemist in 1691, when Locke became responsible for his literary and scientific remains[2]. Their correspondence shows us Locke carrying out experiments under the direction of his friend, and communicating to him his observations of remarkable phenomena, lists of foreign books and accounts of scientific instruments seen by him abroad. In view of the relations of the two men, and of the position of authority occupied by Boyle in questions relating to the natural sciences, it would have been strange if Locke's views on the subject had not been influenced by him, as we have seen his theory of space was by Newton.

The results of our demonstrations in physical science can never, Boyle maintains, possess the full or 'metaphysical' certainty of absolutely necessary truth. The most that we can attain to in respect of them is 'physical certainty,' or certainty based on the assumption of certain physical principles, which are not themselves certainly known to be true. Thus, the maxim, *ex nihilo nihil fit*, is one which is rightly accepted as a hypothesis in physics; but it cannot be seen to be necessarily true, and is, Boyle thinks, if taken as an ultimate principle, actually false[3]. In support of his theory of the imperfection inherent in

[1] Epistle to the Reader. [2] Fox Bourne, vol. II. 223.

[3] *The excellency of Theology compared with natural philosophy*, *Works*, vol. III. p. 433.

our physical knowledge, he urges the difficulties in the way of arriving at a non-contradictory and satisfactory conception of matter. Attention has already been called to his reference to the problem of infinite divisibility in this connection. In opposition to Descartes' theory of matter, he uses the argument, which we find subsequently in Locke, that if extension constituted the essence of body, it would be impossible for God to annihilate a portion of matter, without at the same time creating a new matter to take its place[1]. He finds a further set of obstacles, to the construction of a completely satisfactory physical science, in the impossibility of understanding the nature of sensation, or of the sensible qualities of which it affords us cognisance. The difficulty to which he particularly draws attention is that of explaining our 'particular distinct sensations,' as distinguished from the more general and generally recognised difficulty of understanding how a material and an immaterial substance can be united at all, or how the former can act upon the latter. He holds, of course, the general view that sensible qualities depend upon the 'primary and catholic' affections of the minute portions of matter, and it seems to have been from him that Locke derived the names for this distinction, to which the *Essay* gave such an extended currency. But even if we knew upon what primary determinations a sensible quality depended, we could not, he insists, see how the former give rise to the latter. One kind of motion, we find, occasions a visual, and another an auditory perception; but all that we can say, in each case, is that it is 'the good pleasure of God to have it so[2].' Boyle here indicates what Locke subsequently signalised as the most irremovable of all the bars to a demonstrative science of nature[3].

[1] *op. cit.* p. 432. [2] *op. cit.* p. 434. [3] IV. 3. 12.

Another point on which Boyle anticipates the position of Locke is in his insistence upon the presence of a subjective and conventional element in all our classifications of natural objects; although, it must be remarked, he does not bring his view on this subject into such direct relation with the imperfection of physical science as we find in the *Essay*. His treatment of the subject, like that of Locke, is developed in opposition to the scholastic theory of classification by reference to substantial forms. 'Whatever men talk in theory of substantial forms,' he declares, 'yet that, upon whose account they really distinguish one body from others, and refer it to this or that species of bodies, is nothing but an aggregate or convention[1] of such accidents as most men do by a kind of agreement (for the thing is more arbitrary than we are aware of) think necessary or sufficient to make a portion of the universal matter belong to this or that determinate species of natural bodies[2].' He goes on to suggest that a new meaning may be given to the term 'form,' consonant both with the principles of the corpuscular philosophy and with sound views about classification. 'Since an aggregate or convention of qualities is enough to make the portion of matter it is found in what it is, and denominate it of this or that determinate sort of bodies; and since those qualities, as we have seen already, do themselves proceed from those more primary and catholic affections of matter—bulk, shape, motion or rest, and the texture thence resulting—why may we not say that the form of a body, being made up of those qualities united in one subject, doth likewise consist in such a convention of those newly named mechanical affections of matter as is necessary to constitute a

[1] *i.e.* collection.

[2] *The origin of forms and qualities according to the corpuscular philosophy*, p. 41.

body of that determinate kind[1]?' If translated into the language of ideas, and with a still greater emphasis on the difference between sensible qualities and the unknown primary determinations on which they depend, we have here the main features of Locke's theory of essences, nominal and real.

It may be noted in conclusion that it is not only on topics connected with the natural sciences, on which Locke might be expected to follow the lead of his distinguished friend, that Boyle anticipates in his published writings characteristic positions of the *Essay*. He holds that 'we men mistake and flatter human nature too much, when we think our faculties of understanding so unlimited, both in point of capacity and extent, and so free and unprepossessed, as many philosophers seem to suppose[2].' Our capacity for knowledge, he declares, is proportional to God's design in making us, and consequently does not extend to many truths which it is 'unnecessary for us to know here.' He holds, on the other hand, that 'the fundamental and necessary articles of religion' are 'both evident and capable of a moral demonstration.' In order that we may apprehend divine truths, however, our active co-operation is necessary. Some men fail, in this respect, through their incapacity for 'lasting and attentive speculation'; others are so absorbed in 'their secular affairs and their sensual pleasures' that they have neither disposition nor leisure for such thoughts; while others, again, are so biassed by their interests and blinded by their passions, that they are incapable of a 'clear discernment and right judgment of divine things[3].' Although the metaphysical

[1] *op. cit.* pp. 43-4.
[2] *A Discourse of things above reason*, *Works*, vol. IV. p. 42.
[3] Preface to *The Christian Virtuoso*, *Works*, vol. V. p. 38.

and religious positions here indicated were such as found an extensive acceptance in contemporary English thought, the similarity of these passages to the views put forward in the *Essay* is sufficient to lead us to suspect something more than a casual coincidence. It is at least suggestive to remember in this connection that in Locke's Oxford days both he and Boyle had been members of one of those circles for discussion, of which he was so fond. It was, we know, in a later meeting of a group of this kind that the problem of the *Essay* first occurred to him, as the result of a discussion about 'the principles of morality and revealed religion.' It may thus well be that any dependence which may exist is of a different and less one-sided character from that which would be suggested by the priority of publication.

§ 11. In the present chapter an attempt has been made to indicate the principal points on which Locke's work comes into contact with that of his contemporaries in England, in respect of several of which it appears that he was directly influenced by them. Even more important than such particular points of resemblance is the community of spirit and outlook, which unites Locke both with the Cambridge Platonists and with his scientific friends, Newton and Boyle. For, although the *Essay* was the first systematic attempt to delimit the boundaries of the knowledge possible to man, the limited capacity of the human mind is a common theme to all these writers. Regarding Descartes as the inaugurator of a new period in the intellectual world, they are at one in refusing to accept the more dogmatic side of his system and his purely rationalistic method. Our ability to conceive, they all insist, cannot be taken as a measure of reality. They all reject the Cartesian theories of the nature of matter and of the possibility of explaining all physical processes in mechanical terms, which they regard as merely preparing the way for the materialism of Hobbes. In all of them we find the conviction that reason can vindicate the basis of the moral and religious life, although it is unable to reveal to us the whole secret of Nature.

It is not, however, to be inferred that either such agreement as we have found on points of detail, or this identity of outlook, detracts from the importance and genuine originality of Locke's work. Originality does not lie in detachment from the intellectual life of one's age, but in a transformation of it which implies its complete absorption. In particular, a theory of knowledge must stand in the closest relation to the stage which has been reached in the development of the sciences. Alike in the central position which he assigned to this enquiry, the completeness with which he sought to deal with it, his attempt to disentangle it from metaphysical assumptions, his criticism of fundamental conceptions, and his method, Locke is far removed from the writers in question. Nor are the permanent value and significance of the *Essay* diminished if, in its general attitude to life and the things of the mind, it is at once the most complete and the most reasoned expression of the spirit of the age and country to which it belongs.

CHAPTER XI

LOCKE AND LEIBNIZ

§ 1. In this and the following chapter I propose to consider the light which is thrown upon the historical significance of the *Essay concerning Human Understanding*, by the elaborate commentary and criticism contained in the *Nouveaux Essais sur l'Entendement Humain* of Leibniz, and to make some comparison between the theories of knowledge of the two writers. We must not, indeed, expect to find in the work of Leibniz an attempt to lay bare the fundamental principles of the philosophy he criticises, or to show in what respects these need correction, or wherein there is a failure in their consistent development; for criticism of such a kind would have been an anachronism in the eighteenth century. The aim of Leibniz is rather to develop and set forth his own views on the questions which arise, under the stimulus afforded by the thought of another. We must, too, at the outset, disabuse our minds of the prepossession which would see nothing but an irreconcilable opposition between the positions of the two. Even if we are not prepared to maintain with Hartenstein[1] that the differences between them concerning the foundations of human knowledge are of less importance than the agreement, we shall at least find a large area of common doctrine, within which Leibniz is prepared simply to accept the views put forward in the *Essay*. And although,

[1] *Locke's Lehre von der menschlichen Erkenntniss in Vergleichung mit Leibniz's Kritik derselben.*

from the nature of the case, it is the points of difference which he emphasises and seeks to develop, he does not fail upon occasion to give expression to his agreement and to his appreciation of the work of the older writer. Even when he considers that his own thought works at a deeper and more philosophical level, he is prepared to recognise the worth and relative validity of what he regards as the more superficial doctrine.

§ 2. Had his attitude been a different one, some excuse for it might have been found in the contemptuous reception given by Locke to the short paper of reflections on the *Essay*, written by Leibniz at the time of his first reading of it. This paper was sent by Leibniz some time later to Thomas Burnet, with permission to show it to others, and with the evident desire that it should ultimately reach the author of the *Essay*. After some delay it was communicated to Locke, who never made any direct acknowledgment, but expressed his poor opinion of its value in a letter to Molyneux, which was published shortly after his death. 'I must confess to you,' he wrote, 'that Mr L.'s great name had raised in me an expectation which the sight of his paper did not answer, nor that discourse of his in the *Acta Eruditorum*, which he quotes, and I have since read, and had just the same thoughts of it when I read it as I find you have. From whence I only draw this inference, that even great parts will not master any subject without great thinking, and even the largest minds have but narrow swallows[1].' At this hostile judgment Leibniz professed himself as not surprised, on the ground that they differed too much in principles, and that consequently the views advanced by him appeared paradoxical to Locke[2]. And indeed many of these 'reflections,' given as they are without

[1] *Works*, vol. IX. p. 407.

[2] Letter to Remond, March 14th, 1714.

reference to their grounds in his philosophical system, were well calculated to produce such an impression. While it is maintained that in addition to the Law of Contradiction only experiences should be accepted as primitive principles, primitive ideas are straightway identified with attributes of God. We are told that we have perceptions which we are not conscious of having, and that it is demonstrable that the soul thinks always. Not only is there something solid in what Plato called *reminiscentia*, but we have a 'presentiment' of all our future thoughts. All our ideas, including our sensations, have their origin in our own souls. Our ideas of sensible qualities are on the one hand condemned as inadequate, on the other hand declared to be capable of real definition. While the view of Locke, that we can have no positive ideas of an infinite space, time or number, is accepted, reference is made to a 'true infinite,' which is not a whole composed of parts and is found in the Absolute. Less paradoxical, because more familiar, but at least equally perverse, in view of the contents of the *Essay*, would appear to Locke the assertion of the value of identical propositions, of axioms and the forms of the traditional logic. It is clear that we cannot ourselves profitably consider Leibniz's criticism of Locke, or examine the relations between their theories of knowledge, without dealing, however briefly, with the way in which Leibniz's views on the question had come to be formed, and without considering the relation of these views to the rest of his philosophy.

§ 3. One of the reasons which Leibniz subsequently gave for having written the paper, which had such an unfortunate reception, was that he had himself already 'meditated deeply upon the subject of the foundations of knowledge,' before reading the *Essay*. Now these meditations had proceeded along two distinct lines; he had approached the question of knowledge on the one hand from a formal and logical, and on the other hand from a real and metaphysical point of view. From the former standpoint he had early sought to determine the true method of scientific knowledge, and to exhibit the ideal of perfect intelligibility which it implied. The first outcome of his reflection, working along this line, had been to render still more fixed and rigid the abstract method of the Cartesian rationalism, and still more pronounced the acceptance of the formal Law of Contradiction as the supreme principle of rational knowledge. Starting with a division of notions into 'primitive' and 'composite,' he maintains that, by means of what he calls the *Ars Combinatoria*, 'all the composite notions in the whole world are reduced to a few simple ones as their alphabet; and by the combination of such an alphabet a way is made of finding, in time, by an ordered method, all things with their theorems and whatever is possible to investigate concerning them[1].' By taking suitable characters to represent these elementary constituents of thought, and by determining the operations which can be performed upon them, a universal method can be formulated, which will accomplish for all the sciences what Descartes and others have done for arithmetic and geometry by means of algebra. Descartes and Spinoza had both found the analogue of their philosophical method in the procedure of geometry; Leibniz insists on looking to the still more abstract science of number for his type and ideal of rational knowledge. For while the geometer is no doubt justified, from the point of view of his science, in taking for granted

[1] Gerhardt's edition of Leibniz, vol. I. p. 57. Quoted in Russell's *Leibniz*, p. 283.

the axioms which form its starting point, Leibniz considers that these axioms are not themselves perfectly simple truths, but stand in need of further analysis, or, in other words, themselves require proof. If the ideal of rational intelligibility is to be attained, the process of analysis must be carried back until we have left on our hands nothing but perfectly simple notions, from which every trace of composition or synthesis has been eliminated, as in the merely self-identical units of arithmetic. Our apprehension of these 'irreducible notions,' which constitute the ultimate data of our rational knowledge, will, in fact, find expression in a series of identical propositions, the distinction between the notion and the proposition here reaching its vanishing point. Such then was, and such always remained, Leibniz's ideal of rational knowledge; although it might be a matter of doubt to him whether the perfect analysis of notions which it involved could be successfully carried out by us.

§ 4. Now, while Descartes had proclaimed clearness and distinctness of thought as the criterion, by means of which we might distinguish absolutely certain knowledge from everything that was doubtful or erroneous, he had never, as we have seen, defined with precision these characteristics of the contents of the 'natural light.' In consequence of this omission, the self-evidence of certain propositions had, Leibniz complains, too often been assumed without warrant by Descartes himself, and to a still greater extent by his followers, culminating in the loose appeal to innate 'ideas' and 'principles' which constituted, in his opinion, a partial justification for their rejection by Locke. To correct this defect in the Cartesian theory was the chief purpose of the *Thoughts on knowledge, truth and ideas*, to which Leibniz referred in his first rough notes on the

Essay, and in which Locke found so little to admire. Regarding a notion as *clear* (as opposed to obscure) when it is sufficient to enable us to recognise the thing it represents; and a composite notion as *distinct* (as opposed to confused) when we are able to enumerate a sufficient number of distinctive characters to distinguish the thing thought of from all others, he declares that such a notion is only *adequate* when this process of analysis has been completed, by the resolution of the complex notion into its primitive constituents. He introduces the further distinction between *intuitive thought*, in which all these constituents are themselves together present to our mind, and *symbolical thought*, which employs signs to represent some of them; and maintains that we should only be said to conceive an idea when we make use of the former. Again, while the enumeration of characters which renders a notion distinct is sufficient to constitute a *nominal definition*, a definition is only *real* when it carries with it the possibility of the thing defined. Now such possibility is known *a priori* in the case of adequate notions. Being analysed into elements which are themselves simple identities, no violation of the Law of Contradiction can be involved; and what is not contradictory is possible. Where, however, analysis has been less thorough, contradiction may lurk; though its absence, and the consequent possibility of the notion, may be known *a posteriori*, if experience shows us that the thing actually exists; since the actual must obviously be pronounced possible. As a matter of fact, we are told, our usual starting point is the acceptance of certain notions from experience, which are then employed for the composition of others, although they may possess only a relative and not an absolute simplicity, such as is required in the data of rational knowledge.

§ 5. Descartes, too, had been compelled to admit the legitimacy of such a resort to experience. For him, however, this was only a temporary expedient in the process of scientific construction, which, like a scaffolding, will be no longer needed when the building is complete. But Leibniz, insisting on a stricter interpretation of the principles of the Cartesian rationalism, finds that a definite limit must be set to their applicability; since, as a matter of fact, all our knowledge is not reducible to the form described above. While maintaining that the Law of Contradiction is the supreme principle upon which depends the justification of all 'truths of reason,' he recognises a second kind of truth, viz., 'truths of fact,' for the comprehension of which it does not suffice. The distinction between the two kinds of truths meets us first in an appendix to the dissertation on the *Ars Combinatoria*, published when Leibniz was only twenty years of age, and soon becomes a central feature of his philosophy. Truths of reason are necessary propositions, *i.e.* their opposites involve contradiction, and are therefore impossible; truths of fact are contingent, *i.e.* their opposites are free from contradiction, and are therefore as conceivable and as possible as these truths themselves. Their contingency, however, must not be understood to imply an absence of determination. For such truths are all governed by the Law of Sufficient Reason, which asserts that 'no fact can be found real or existing, no statement true, unless there is a sufficient reason why it should be so and not otherwise, although these reasons very often cannot be known by us.' By a perfect intelligence any given empirical matter of fact would be seen to be determined by real conditions, from a knowledge of which its occurrence could have been predicted. Thus, to take the illustration to which Arnauld took such strong exception, we are told that 'all human events follow with hypothetical necessity from the single supposition that God created Adam[1].' It would, however, be equally erroneous to suppose that the distinction between th two kinds of truths is in the last resort a merely relative one, due to the incapacity of our finite minds for the infinite process of analysis, which would be required for the full comprehension of the way in which any particular fact of experience is grounded in the system of reality. For, however securely the particular fact may be connected with other elements of reality, so that an alteration of any one element would involve an alteration in all the rest, neither these connections nor the existence of the actual system of reality is necessary, in the sense required by Rationalism. As to the connections, they are only hypothetically necessary, *i.e.* they are only necessary on the supposition of the existing system of reality. But other orders of nature are conceivable and possible. A reason there must be, indeed, why just this system of things is realised and not another; but this reason is teleological in character, consisting in the superior value of the present system, in virtue of which it has been chosen by God. Except in the case of the affirmation of the existence of God, which Leibniz regards as a necessary proposition, all predications of existence are contingent; and all contingent propositions directly or indirectly imply an assertion of existence. If, therefore, the analysis of a truth of fact into its simple constituents could be completely carried out, we should have on our hands, not merely a number of identical propositions, in which each simple content is affirmed of itself, but a further proposition affirming the existence of the complex, which could never be

[1] Gerhardt's edition of Leibniz, vol. II. p. 37.

justified by an appeal to the Law of Contradiction. The sphere of contingency being thus defined, all propositions which do not predicate existence, are regarded by Leibniz as both necessary and analytical. It appeared to him as axiomatic, that a proposition which predicates any content of a subject cannot be true unless this content forms part of the notion of the subject.

§ 6. It is clear that even these logical and formal reflections concerning knowledge are not unconnected with Leibniz's theory of reality. Thus, the point of view from which the distinction between the two kinds of truths is drawn is metaphysical rather than epistemological. It is taken for granted that the difference of modality on which it rests is a difference *in rerum natura*. Again, the distinction between the simple and the composite is applied by Leibniz with equal confidence to notions or truths on the one hand and to substances on the other. The theory of the analytical nature of all propositions which characterise a subject by a predicate has its counterpart in his metaphysics, in the theory of substance as containing in itself the ground of all its changes of state[1]. These reflections, nevertheless, form the nearest approach in Leibniz to the unfettered consideration of knowledge which Locke demanded. The attempt to investigate the nature of knowledge as a preliminary to the construction of a theory of reality was entirely foreign to the conceptions of the continental thinker. Long before he read the *Essay*, he had worked out a theory of reality from which certain consequences concerning the mind and its knowledge, including the principal points on which he dwells in his criticism of Locke, were a

[1] I cannot, indeed, accept Russell's view that the fundamental positions of Leibniz's metaphysics are nothing but a development of his logical doctrine.

deduction. This fundamental contrast in presuppositions and point of view must be constantly kept in mind in any comparison that is made between the two thinkers, for it is the key both to the strength and to the weakness of each.

§ 7. Turning, then, to the consideration of the direct influence of Leibniz's theory of reality upon his theory of knowledge, it would, at first sight, seem difficult to conceive a less promising basis for the treatment of knowledge, than the main principles of his metaphysics. The resolution of reality into a system of monads, each of which develops its own states and determines its own changes entirely from within, effectually cuts off the mind from all commerce with a reality beyond itself. It is not only confined to its own ideas, as the immediate objects of its thought, as Locke had taught, but these ideas arise simply as steps in its self-evolution, undetermined by anything without it. The unity of the system of monads having been saved by the *tour de force* of the Pre-established Harmony, nothing remained but to interpret knowledge as a mode of expression, by which what takes place in the individual monad corresponds to the content of the rest of the system. And since this correspondence is not limited to particular points, but is universal, not only must the soul contain in itself the ground of all its own future states, but the whole content of the universe must be somehow actually mirrored in its cognitive faculty.

§ 8. The general conception of knowledge outlined above, to which Leibniz was committed by his theory of reality, is one which it is impossible to rid of the appearance of arbitrariness and artificiality. But it clearly cannot be so much as entertained, if the only mental functions which are recognised are those which involve self-consciousness.

Thus, by the necessities of his metaphysical position, Leibniz was driven to that extension of the conception of mental activity, which constituted his one great contribution to the development of Psychology, and furnished the basis of his principal criticisms of Locke. In opposition to the Cartesian identification of mental function with self-conscious thought, which Locke had accepted as axiomatic, and had merely endeavoured to apply with greater consistency, Leibniz was led to distinguish between mere perception and apperception, or the consciousness that we perceive; and further, to recognise the existence of 'minute perceptions,' the contents of which cannot be separately discriminated, but which nevertheless play an important part in our mental life. Thus, while the course of Leibniz's logical reflections led to a still further sharpening of the abstract rationalism of Descartes, in his attempt to formulate the ideal of rational knowledge, his new conception of mental function involved an emphatic insistence upon the part played by the dim and obscure in the actual life of mind.

§ 9. From the point of view of psychology, the above distinctions undoubtedly mark an important advance. The hampering effect of their absence in Locke is very apparent on this side of his work. For, with all his resolution, he had not been able to carry through the view that nothing is present to, or contained in the mind, which is not, at once, an explicit object of discriminative consciousness, and accompanied by the recognition that we are conscious of it. At times he is found tacitly to abandon this principle, without seeming to be aware of his inconsistency, as when he admits that it may not be 'so easy, nor perhaps possible for us to distinguish betwixt two approaching ideas, which yet are really different[1].'

[1] II. 16. 3.

When dealing with psychological problems he sometimes approaches to the verge of admitting the existence of what are now usually called sub-conscious mental processes; though still formally denying them, and seeking some other explanation of the facts in question. Thus, when discussing the degrees of attention, he tells us that when this function is at its lowest the mind lets its ideas 'pass almost quite unregarded, as faint shadows that make no impression[1].' Again, his analysis of our acquired perceptions leads him to remark that 'the ideas we receive by Sensation are often in grown people altered by the judgment without our taking notice of it.' Thus, when Sensation presents us with the idea of a surface variously coloured, we frame for ourselves the quite different idea of a convex figure uniform in colour. In such cases the immediate idea of Sensation 'serves only to excite the other and is scarce taken notice of itself; as a man who reads or hears with attention and understanding takes little notice of the characters or sounds, but of the ideas that are excited in him by them[2].' A considerable strain is evidently here laid upon the principle, which Locke so strenuously maintains, that 'thinking consists in being conscious that one thinks'; though it is clear that it is not intended to be abandoned. However faint and transient our ideas may be, they still, it is assumed, receive some amount of 'notice' and 'attention,' of which we must be at the moment conscious. Our acquired perceptions are explained as due to the rapid substitution by the mind of one idea for another, of which, however, we must have had an equally definite, though merely momentary awareness.

§ 10. But while Leibniz is ready enough to take advantage of his new principle for the explanation of empirical

[1] II. 19. 3. [2] II. 9. 9.

facts, which had proved baffling to Locke, it is not so much in these, as in the more speculative uses which can be made of the principle, that he is really interested. Starting with the realistic conception of the mind as a substance, having its own definite nature and constitution, Locke had found himself compelled to relegate this substance to the region of the unknowable, and to treat the mind as only empirically cognisable, through and in relation to its definite thoughts or experiences. As Leibniz considers activity, of which 'representation' or perception is the fundamental form, to constitute the very essence of substance, the character which the mind possesses, apart from the content of its explicit consciousness at the moment, and even in the entire absence of such content, consists for him of the mass of sub-conscious perceptions, by which, in its own way, and from its own point of view, it represents, however dimly, the universe. Agreeing with Locke that moral personality depends upon the possession of self-consciousness, he finds in the continuity of the sub-conscious life of the soul a 'real' as distinguishable from this 'moral' identity, for which there was no place in Locke's theory. The doctrine that the mind is always active, which Leibniz accepts on *a priori* grounds, can no longer be assailed on the ground that it is not always exercising self-conscious thought. The new conception is also used to explain the latency which seems to be involved in memory, and in the permanent possession of knowledge, which is not perpetually present to our mind as such. And if the experiences of our past life are still present in the form of sub-conscious activities, although they are no longer definitely cognised, we may also suppose that this obscure region of our being contains similar functions which have not yet been raised to the level of conscious thoughts. A new interpretation can thus be given to the doctrine of innate principles and ideas, which avoids Locke's dilemma, that unless they are explicitly present to self-consciousness from the start, they amount to nothing more than a bare faculty or capacity. Finally, so far from confusion in an idea being a contradiction in terms, as Locke had maintained, it is present in all complex ideas of which the simple constituents are sub-conscious. Some degree of confusion, indeed, is for Leibniz inseparable from the nature of a mind which, though finite, contains in itself a representation of the whole system of reality.

§ 11. His restatement and defence of the theory of innate ideas and principles is placed by Leibniz in the forefront of his reply to Locke, and since it bears directly upon the question of knowledge, it must receive more than passing notice. It may be said at once that Leibniz's position is by no means free from ambiguity and inconsistency, whether we enquire as to the meaning of innateness, or as to the ideas and principles for which innateness is claimed. Innateness is generally conceived by him as an original active disposition or tendency to form the idea of a certain object. At times, however, he is found to urge that it is just because ideas are themselves objects of thought that they are capable of existing both before and after the thoughts which refer to them[1]. Leibniz, in fact, seems to carry over into the region of sub-consciousness Locke's view of the idea as at once an activity of the thinking mind and the object of its thought. The peculiar difficulties of this position, when applied to the sub-conscious, were doubtless hidden from him by his assumption

[1] *Nouveaux Essais*, II. I. I. This work is for brevity referred to below as *N. E.* In quoting from it I have made some use of Langley's translation.

that mental functions were essentially representative, and by his easy identification of the relation of knowledge to its object with that of a bare correspondence.

§ 12. To the question as to what ideas are innate, Leibniz gives a two-fold answer. His metaphysical position required him to regard the whole of the individual's knowledge and experience as from one point of view nothing but the self-evolution of his own nature; evolution being conceived as a process of unfolding or laying bare that which was actually present in a less recognisable form from the beginning. Hence, all the ideas which the mind will ever form, and all the propositions to which it will ever assent, must be innate. It was in this, its only consistent form, that Leibniz had presented his position in his first reflections on the *Essay*. While the same position is occasionally re-asserted in the *Nouveaux Essais*, it is not in this form that the theory of innateness is there defended against Locke's attack. A distinction of origin is now drawn between intellectual ideas, and the necessary truths which depend upon them, on the one hand, and sensible ideas, and the truths of fact into which they enter, on the other; and it is contended that while the latter can be explained as the result of experience, the former must be regarded as purely innate.

§ 13. It becomes necessary, therefore, to enquire as to the grounds on which it is maintained that innateness is a characteristic of a special class of ideas and truths. What reasons does Leibniz consider there are for holding that the Law of Contradiction, or the idea of substance, must be regarded as having its origin in the mind, which do not apply to the idea of red, or to the statement that sugar is sweet? To this question it is impossible to obtain any single and consistent reply from Leibniz. Ideas of sense, we are often told, are characterised by obscurity, whereas the intellectual ideas are clear and distinct; but clearness and distinctness cannot for Leibniz, as for Descartes, be actual marks which point backwards to an origin in the mind itself. For, according to him, the obscure and the confused belong to the mind no less than the clear and distinct, and indeed the actual existence which is claimed for the innate, before it is consciously apprehended, consists in its presence in the obscure region of sub-consciousness. This use of the conception of sub-consciousness implies that the same idea can be at one time obscure or confused and at another time clear and distinct. But such a view is fatal to the employment of clearness and distinctness as a criterion of origin.

At other times Leibniz writes as if the ideas and principles for which a peculiar innateness may be claimed were those involved in the knowledge of the mind itself, as distinguished from other things. We are, he is fond of saying, innate to ourselves. To the old saying, *Nihil est in intellectu quod non fuerit in sensu*, he makes the well-known addition *nisi ipse intellectus.* Since the mind is itself a substance, possessing unity and identity, enduring and acting; the ideas of substance, unity, identity, duration, action, and many others of a similar nature, can be apprehended by the mind without considering anything but itself. From this point of view, Leibniz remarks, Locke's doctrine is not so unlike his own after all; for, according to the *Essay*, Reflection is a distinct source of ideas from Sensation. The conception of Reflection requires, indeed, he maintains, to be extended, so as to include ideas of the mind's essential nature, as well as the ideas of its operations, to which it is confined by Locke. There still remains, however, the claim that these ideas involved in our knowledge of self had an existence in the mind before they were consciously apprehended by it. For this he can find no better ground than the immediacy with which the mind is present, and always present, to itself. Thus, while rejecting the consequence which Descartes and Locke had drawn from this conception, viz., that explicit self-consciousness necessarily accompanies all states and activities of the mind, he assumes that the mind must always at least have some dim awareness of its own metaphysical nature.

Elsewhere we find Leibniz urging that the necessity of certain truths is a proof of their innateness. The argument upon which he frequently relies is that these truths cannot be proved by experience, which only furnishes us with particular examples, from the consideration of which we can form inductive generalisations, but from which we cannot derive strictly universal or necessary truths. So far, of course, there is nothing in the argument to which exception would have been taken by Locke, who had asserted, even more emphatically than Leibniz, the inadequacy of an appeal to particular experiences, for the purpose of justifying the universal propositions which constitute our scientific knowledge. Hence Leibniz is again led to remark that the view of the *Essay* is not, after all, so different from his own. What Leibniz has to do, in order to maintain his position, is to show that the intuitive apprehension of such propositions, which Locke admits, implies their innateness, which he denies. This, however, the argument, as stated by Leibniz, merely takes for granted.

There is yet another way of seeking to make out a case for the innateness of a certain kind of knowledge, which we find in Leibniz. Instead of merely insisting that the knowledge of certain truths is innate, because they cannot be proved by experience, he now argues for the innateness of the principles upon which the proof of all other truths depends. Instead of maintaining the innateness of the ideas and propositions concerned in the knowledge of self, the innateness of certain ideas and principles is now grounded on their being involved in all our knowledge, whatever its object may be. 'The ideas of *being*, of *possibility*, of *identity*,' we are told, 'are so thoroughly innate, that they enter into all our thoughts and reasonings[1].' It is true that they are not always explicitly apprehended by us, and do not constitute in order of time the first objects of our conscious thought. The 'order of nature,' however, is different from the order of our experience, since the proof of the particular depends upon the universal. Hence, when we would consider what is in us virtually before all apperception, we are right in insisting on the latter. 'For the general principles enter into our thoughts, of which they form the soul and bond of connection. They are as necessary to them as muscles and sinews are for walking, even though we do not think of them at all. The mind relies upon these principles at every moment, but it does not manage so easily to distinguish them, and to represent them distinctly and separately[2].' Or, as he elsewhere puts it, innate principles play the part of the suppressed major premise of an enthymeme, without which the conclusion could not be obtained.

This final form of the theory of the special innateness of a certain kind of proposition has sometimes been held to involve a suggestion, if not an anticipation, of the Kantian doctrine of the *a priori*. The resemblance between the two, however, is in reality very slight. For, according to the view of Leibniz, the mind furnishes us with a definite

[1] *N. E.* I. 3. 3. [2] *N. E.* I. I. 20.

kind of knowledge apart from experience, and not merely with forms and categories, which require a filling from a different source. Hence, although sense-experience is required to enable us to think of the truths of reason, these do not carry with them any necessary reference to sensible phenomena. Nor are the truths for which innateness is claimed regarded by Leibniz as the formulation of synthetic functions constitutive of our world, but as first principles from which deductions of an analytical character can be made.

The argument that the ultimate truths, upon which the proof of all other propositions depends, must be innate, clearly depends for its validity upon an identification of the psychological and the logical orders in thought. While recognising and insisting that the 'natural' or logical order differs from the temporal order of our explicit or apperceptive consciousness, Leibniz assumes that when the sub-conscious life is taken into account this can no longer be the case. The logically prior universal must have been actually present in the mind before the particular which falls under it, and on the apprehension of which it exerts a real though hidden influence. The presupposition of an identity between the logical and the psychological orders was, indeed, common to Locke and Leibniz; though it was understood and applied so differently by each. Interpreting it exclusively with reference to the only kind of mental functions which he recognised, viz., those of our explicit consciousness, Locke was led to disparage the logical value of such 'maxims' as the Laws of Identity and Contradiction, on the ground that they are 'not the truths first known to the mind[1].' Leibniz, maintaining their logical implication in all truths as such, and indeed

[1] IV. 7. 9.

holding that all other truths of reason can be demonstrated from them, regards them as a pre-eminent example of the knowledge which is innate.

§ 14. We must now turn from Leibniz's theory of innateness, to consider his account of the ideas which, in a relative and popular sense, he regards as derived from experience. What experience itself is, from the more ultimate point of view, he never seems to have enquired; nor would it be easy to find a meaning for it consistent with his system. Putting aside this difficulty, which does not concern us here, we find him maintaining that Locke's simple ideas of Sensation are only simple in appearance. For, as we have seen, all sensible ideas are for him confused, and their confusion consists in the presence in them of a sub-conscious or undiscriminated plurality. Leibniz in fact maintains on general grounds that, although these ideas are simple and unanalysable to our apperceptive consciousness, they must in reality be complex and capable of analysis. As to what these grounds were, we must now enquire.

In his early *Thoughts on knowledge, truth and ideas*, Leibniz had contented himself with the remark, that our notions of sensible qualities are certainly composite, since they have their causes. There is implied in this *dictum* an implication of the composition theory, which always underlay his treatment of the subject, viz., the assumption that causation is composition, and that consequently every effect contains in itself the plurality of conditions upon which it depends. It follows that a distinct idea of an effect would enable us to detect in it this plurality. Hence, when, as in the case of the so-called simple ideas of Sensation, we cannot do this, our idea must be confused, and must contain an undetected plurality. Now our ignorance of the causes of these ideas appears in different ways, according to the level of reflection which we occupy. If we seek to place ourselves at the point of view of ultimate truth, we must recognise that our sensations arise entirely from conditions in the mind itself. But since we are not conscious of any causal activity in reference to them, these conditions must be found among the *petites perceptions* of sub-consciousness. The theory of the self-evolution of the individual mind and the conception of sub-conscious mental functions having once been accepted, this application follows easily enough. If, however, we would treat the question from the more popular level, which Leibniz occupies throughout the greater part of his criticism of Locke, and from which we regard our sensations as caused by external conditions, we find ourselves immersed in serious difficulties. For, while we can only regard these conditions as imperceptible mathematical determinations of body, we are not only ignorant as to what they are, but we cannot even conceive how such conditions could give rise to our perceptions. Thus, the very reasons which led Locke to declare that matter, as exhibiting secondary qualities, is incapable of scientific treatment, are regarded by Leibniz as proofs of complexity in the apparently simple ideas of these qualities, which come to be enshrouded in a mystery almost as inscrutable as that which envelopes the Lockian idea of substance. 'It is,' he declares, in reference to these ideas, 'an *I know not what* of which we are conscious, but for which we cannot account[1].' Even in the few cases in which we have definite grounds for

[1] Letter to Queen Charlotte of Prussia. Gerhardt's edition of Leibniz, vol. VI. p. 498. This letter will be found to contain the fullest expression of his views on the whole subject.

supposing the presence of certain factors, we are in reality no better off. Since green arises from a mixture of blue and yellow, we may, he thinks, regard the idea of green as composed of the ideas of these colours; but we cannot detect the latter in the former, or generate the idea of green by an intellectual combination of the ideas of blue and yellow. Although the real complexity of the cause may in this case be experimentally verified, the apparent simplicity of the effect is as evident and as baffling as ever[1].

§ 15. In his explanation of the meaning of innateness, and of the complexity which he maintains is involved in Locke's simple ideas of sensible qualities, we have seen Leibniz applying his new conception of mental function to the reinterpretation and defence of two of the fundamental positions of rationalism.

Apart, however, from his insistence upon the non-empirical origin of certain ideas, and upon the complexity and confusion of our ideas of secondary qualities, Leibniz has little to offer in the way of criticism of Locke's general theory of the formation and constitution of our ideas, as developed in Book II of the *Essay*. He was himself far too deeply committed to the composition theory for an effective handling of this part of the subject. Locke's procedure presented itself to him as a legitimate and useful manner of expounding the content of our ideas, lacking indeed in philosophical depth, since no attempt is made to push the analysis up to the simple intellectual notions, which constituted for him the primary data of knowledge. But while we may pass over the bulk of Leibniz's comments on Book II of the *Essay*, as unimportant in themselves and irrelevant to our purpose, some attention must be paid to his treatment of our

[1] Cf. *N. E.* II. 2. 1.

ideas of space and substance, both on their own account and as illustrating the relation of his position to that of Locke.

§ 16. To Leibniz our spacial ideas prove distinctly embarrassing. His general intention is to assign to them a position intermediate between the distinct and innate ideas by which the mind cognises its own nature, and the confused ideas which it derives from sensible experience, thus meeting the requirements of the Principle of Continuity. But to carry this conception out in detail, in a way which shall be consistent with his other positions, proves to be no easy matter; whether we consider the degree of distinctness possessed by these ideas, or the source to which they are to be assigned. As constituting the basis of the demonstrative science of geometry, they would seem to be pre-eminently distinct. From a metaphysical point of view, however, they must be pronounced to involve confusion; since reflection shows that what we cognise as an external world is in reality non-spacial, and that the appearance of extendedness would disappear could our thought attain to a sufficient degree of distinctness. Thus, the ideas which Locke regarded as possessing a perfect intellectual transparency are for Leibniz less distinct than the ideas of substance and identity, in the exposition of which Locke had found his most puzzling problems.

Still greater difficulties arise when Leibniz seeks to refer these ideas to their source. To regard them, as Locke had done, as ideas derived from more than one sense, would have been, in his opinion, to degrade them to the level of our ideas of secondary qualities, and to plunge them in the still greater confusion which these involve. On the other hand, they cannot be innate in the same sense as the metaphysical conceptions by which the mind apprehends its own nature, since extendedness is emphatically not a characteristic of the self. From this dilemma, Leibniz seeks to escape by assigning these ideas to 'the common sense[1].' But since the common sense is admittedly not a sense at all, this is, he recognises, equivalent to their derivation 'from the mind itself.' They are, then, he declares, 'ideas of the pure understanding,' but 'related to the external.' A position such as is here suggested can, however, find no place in his system without disastrous results, either to his view of what constitutes pure understanding, or to his theory of the real nature of that which we apprehend as external. For pure understanding must apprehend reality as it is, and reality is a non-spacial system of monads.

These difficulties in classifying and referring to their source the ideas which lie at the basis of geometrical science are independent of the distinction which Leibniz draws between extension as a property of bodies and our conception of space itself, important as this is from the metaphysical point of view. While endeavouring to represent the extension of body as due to our imperfect apprehension of a plurality or repetition of unextended monads, space is declared to be merely an abstract system of relations, or an order of possible existences. Leibniz thus adopts and develops the purely relational theory of space, which we have seen that Locke at one time entertained, but which he abandoned in favour of the theory of More, also adopted by Newton, that space must be conceived as real apart from body, and as pertaining to the Divine Being. In his criticism of the *Essay* Leibniz merely

[1] *N. E.* II. 5. I.

indicates this difference of view. The full statement and defence of his position are contained in his correspondence with Clarke.

§ 17. While substance constituted the fundamental metaphysical category both for Locke and for Leibniz, each had been brought, in his own way and from his own point of view, to a critical examination of its significance. Locke, directing his criticism from the point of view of conscious experience was, as we have seen, unable to find in the conception anything but a necessary point of reference for the contents of experience. The realistic presuppositions of his unconscious metaphysic had, however, prevented his thorough-going adoption of this conclusion, and hopeless perplexities had arisen from the assumption to which they led, that substance must still have a content of its own, which from the nature of the case we cannot grasp. The chimerical nature of these difficulties Leibniz had no difficulty in exposing. They arise, he points out, from our first abstracting the bare idea of substance from all determinations, and then requiring that it shall nevertheless possess determinations. Thus the complaint of our ignorance of its nature 'arises from our demanding a kind of knowledge of which the object does not admit[1].' Not indeed that he would himself reduce substance to a bare point of reference. Proceeding on more metaphysical lines, his own criticism had reached a very different result. Taking its point of departure from his dissatisfaction with the consequences which seemed to him to have been correctly drawn by Spinoza from the Cartesian conception of substance, it had led to a transformation of that category. Instead of conceiving substance statically, as an independent existent, we must

[1] *N. E.* II. 23. II.

view it dynamically, as an independent principle of activity. Now the nature of this activity is revealed to us in our own inner experience. Thus, while Locke, endeavouring to find a meaning for substance from the point of view of experience, ended by treating it as purely transcendent, Leibniz, as the result of his metaphysical analysis, presents us with the conception of substance as an immanent principle of experience, involving a teleological unity. Unfortunately, the fruitfulness of this new idea was largely nullified by his continuing to identify the conception of substance with that of a logical subject in the notion of which all its predicates are contained. For this identification led directly to the conversion of the principle of activity into the principle of the isolation of substances, and to the denial of any real communion between them. Of the real point of vantage with which the new conception provided him in his criticism of Locke, Leibniz, at all events, shows himself almost unaware. Instead of developing his own conception, and setting it over against that which he found in the *Essay*, he contents himself with the bare assertion that the conception of substance is not so empty and sterile as Locke had supposed, and that numerous *a priori* metaphysical truths can be derived from it.

§ 18. While Locke and Leibniz differ thus fundamentally in their views concerning the meaning of substance, they are at one in accepting the view that relations can have no place *in rerum natura*, but are *entia mentalia* dependent upon the activity of a comparing mind. Having expressed his concurrence with Locke's division of the objects of our thought into substances, modes and relations, Leibniz proceeds at once to affirm the metaphysical inferiority of the last-named category. 'I believe that qualities are only modifications of substances, and that the understanding adds to them the relations[1].' He is, indeed, careful to add that they must not be regarded as on that account entirely groundless or unreal. They are not mere fictions of our understandings, but are ultimately grounded in the divine understanding, the 'supreme intelligence which determines them all for all time[2].' A dogmatic solution of this kind was, of course, opposed to the spirit of Locke's enquiry. Nor does it remove, but rather intensifies, the difficulty of comprehending how relations can arise in the apprehension of a reality to whose nature they are foreign.

We have now endeavoured to indicate the different motives which underlie Leibniz's treatment of knowledge, and to trace their working in his criticism of some of the main positions of the earlier books of the *Essay*. It still remains to make a comparison between the views of Locke and Leibniz concerning the general nature, kinds and extent of our knowledge. To this we shall proceed in the following chapter.

[1] *N. E.* II. 12. 5. [2] *N. E.* II. 30. 4.

CHAPTER XII

LOCKE AND LEIBNIZ (*continued*)

§ 1. Between the views of Locke and Leibniz concerning the questions which are discussed in the concluding book of the *Essay*, there is at first sight a considerable amount of agreement. With many of the presuppositions and general views of his predecessor Leibniz has, at all events, no quarrel. That knowledge is primarily concerned with ideas which, while mind-dependent, represent a reality beyond the individual mind; that in its most perfect form it is reducible to self-evident propositions, which are apprehended by intuition; that demonstration consists in a concatenation of such intuitions, by which connections of ideas which are not self-evident are mediately brought to light; that while the typical examples of this procedure are to be found in mathematics, it is not limited to quantity; that by means of such perceptions of connections of content among our ideas, immediate and mediate, we are furnished with propositions which are universal and necessary; that such knowledge could not be obtained by any process of empirical generalisation, and does not assert or imply real existence; that the only existence which is immediately known is that of the mind itself, but that the existence of God can also be known with absolute certainty, by demonstration; that our knowledge of the existence of external things, though theoretically falling short of the requirements of a perfect apprehension of truth, must yet be accepted as practically indubitable: in all these positions Leibniz follows Locke. A difference of first rate importance manifests itself, however, when we enquire as to the contents of the fundamental truths of rational knowledge, which intuition apprehends. With this difference we shall begin our comparison of the theories of the two thinkers. Having followed out this divergence as to the nature of rational knowledge, we shall consider their treatment of the relation of rational knowledge to the truths made known by experience.

§ 2. Notwithstanding Locke's insistence upon the synthetic character of all instructive propositions, Leibniz continued to hold the view, at which we have seen he had early arrived, that the ideal of rational knowledge can only be attained by the reduction of all propositions to statements of identity. 'The primitive truths of reason,' he still declares, 'are those which I call by the general name of *identicals*, because it seems that they do nothing but repeat the same thing, without teaching us anything[1]'; an appearance which is certainly not belied by such examples as '*A* is *A*,' '*B* is *B*,' 'the equilateral rectangle is a rectangle.' To definitions and identical propositions, he still thinks, all other necessary truths can be reduced. The significance of Locke's exposure of the futility of such a procedure he entirely failed to grasp. Even if it be frivolous to repeat, 'Oyster is oyster,' the value of identical propositions will appear, he assures us, as soon as we consider how other truths can be reduced to them[2]. Instead, however, of endeavouring to give examples of such reductions or demonstrations, he confines himself to pointing

[1] *N. E.* IV. 2. I.

[2] *N. E.* IV. 8. 3.

out that the proof by *reductio ad impossibile*, as employed by geometers, involves the use of the Law of Contradiction; and to attempting to show that this principle by itself suffices to justify the logical process of conversion, and the reduction of the indirect moods of the syllogism to the first figure. It is unnecessary to dwell upon the inadequacy of this defence; since it is evident that conversion would be meaningless, and the syllogism impossible, if we started with merely identical propositions. Holding, then, to the positions at which, as he says, he had arrived in his youth, Locke's contention that identical propositions are 'trifling' seemed to him to indicate 'a want of having thought sufficiently on these matters[1].' Regarding Locke as working at a comparatively popular and superficial level, he considered his admission of the immediate certainty of propositions expressing synthetical connections of ideas as an indication of his failure to attain to the conception of a 'perfect analysis.' 'You see, then, sir,' his own representative in the dialogue is made to say, 'that what you and your friends have said concerning the connection of ideas, as the genuine source of truths, needs explication. If you are willing to content yourself with a confused view of this connection, you weaken the exactness of demonstration....Yet, if you wish this connection of ideas to be distinctly seen and expressed, you will be obliged to recur to definitions and identical axioms[2].'

§ 3. An interesting illustration of Leibniz's point of view is afforded by his treatment of the four kinds of agreement or disagreement of ideas into which our knowledge is divided by Locke. After remarking that relation 'taken generally' covers all forms of agreement, he proceeds

[1] *N. E.* IV. 2. 1.

[2] *N. E.* IV. 12. 6.

to distinguish two kinds of relation, viz., relations of comparison and relations of concurrence. The former, he tells us, comprise 'identity and diversity, either in whole or in part, by which are constituted *the same* or *the diverse*, *the like* or *the unlike*.' Relations of concurrence include Locke's coexistence, and may be extended, we are told, to cover our knowledge of the existence of objects, since the existence of an object may be regarded as its concurrence with the *ego*. 'Thus I believe it may be said that there is only comparison and concurrence; but that the comparison which marks identity or diversity, and the concurrence of the thing with the *ego*, are the relations which deserve to be distinguished among others[1].' It will be seen that while three of Locke's varieties of agreement or disagreement are here accounted for, the one which he had denominated 'relation,' in the strictest sense of the term, disappears altogether. Those special connections of content which Locke had regarded as synthetic, must, according to Leibniz, be brought under the head of total or partial identity, or degraded to the level of mere factual concurrence.

§ 4. Locke's favourite examples of such synthetic, yet self-evident and necessary truths, had been drawn from the mathematical sciences, and these Leibniz repeatedly and expressly declares are capable of reduction to definitions and identical propositions. This reduction, he thinks, has been most successfully effected in the case of arithmetic. $3 = 2 + 1$ is not, as Locke supposed, an example of intuitive knowledge; for it is not a truth, but a definition. On the other hand, while $2 + 2 = 4$ is a truth, it is not self-evident, but requires to be demonstrated by means of the definitions which lie at the basis

[1] *N. E.* IV. I. 7.

of the science[1]. Against the reduction of arithmetic to a merely verbal system, Leibniz thinks to guard himself by the contention that these definitions are not nominal but real, *i.e.* they imply the possibility of the thing defined. For, according to the rationalistic principle of possibility, which Locke had employed and Leibniz expressly formulates, ideas which are through and through distinct, or which are adequate, can thereby be known *a priori* to be ideas of possible existents; for their transparency can harbour no contradiction, and the non-contradictory is possible. Hence the definitions of arithmetic, being adequate, contain the 'concealed statement' that the ideas in question are possible, which is a matter of intuitive knowledge.

In the case of geometry it is admitted that the reduction to distinct definitions and identical propositions, which the 'perfect analysis' requires, has not yet been carried out. The science, as we have it, rests upon secondary and provisional axioms which can be, but have not been, resolved into mere identities. Nor should the definitions it employs be accepted as final. For we are here immersed in the perplexities of the continuous, with its confused infinity. As he says elsewhere, geometers have not even a sufficiently clear idea of the straight line, for they cannot analytically derive all its properties from its definition. In other words, Leibniz recognises his own inability to eliminate synthetical propositions from geometry, though he continues to proclaim the possibility of such elimination, as involved in the conception of the science as consisting of necessary truths.

§ 5. Holding that the mathematical sciences consisted of truths which were really analytical, even where their reduction to this form had not been actually effected, Leibniz

[1] *N. E.* IV. 7. 10.

is in hearty agreement with Locke's view that demonstration is not limited to the sciences of quantity. Logic, ethics and metaphysics are all included within its sphere. Ethics, which Locke had alone singled out, is not merely as capable of demonstration as geometry, but more so. For in it we are dealing with purely intelligible ideas, and are no longer troubled by the infinity which is involved in continuous quantity[1]. Without apparently perceiving the inconsistency with his general position, he attributes the superior success which has actually been achieved by geometry to the fact that in it 'experience is able to guarantee the reasoning at every moment,' whereas in ethics and in metaphysics 'this parallelism of reason and experience is no longer found[2].' His view of the part played by the diagram in geometrical reasoning is, in fact, the same as that of Locke. While demonstration is independent of diagrams for its validity, and could proceed without their aid, they are useful 'to facilitate the comprehension of what we wish to say, and to fix the attention[3].' He had, too, for long been of Locke's opinion that artificial means may be found which will compensate for their absence in other sciences. The *characteristica universalis*, upon the possibilities of which he so often dwells, involves as one of its features the representation of all our notions by visible characters, thus securing as far as possible for other subjects the service which the diagram performs in geometry; while the *ars combinatoria* has to reduce all human thoughts to their simple constituents, as to an alphabet, and work out the formal rules of their combination, after the manner of a universal algebra. Could this ideal be attained, disputation would be as unnecessary in philosophy as

[1] *N. E.* IV. 3. 19. [2] *N. E.* IV. 2. 13. [3] *N. E.* IV. 1. 9.

in the adding up of an account. Philosophers who found themselves in disagreement would only need 'to take their pencils in their hands, to sit down to their slates, and to say to each other (with a friend to witness, if they liked): Let us calculate[1].'

§ 6. While Leibniz's conception of the perfect form of knowledge is rationalistic, in the narrowest sense of the term, another motive makes its appearance in his treatment of the nature of knowledge in general, and of the relations between its different varieties. If he regards Locke's account of intuitive and demonstrative knowledge as too lax, since it accepts as ultimate the apprehension of synthetical connections of ideas, he complains, on the other hand, that his view of knowledge in general is too stringent. So far from allowing too little to the rational factor in knowledge, he complains that Locke, in his definition of knowledge, insists upon it over much, thus unduly limiting the sphere of knowledge. He rejects, in the first place, Locke's identification of knowledge with certainty, and its consequent distinction from even the highest degree of probability. Opinion based on probability may also, he thinks, be called knowledge[2]. To Locke's three 'degrees' of knowledge—intuitive, demonstrative and sensitive—he would therefore add a fourth, viz. the knowledge of the probable[3]. And certainty itself, he would interpret, not as theoretically excluding the very possibility of doubt, but as that which is incapable of being doubted for practical purposes, as long as we retain our sanity[4]. Or, as he elsewhere puts it, we must recognise the moral or

[1] Gerhardt's edition of Leibniz, vol. VII. p. 200. Quoted in Russell's *Philosophy of Leibniz*, p. 170.

[2] *N. E.* IV. 2. 14. [3] *loc. cit.* [4] *N. E.* IV. 11. 10.

physical certainty, which has its source in unvarying experience, as well as the metaphysical certainty, which is found in our apprehension of necessary truths[1]. He objects to Locke's definition of knowledge, as the perception of the agreement or disagreement of our ideas, that we may have knowledge though we do not perceive such an agreement or disagreement, but only 'feel it confusedly without apperceiving it[2].' Finally, he will not even accept the limitation of knowledge to judgments. Though the apprehension of truth is impossible apart from judgment, knowledge, he holds, has a wider signification than this, according to which it is to be found in ideas and terms, prior to the formation of propositions[3].

§ 7. The motive which underlies this widening of the conception of knowledge finds still further expression in Leibniz's treatment of the relations between the different kinds of knowledge. What he in principle desired to do was to exhibit these as continuous stages in the evolution of our cognitive consciousness; an evolution which, beginning at the level of merely subconscious apprehension, would find its completion in the most perfect form of intuitive knowledge. Now 'evolution,' it must be remembered, whether biological or psychological, meant for him 'preformation.' It was not conceived as a process of development in and through which genuinely new forms of being, or contents of consciousness arise, but as the rendering patent or obvious of something which was really present, though in a less obvious form, from the start. Such a conception of evolution is indeed but the counterpart of the composition theory. As the latter maintains that the conditions which constitute a cause exist unmodified in the effect, which is merely their sum; so, the former

[1] *N. E.* IV. 6. 13. [2] *N. E.* IV. I. I. [3] *N. E.* IV. I. 2.

considers that nothing can emerge in the course of evolution which was not present in some hidden way from the first in the evolving being. Applied to the mind, it implies that no addition is ever made to its initial content, and that the various stages of our cognitive consciousness are but the different degrees of clearness and distinctness with which the same content is apprehended. If Leibniz was guided by a true instinct in his desire to mediate between the different forms of knowledge, the inherent unworkability of this conception of evolution prevented him from doing more, in most cases, than to blur the outlines of the distinctions he criticised.

§ 8. The most fundamental distinction which Locke recognises among the propositions which constitute our 'real instructive knowledge,' is that between propositions concerning the existence of particular things and universal propositions concerning the relations of our abstract ideas. To one or other of these the various kinds of knowledge are found, in the end, to reduce themselves. This classification of instructive propositions has obvious points of contact with the Leibnizian distinction between truths of fact and truths of reason, with which Leibniz himself compares it[1]. Both Locke and Leibniz recognise the exceptional position of the predication of existence, and the hypothetical character of the universal proposition. For both the final distinction within knowledge is that between an apprehension of particular facts as revealed by experience, and a knowledge which is universal and necessary, but formal and abstract. Apart, however, from their opposed views as to the nature of this latter type of knowledge, their fundamental difference of standpoint shows itself in the way in which the distinction is

[1] *N. E.* IV. II. 13.

drawn. While Locke's division of propositions is simply put forward as the result to which he has been brought by his examination of knowledge; the Leibnizian distinction, though originating in reflection on knowledge, and applied to the classification of knowledge, is really drawn from a metaphysical point of view. The distinction between the necessary and the contingent is interpreted objectively, as a difference in the truths themselves, apart from our knowledge of them or their relations to the knowing mind. Necessary truths, being dependent on the Law of Contradiction, have their basis in the divine understanding; contingent truths are an expression of the divine will, working through its choice of the best. We may even, it would seem, recognise that a proposition formulates a necessary truth, without being able to see that it is necessarily true. For the axioms of geometry are treated as necessary truths, although it is held that we have not yet succeeded in meeting the requirements of the 'perfect analysis' with reference to them; and until this has been done we cannot see with perfect certainty that their opposites involve contradiction.

§ 9. The Leibnizian distinction, then, is primarily metaphysical rather than epistemological. Interpreted in its ultimate terms, as resting upon the contrast between the Law of Contradiction and the principle of the Choice of the Best, it resists all his skill as a mediator, and constitutes an unresolved dualism underlying his theory of knowledge[1]. Within the region of knowledge, however, Leibniz is not prepared to accept as final the mere setting beside each other of a knowledge of particular existences and a knowledge of universal truths. His own direct comments on Locke's position are, indeed, not very impressive.

[1] Cf. Adamson, *Development of Modern Philosophy*, vol. I. p. 102.

Propositions of fact, he declares, may become general in a way, by induction; besides the universal truths which are necessary, reason, he thinks, furnishes us with some truths which are not absolutely universal, but only probable, 'as for example, when we assume an idea to be possible until its contrary is discovered by a more exact investigation[1].' But as he admits that the generality achieved by induction is not 'perfect,' since we cannot see its necessity; and as an assumption which is subsequently refuted can hardly pass for knowledge, these considerations do not take us far. It is more helpful to call to mind Leibniz's insistence that the contingency of truths of fact does not imply the absence of determination, or the impossibility of their scientific treatment. Though in the last resort inexplicable without reference to the Choice of the Best, each fact of experience has its proximate ground in other facts of the same kind, with which it is systematically connected. Owing to the infinity which pertains to every element of the real, there is thus opened up a field of investigation which is unlimited. Instead of referring factual connections which we cannot explain, such as that between body and mind, directly to the 'good pleasure of God,' we must regard them as in principle capable of rational comprehension, could we only carry our analysis far enough. Instead of looking, as Locke had done, for a criterion of the existence of sensible things in a characteristic of sensation, such as its force and vividness, we must seek it in the connection of phenomena with one another. Moreover, the truths of reason are themselves the principles according to which the facts of experience are connected. They are thus implicit in our empirical knowledge, though its content can never be completely deduced from them

[1] *N. E.* IV. II. 13.

alone. In such views there is much that is suggestive. It is clear, however, that the desired conciliation cannot be effected as long as the truths of reason are conceived as identical propositions. As such they cannot furnish the bonds of connection between phenomena; indeed, from the point of view from which identical propositions are the ideal of knowledge, these connections must remain as unintelligible as the phenomena themselves would be in isolation.

§ 10. A similar difference shows itself when we compare the views of Locke and Leibniz upon the relation of the mathematical and the physical sciences. For Locke, as we know, while mathematics consists of universal propositions concerning relations of ideas, our knowledge of natural phenomena is in the main restricted to the contents of particular experiences. From these we may, indeed, obtain conclusions of a more general kind, possessing a high degree of probability, but lacking the certainty of knowledge; and it would, he thinks, be 'lost labour' to seek after 'a perfect science of bodies[1].' In so far as Leibniz's rejection of this position depends upon his laxer interpretation of the meaning of knowledge, we need not dwell upon it further. To that extent, indeed, the question is in part a verbal one. To Locke's contention that we can only know the nominal and not the real essences of substances, Leibniz replies that a thing can have but one essence, though it may have many definitions, each of which more or less perfectly expresses this essence. As the sciences advance, therefore, our nominal definitions become more and more adequate to the substances defined. A knowledge of the essences of substances presents itself to him, therefore, as a goal towards which we may approach,

[1] *Essay*, IV. 3. 29.

rather than as something from which we are for ever cut off. Nor will he admit that there is any fundamental difference, as regards the conditions of their reality, between our ideas of substances on the one hand and of modes and relations on the other. For, he maintains, reverting once more to the standpoint of dogmatic metaphysics, they all alike have their archetypes in the divine mind.

It was, however, in the nature of the immediate contents of our sense-experience that Locke had found the final and insuperable bar to the scientific treatment of natural phenomena. Between these he could directly discover little or nothing in the way of necessary connections, while the possibility of their indirect connection, through the primary qualities of the minute parts of body, upon which they are thought to depend, seemed to him to be blocked, not only by our actual ignorance of these primary qualities, but by our total inability to conceive how the contents of our sensible experience could result from them. That we are here in the presence of an obstacle which is absolute and final, Leibniz will not allow. Denying the simplicity of our ideas of secondary qualities, the confusion, which on his theory they involve, is taken to imply the possibility of their analysis, and consequently their theoretical intelligibility. Holding on *a priori* grounds the commensurability of the mental and the material, he maintains that our ideas of sensible qualities must correspond precisely to their physical causes. Could we reach the internal constitution of a body, we should be able to see why it has the qualities which experience presents, or rather they would be reduced to their intelligible reasons. That they should, nevertheless, still be experienced as sensible, is inconvenient for his theory, but need not concern us here. Ultimately, indeed, there exists for

Leibniz, as well as for Locke, a fundamental difference between the mathematical and the natural sciences. For while mathematics, he thinks, rests entirely on the principle of Contradiction, 'in order to proceed from mathematics to natural philosophy, another principle is requisite[1],' viz., the principle of Sufficient Reason, which in the last resort means the principle of the Choice of the Best. Thus, ideally, 'the true physics must be derived from the source of the divine perfections[2],' instead of being based upon simple and necessary truths, such as form the foundation of the mathematical sciences. In the meantime, working from the other end, there is before us an infinite field for investigation by empirical and analytical methods.

§ 11. If we endeavour, in summing up, to form an estimate of the value of Leibniz's elaborate commentary upon and criticism of the *Essay*, it must, I think, be said that, apart from its frequent suggestiveness upon particular points, it makes no really substantial contribution towards the solution of the problems to which Locke had directed attention; nor does it grapple sufficiently closely with Locke's point of view to lay bare its shortcomings and correct its defects. Leibniz never appreciated the significance of the attempt to treat knowledge from the standpoint of an immanent criticism, which, however imperfectly carried out, constituted the true importance of the *Essay*. On the general validity or invalidity of such a procedure he has nothing to say, and proceeds as if the question had never been raised. If the possession of a more developed metaphysical theory saved him from some of the more obvious crudities of Locke's thought, his constant employment of it for the dogmatic solution of questions of

[1] Second Letter to Clarke. [2] Letter to Boyle.

epistemology, without explanation or defence, shows how completely impervious he remained to the new point of view. Nor, had his attitude towards it been other than it was, could he have contributed much towards its elucidation or development, since he accepted without questioning two of the chief sources of weakness in Locke's theory of knowledge, viz., the view that the immediate objects of knowledge are ideas, and the composition theory. Moreover, the distinctive features of his own metaphysical system were not of a kind to throw light upon the theory of knowledge. From this point of view, at least, the theory of monads, with its implication of mental preformation and the development of all our ideas and experiences from within, must be pronounced a veritable *cul de sac*. Even Leibniz himself realises the impossibility of a fruitful discussion of the preformation theory of knowledge with one who does not accept the metaphysics from which he deduces it, and in consequence leaves it on one side in his defence of innate ideas and principles.

Turning from the relation of his theory of knowledge to his metaphysics, to the content of the former, we find Leibniz again failing to apprehend the significance of Locke's work on a matter of prime importance. He passed by without serious consideration Locke's demonstration of the futility of identical and analytical propositions, and continued to exalt as the ideal of knowledge the narrowly rationalistic conception which he had inherited and developed. By insisting on the synthetic character of 'instructive' propositions, including those which are necessary and universal, Locke had raised a problem of the full significance of which he was not himself aware, but which for his critic simply did not exist. For the pure formalism of his theory of rational knowledge.

Leibniz's clearer perception of the function of the universal is not a sufficient compensation. The one result of first rate importance, which emerges from his criticism of the *Essay*, is the superseding of the Cartesian identification of mental function with self-consciousness, and the establishment of the conception of sub-consciousness. To the advantage which this gave to Leibniz in the treatment of questions of psychology, attention has been drawn. But from its speculative employment, in defence of his preconceived metaphysical positions, nothing but confusion did or could result.

CHAPTER XIII

LOCKE AND KANT

§ 1. Our undertaking in the present chapter is of a very different character from that in which we have been engaged in the last two. In considering the relation between the theories of knowledge of Locke and Leibniz, we were in the main concerned with the detailed criticism of the former writer by the latter. In dealing with the relation of the doctrine of the *Essay* to that of the *Critique of Pure Reason*, the problem is of quite a different kind. Kant makes but the scantiest of references to the work of Locke, with which, indeed, he was only superficially acquainted. We must seek, therefore, to bring together for ourselves the essential features of the thought of the two writers concerning the problem of knowledge, and to institute a comparison between them. In doing so, we shall be led to deal more fully than we have yet done with some of the fundamental positions of the *Essay*, and with the place which it occupies in the development of modern philosophy.

To indicate with brevity the relations between the accounts of knowledge which are given by Locke and Kant is a matter of no little difficulty. For while nothing is easier than to institute a comparison between particular statements or partial doctrines of the two writers, such a procedure is in this case more than usually unprofitable and misleading. The *Essay* and the *Critique* are both expressions of complex and unstable thought positions, which do not admit of enunciation in a small number of simple propositions. Both works contain the record of an intellectual development, rather than the finished product of a course of coherent reflection; and both are infected by the inconsistencies which arise from the transcendence of initial assumptions, which are yet not explicitly abandoned. Nor are these resemblances to be regarded as merely accidental. They are due to the fact that each of these thinkers is seeking to approach the problems of philosophy from a new point of view, the significance and implications of which he has not succeeded in fully realising. The originative and dominant force in the thought of each is to be found in the attempt to apply to our knowledge and experience the principle of an immanent criticism, which, however, neither is able to do with complete consistency. It is of course to be expected that the philosophy of Kant will show an advance upon that of Locke, in a clearer consciousness of what is involved in such an undertaking. Not only does it presuppose another century of philosophical development, but it has behind it a longer and more thorough course of philosophical reflection on the part of its author. Up to the time at which the problem of the *Essay* first presented itself to him, Locke does not seem to have devoted much thought to a serious grappling with philosophical questions, and the first draft of his reflections upon the subject is marked by extreme crudity. The *Essay*, even when completed, takes its start from and makes its appeal to the mind of the educated man of the period, rather than the professional philosopher. The *Critique of Pure Reason*, on the other hand, is from the outset the product of a mind for long concentrated upon the technical problems of philosophy. We may, nevertheless, find reasons for holding that in certain important respects the more naif doctrine of the earlier writer is susceptible of a more satisfactory development than the highly artificial system of the thinker of Königsberg.

§ 2. The similarity of Locke's statement of the purpose of the *Essay*, in its Introduction, to the most general form in which Kant describes the problem of the *Critique* has often been noticed. Both Locke and Kant announce as their peculiar undertaking the investigation of the nature and extent of the knowledge which is possible for us. They both find in such an enquiry the only safeguard against the equally fatal dangers of dogmatism and scepticism. They both proclaim that this examination of knowledge is to be undertaken apart from any investigation of reality, or the assumption of any theory concerning it. They thus call a halt to the dogmatic metaphysician, who had taken for granted the competency of thought to determine the nature of reality, which he nevertheless conceived as entirely independent of and discontinuous with the knowing mind. But in insisting upon the postponement of all such attempts, until their legitimacy has been established by an examination of the conditions of knowledge, both Locke and Kant commit two fatal but complementary errors. On the one hand, they tacitly take for granted the dogmatic conception of reality; on the other hand, they divorce knowledge from the apprehension of reality, in which its life consists. The result is that each is haunted by the spectre of a reality which is in its intrinsic nature unknowable; while, notwithstanding their efforts to avoid such a result, knowledge has for each, in the last resort, the appearance of a merely formal function. The former position appears in its most conscious and developed form in the Kantian doctrine of the thing in itself. And although Locke starts with the popular assumption, that the reality foreign to and absolutely independent of the knowing mind is to be found in material existence, characterised by the primary qualities, he is in the end forced to a position very similar to that of Kant. For behind the perceptible body there exists for him the unknown real essence, upon which all its perceptible qualities depend; while behind and implied in both the perceptible body and its real essence is the unknowable *substratum*. This, like the Kantian thing-in-itself, represents the empty reference to a reality conceived as wholly disparate from our experience.

But the mere reference to an unknown *x* cannot satisfy the essential requirement which, after all, both Locke and Kant are unable to ignore, viz., that knowledge has in some sense and in some sort reality for its object. We find, accordingly, in both the admission of a secondary kind of reality, of which knowledge can be obtained. This appears in the Kantian theory of the reality of the phenomenal object, as involving constituents drawn from experience and determined by the categories, and in Locke's contention that although our knowledge is concerning ideas, and cannot consequently penetrate to the being of things, yet, in so far as the ideas which it involves are received from experience, they and the knowledge into which they enter must be pronounced to be 'real.' This secondary kind of reality, it must be observed, is in each case conceived as directly dependent upon the functioning of the mind. Although neither the 'phenomenon' of Kant nor the 'idea' of Locke is correctly designated as a subjective state, neither can have any existence apart from the mental function by which it is apprehended. It is the synthetic activity of the subject which constitutes phenomena; and ideas 'cease to be anything when there is no perception of them.' But a reality which only exists in and through the act by which it is cognised is as unable to satisfy the conditions of knowledge as a reality which is entirely beyond its reach. To avoid such pitfalls criticism must take its start from the recognition that knowledge essentially involves a relation of the mind to a reality, which has a nature and an existence independent of our cognition of it, but is nevertheless continuous with our experience. It is not such an admission, but the attempt to postpone all considerations of reality, and to treat knowledge in complete abstraction from it, which leads us eventually back into the slough of dogmatism.

§ 3. The difficulties of their position show themselves in a still more conspicuous manner in the accounts which our authors give of the reality of the mind itself. As we have seen, the intention of Locke's 'historical, plain method,' was to consider the mind only as it is employed about ideas; but the tacit assumption remained that the mind is in itself a transcendent entity, lying beneath or beyond experience. Notwithstanding the exceptional perplexities which he finds in the attempt to bring what we experience of its nature and function under the category of substance[1], Locke continues to speak of the mind as involving a *substratum*, which lies beyond the reach of experience or knowledge. Finally, since the innermost being of mind and matter are alike unknowable, we cannot, he tells us, be sure that they are not determinations of a single substance. While less crudely stated, and with a clearer consciousness of the difficulties involved, and a more strenuous endeavour to avoid them, all of these positions

[1] Cf. above, ch. I. § 13.

continue to have their place in the thought of Kant. Although he exposes with triumphant thoroughness the transcendental illusion involved in the attempt to represent the soul as a substance, he still thinks of our consciousness as involving an unknown and unknowable ground or basis. Behind the 'phenomena' of the 'internal sense,' by which the 'empirical self' is cognised, there lies a noumenal something, which we cannot make an object of knowledge. And hence, we are told, we must admit the possibility that the noumenon which forms the foundation of our perception of our self may be the same as that of which material existence is an appearance. The closest parallel of all is to be found in the curious speculation which Locke and Kant both employ to refute the dogmatic interpretation of our consciousness of personal identity, as signifying a sameness of underlying substance. Against this theory both urge that it is impossible for us to know that such consciousness, with the memory it involves, cannot be transferred from one such substance to another[1]. While this argument constitutes in reality a *reductio ad absurdum* of the whole dogmatic theory of the soul, from which both Locke and Kant are seeking deliverance, neither of them goes so far as to reject the conception of conscious experience as a particular determination of an underlying ground or *substratum*, which has a nature of its own apart from experience, as intrinsically unintelligible; both merely maintain that the identity of such an ontological ground cannot be known, or shown to be necessarily involved in our consciousness of identity.

Finally, when both the mind and the reality from which

[1] See above, ch. v. § 20, and cf. Kant's note on the third parallogism, in which he employs the analogy of an elastic ball communicating its whole motion to another.

it is distinguished have been admitted to the position of entities discontinuous with our experience, the temptation is irresistible to regard experience and knowledge as an effect of some kind of interaction between them. Instead of constituting our ultimate datum, to be supplemented and interpreted by reference to that which is more complete, but continuous with itself, experience comes to be represented as the product of two factors, which are essentially incapable of being experienced. While Locke and Kant differ profoundly on the further question of the nature of the contributions made by the two factors, each in his own way accepts this view of experience as a manufactured product, although it is a sheer reversion to the dogmatism they both repudiate.

But the mind which lies behind experience, whether its rôle is the relatively active one of synthesising sense elements, or the relatively passive one of perceiving ideas, is not the self of our everyday knowledge. This latter clearly must be assigned to the realm of secondary or phenomenal reality, and is thought of by both Locke and Kant after the analogy of a material thing, although sharply distinguished from such as far as its nature is concerned. Thus we have in Locke the distinction between material substances, characterised by the most fundamental determinations of our ideas of Sensation, and mental substances whose distinguishing content consists of ideas of Reflection; while Kant still more definitely seeks to work out the misleading conception of an inner sense as supplying the data for the cognition of the empirical self.

§ 4. We have been tracing the short-comings and inconsistencies which follow, for both Locke and Kant, from their conception of their problem as an examination of knowledge in complete abstraction from reality. We have seen that in each the attempt to postpone all consideration of reality involves a latent dogmatism, which finally asserts itself in a way which is destructive of the whole standpoint of an immanent criticism. It remains true, nevertheless, that the chief significance of each is to be found in the attempt to secure and maintain such a point of view. In order to compare their positive contributions to such a result, we must consider the more special forms which the problem of knowledge assumes in their hands and their methods of dealing with it.

The knowledge which above all seemed to Kant to stand in need of examination was that which finds expression in propositions asserting connections which are universal and necessary. Hence, in the forefront of his investigation he places the question, 'How are synthetical *a priori* judgments possible?' Now Locke, and Locke alone before Kant, had realised the significance of the distinction here implied between analytical and synthetical judgments. Kant, indeed, himself draws attention to the *Essay* in this connection[1], but shows, in doing so, that he is quite unaware of the fullness with which Locke had anticipated him on this particular point, in his account of the distinction between 'trifling' and 'instructive' propositions. Locke, moreover, had recognised the fundamental importance for our knowledge of judgments which, besides being synthetic, are universal and necessary. Such judgments, and such judgments alone, formed for him the content of science, and it was to their consideration that he had specially addressed himself. He was as fully convinced as Kant that universal and necessary judgments cannot find their justification in an appeal to particular experiences. Finally,

[1] *Prolegomena*, § 3.

Locke had not failed to recognise the synthetical character of mathematical judgments, a thing which Kant thought had 'hitherto altogether escaped the observation of those who have analysed the human reason[1].' It may in fact be said, that the attempt to explain the possibility of synthetical *a priori* judgments, the typical examples of which are furnished by the mathematical sciences, occupies almost as prominent a position in the *Essay* as in the *Critique*.

§ 5. Before proceeding to the consideration of the solutions, which Locke and Kant offer, of the problem to which they both call special attention, it may be well to compare briefly their accounts of the knowledge for which an *a priori* character is not claimed. Such knowledge is contained for Kant in his *a posteriori* judgments, and for Locke in particular propositions concerning existence, as contrasted with the universal propositions concerning the relations of our abstract ideas, which alone constitute science. While both writers start with the presupposition that knowledge of this kind arises directly from our perceptual experience, and calls for no further explanation, they are both in the end led to abandon this position. For such knowledge is found to imply an objectivity which cannot be accounted for by the mere existence of affections of the mind, or even by the apprehension of experiential contents as objects of thought. The difficulty presents itself to Locke in the form of a reference by the mind of these contents to the independent external reality. In the end, as we saw, he is forced to the admission that of such a relation there cannot be knowledge in the strict sense of the term, but only an assurance which is practically equivalent to it. While maintaining the existence of a thing

[1] *Prolegomena*, § 2.

in itself, wholly independent of the mind and its experience, Kant came to see that the reference beyond the mind and its ideas, which is involved in knowledge, cannot be a reference to this unknown *x*. He explains it as consisting of a synthesis of the particular content in question with others in the systematic whole of phenomenal reality. Now the modes in which this synthesis is effected are *a priori*, since they are logically presupposed in our cognition of the particular fact, the objectivity of which is constituted by the synthesis. Thus it turns out that the *a posteriori* judgment itself involves *a priori* determination.

But if Kant in this way transcends Locke's theory of two absolutely different and unrelated forms of knowledge, it is only to replace it by an equally absolute distinction between the rational and the empirical factors in knowledge. He holds, that although our knowledge of a matter of fact involves *a priori* determination by a universal, its particular content remains indifferent to this universal. There is thus a purely empirical element in every judgment of fact. When, for instance, we judge that grass is green, or sugar is sweet, we imply an *a priori* determination of our experience in accordance with the conceptions of substance and quality, but the greenness of the grass and the sweetness of the sugar must be accepted as simply given.

Hence for Kant, as well as for Locke, universality always consists in generality. There is no such thing as a concrete universal, *i.e.* a universal which lives in and dominates the particulars to which it is relative. For both, the possibility of science or rational knowledge depends upon our abstracting from certain aspects of the sensible content of experience. Nor is there any serious discrepancy in their views as to the possible extent of such knowledge. The agreement which exists is apt to be hidden by the apparent contradiction between Locke's contention that a science of Nature is impossible, and Kant's confident formulation of the principles of a pure physical science. But the physical science of which Locke denied the possibility was one which would determine *a priori* the relations which actually exist between the qualitative constituents of our experience; and the possibility of doing this Kant repudiates as emphatically as he.

§ 6. In opposition to the dogmatic rationalists, both Locke and Kant hold that there is involved in all knowledge, whether rational or contingent, an essential reference to experience, though the form which this reference assumes is very different in the two cases. For Locke all our knowledge depends upon ideas, the content of which has been originally drawn from experience. Kant, on the other hand, distinguishing a pure from an empirical factor in every cognition, denies that the former can be said in any sense to have an experiential origin. The reference to experience depends, therefore, for him, upon the necessity for supplementing this pure but merely formal function by a material content. This leads to a restriction of knowledge to 'objects of possible experience,' or phenomena conditioned by spacial and temporal relations, which has no place in the theory of the *Essay*. For the doctrine that our knowledge cannot penetrate to the substantial basis of real being does not imply that the objects of which we have a relatively superficial knowledge must all have a place in the spacial and temporal order of existence, or be possible objects of sense perception. We are not debarred, Locke considers, from a knowledge of the existence of

God, however poor and inadequate our comprehension of his nature may be.

§ 7. We must now turn to the consideration of what is for both Locke and Kant the central problem of the theory of knowledge, viz., the possibility of knowledge which is at once synthetic and apodictic. To Locke, such knowledge consists in the perception of relations between the contents of our abstract general ideas. Since the judgments in which such cognitions are expressed are not obtainable by analysis of the single ideas, they are synthetical; since they contain nothing which is not seen to be involved in the intrinsic nature of the ideas, when considered together, they are necessary; while, in reference to the plurality of instances, in which the contents in question may be exemplified, they are universal. Now, whatever we may think of this answer in other respects, it possesses at least the merit of seeking to explain necessary knowledge by exclusive reference to the nature of what is known. It brushes entirely aside the view then prevalent, that the universality and necessity of scientific knowledge must be attributed to some mysterious power in the constitution of the mind, a conception by which Kant himself was largely influenced. In his insistence upon the derivation of all our ideas, including those involved in such knowledge, from data of Sensation and Reflection, Locke at least maintains in principle the continuity of the products of conceptual thought with perceptual experience, which was explicitly denied both by the view then current and by Kant.

§ 8. A position such as Locke's requires, however, to be supported by an adequate theory of the nature of the universal and its relation to experience, and this he was quite unable to supply. In accordance with the presuppositions of the composition theory, which, as we have seen, Locke never formally withdrew or repudiated, the ultimate constituents of our knowledge, as yielded by experience, are represented as so many units, each simple and complete in itself. But unless the universal is in some manner present in the most elementary form of cognitive experience, it can never be elicited from it by any processes of abstraction and 'consideration.' And unless the single idea is from the first implicitly apprehended as belonging to a larger whole, no amount of manipulation by the mind can discover an intrinsic connection between it and any other idea. The attempt to perform either of these feats is doomed to inevitable failure, and can only result in giving to the knowledge which it would explain an arbitrary and artificial character, which is as destructive of its claim to express the nature of a real object as is the appeal to an innate endowment of the mind.

In nothing is Locke more uncompromising than in the statements which he makes concerning the nature of the universality which attaches to our general ideas. Not only are they, like all other ideas, 'particular in their existence,' but the universality which belongs to their signification is represented as something artificial, made by the mind for its own convenience. 'General and universal,' we are told, 'belong not to the real existence of things, but are the inventions and creatures of the understanding, made by it for its own use[1].' When we 'quit particulars, the generals that result are only the creatures of our own making, their general nature being nothing but the capacity they are put into by the understanding of signifying or representing many particulars. For the signification they

[1] III. 3. 11.

have is nothing but a relation that by the mind is added to them[1].' And the motive which prompts the mind to make this addition is merely the inconvenience which would result from the necessity of finding an endless number of names, to stand for each one of our particular ideas[2]. Consistently with this view, our use of general ideas is declared to point to an imperfection in our understanding[3], and universality is said to be after all 'but accidental[4]' to our knowledge.

§ 9. Such being Locke's explicit doctrine, we must next notice the qualifications which it consciously or unconsciously receives in the course of his enquiry. He himself assures us that he does not forget, and still less denies, 'that nature, in the production of things, makes several of them alike[5],' and thus affords us a 'foundation' for ranking them into sorts[6]. It would seem, therefore, that when the mind 'adds' to a particular idea the relation which constitutes generality, the procedure is not after all a purely arbitrary one. As we have seen, too, the simple idea itself comes to be treated as a universal, of which its modes are the different specifications[7]. It turns out, again, that all ideas 'when attentively considered,' are found to contain some relation, although the relation may remain 'secret,' not being made itself an object of thought. But that which includes relations, whether secret or patent, is no longer a mere particular, but a system or universal. Further, when Locke comes to consider the conditions of the comparison which results in the formation of the ideas of relation, he is no longer able to treat the simple idea as something complete in itself. That comparison presupposes something more than

[1] *loc. cit.* [2] II. 11. 9. [3] IV. 7. 9. [4] IV. 17. 8.
[5] III. 3. 13. [6] III. 6. 30. [7] Cf. above, pp. 72–3 and 90.

the arbitrary conjunction of ideas, which have no intrinsic connection, is implied in the recognition that it must be made 'in a certain respect.' For that in respect of which two ideas are compared cannot be foreign to the nature of either, and thus constitutes a universal of which they are particulars. Nor can this universal remain entirely unrecognised, since 'a man, if he compares two things together, can hardly be supposed not to know what it is wherein he compares them[1].' To take an example which Locke himself gives, the relation of whole and part is founded in the nature of number and extension, and it is impossible to have the relative ideas without also having the positive ideas of number and extension, 'to which they properly and immediately belong' and 'of which alone whole and part are relations[2].' Moreover, in the case of the comparisons upon which scientific knowledge depends, this universal must be explicitly apprehended as such. In an interesting passage Locke contrasts the comparing activities of brutes and men. The former, he considers, 'compare not their ideas farther than some sensible circumstances annexed to the objects themselves.' In contrast with this preconceptual power of comparison, as we may call it, it seems to Locke to be 'the prerogative of human understanding, when it has sufficiently distinguished any two ideas, so as to perceive them to be perfectly different, and so consequently two, to cast about and consider in what circumstances they are capable to be compared[3].' But such a power of comparing, 'belonging to general ideas, and useful only to abstract reasonings, we may probably conjecture beasts have not[4].' The 'casting about,' then, which is characteristic of rational comparison, presupposes a general idea of that in respect of which the comparison

[1] II. 25. 8. [2] I. 4. 6. [3] II. 11. 5. [4] *loc. cit.*

is made. What Locke fails, indeed, to notice is that a universal is definitely involved in the mere recognition of ideas as 'perfectly different, and as consequently two,' while it is implicit in those 'sensible circumstances' in respect of which the brute's comparisons are made.

§ 10. Thus, notwithstanding his professed doctrine, Locke is forced in various ways to admit that the universal is something more than an arbitrary fiction of our thought. The inconsistencies which result are such as can only be removed by a radical revision of his original position. It must be recognised that the mental function, upon which the possibility of rational knowledge subjectively depends, does not consist in abstracting from or adding to experience a universal which it does not contain, but in raising experience itself to a higher level, by the explicit recognition of a universal which was previously present though not apprehended as such.

From the reinstatement of the universal as an actual constituent of experience, a certain modification of method would inevitably follow. It is indeed an entire misconception to represent Locke's method as purely psychological, and to signalise on this ground a complete disparity between his problem and his way of dealing with it. Throughout his investigation of ideas he is, as we have seen, concerned with the determination of their objective content, rather than with their psychical existence and temporal genesis. But the simple idea having been accepted as a unit of composition, this content is apt to be regarded as merely a given fact, thus losing its logical character as possessing implications which carry us beyond itself. As soon, however, as it is recognised that the single idea is essentially incomplete, and requires for its comprehension a reference to the whole to which it belongs, it becomes evident that any method of dealing with ideas must possess throughout a logical character. Experience being no longer regarded as a composition of particular ideas, but being seen to contain in itself systematic principles of structure, the most 'historical' and 'plain' account of its contents must seek to render these principles objects of explicit thought, by a new species of logical reflection.

§ 11. To have conceived the possibility of such a real logic, or logic of experience, is the greatest of Kant's achievements, although he failed to free what he called his transcendental method from implications and suggestions which did much to nullify its value. His permanent contribution to philosophical method consists, nevertheless, in his demonstration that a universal structure is logically presupposed in our knowledge of the particular facts of objective experience. The primary datum of knowledge is thus the single whole of experience, and the isolated and purely particular objects from which Locke had thought to take his start are seen to be incapable of being objects of knowledge at all. We can now see Kant's true answer to the question about the possibility of synthetical *a priori* judgments. Since the particular objects of cognitive experience presuppose the universal structure of experience, any propositions which formulate the abstract nature of this structure, and any propositions which can be seen to be entirely dependent upon this structure, will be *a priori*. They will be characterised by strict universality and necessity, and will be independent of specific experiences for their justification. Moreover, as carrying us beyond the particular object and assigning to it a position in a system, such propositions will be synthetic as well as *a priori*.

§ 12. But notwithstanding his triumphant demonstration of the implication of the universal in the simplest facts of objective experience or knowledge, Kant is in the end unable to give a satisfactory account of the relation of the universal to the immediacy and particularity which such experience also involves. He accepts, in fact, the sensationalistic atomism of Hume, the extreme and one-sided development of the assumptions underlying the application of the composition theory to mind; not indeed, as Hume supposed, as a true account of the ultimate constituents of our knowledge, but as an adequate representation of the material in which the universal structure or form of experience has to be realised. Form and matter, the universal and the particular, are thus found in final analysis to be entirely disparate, although both have been shown to be essential to knowledge. We are asked, in fact, to conceive knowledge as arising from the union of a form and a matter which have no intrinsic connection with each other. It only remains to accept the final suggestion, that the form or universal aspect of knowledge is due to the mind, while its particular material content is supplied through the affection of the mind by a completely disparate and independent external reality, to convert the critical philosophy into a new form of dogmatism.

§ 13. It is evident that Kant, notwithstanding his demonstration of the implication of the universal in the object of knowledge, is as little able as Locke to give a satisfactory account of the relation of the universal to the particular aspect of experience. The imposition by the mind of a universal upon a mere manifold of sensation is as impossible a conception as the formation of the universal by an addition made by the mind to an extract from an experience in which it is not involved. Both views rest alike upon an initial denial of the implicit presence of the universal in the content of our immediate experience, the disastrous consequences of which no amount of ingenuity can evade. This denial necessarily affects the method of each, though in different and opposite ways. For where there is no universal Logic cannot move. Accordingly Locke, professing to accept as the ultimate data of knowledge the existence of a number of simple and separate ideas, inevitably tends to emphasise the factual aspect of knowledge at the expense of the logical. The logical moment, which is by no means absent in the *Essay*, exists, and can exist, only in so far as this initial assumption is tacitly abandoned. Kant, on the other hand, having once for all grasped the essential implication of the universals of thought in the simplest facts of knowledge, but holding that they are in no way present in the content of sense, is committed to a logic which, in the last resort, he is unable to bring into contact with immediate experience.

§ 14. We may illustrate the contrast of method, and at the same time indicate the qualifications to which it is subject, by a comparison between the treatment by the two thinkers of the categories, or the conceptions of the fundamental universals involved in our knowledge. For the origin and content of these ideas, as of all others, Locke bids us look to experience. The embarrassments which follow are the inevitable result of the attempt to find a basis for these fundamental universals in an experience which is supposed to be analysable without remainder into a number of simple and separate ideas. The knot is cut by the virtual admission that from the first the data of immediate experience possess implications which carry us beyond themselves. It is found, moreover, that these implications are characterised by logical necessity. We cannot conceive how these simple ideas should subsist of themselves, but are obliged to think of them as determinations of a substance. Similarly, when once experience in the form of willing has yielded the idea of causal efficiency, we find ourselves obliged to assume a cause for every occurrence. What is wanted, and what Locke fails to give, is a close demonstration that these logically necessary relations are but the expression in conceptual thought of features which are essentially involved in immediate experience itself. Owing to this failure, the necessity of thought has in the end the appearance of a mere *addendum* to factual existence.

It is to the empirical character of Locke's treatment of the categories that Kant takes express exception in the only reference to the *Essay* which is contained in the *Critique of Pure Reason*, while the grounds of his objection find frequent expression in other passages. These may be reduced to the following two, which are not, however, very clearly distinguished by Kant. (1) In attempting to trace the historical genesis of our conceptions, Locke is only concerned with a question of fact, the answer to which could throw no light on the validity of these conceptions, or, in particular, upon our right to employ them for the determination of objects *a priori*. (2) In the special case of the categories, no such development from a simpler form of cognition can, from the nature of the case, be traced. In virtue of their *a priori* relation to objects they must be recognised as having a source entirely distinct from the impressions of sense. While it is true that all our knowledge begins *with* experience, it does not follow that it arises *from* experience. On the contrary, our experience of objects must be regarded as a compound, due to the union of impressions of sense with a contribution made by our faculty of thought.

The denial of the possibility of a genetic derivation of the categories rests, of course, upon the assumption, that the universals which our thought finds to be of fundamental significance for our knowledge of objects are entirely disparate from the contents of our immediate experience. While it is valid against an empiricism which regards experience as a composition of simple ideas, it has no force against an empiricism which does not commit this error. Moreover, when once the continuity of our sensational and conceptual experience is admitted, it becomes clear that while it is important to distinguish questions of validity from questions of genesis, it is impossible to keep them entirely apart. The historical origin and development of our conceptions can no longer be regarded as incapable of throwing any light upon their logical content and value. Thus, if Locke is right in maintaining that the idea of active power or efficiency, which is an essential constituent of our idea of causation, is derived from our experience in willing, he has done something to elucidate the ultimate logical content and implications of the conception, as well as to indicate the temporal conditions under which it comes to be formed by our thought. Nor can it be fairly said that Locke failed entirely to notice the relative distinction between the two orders of enquiry. Thus in answer to Stillingfleet's objection, that the derivation of the idea of substance from materials supplied by experience detracts from its rational value, Locke replied that the supposition 'that reason and ideas are inconsistent' is one which 'will not hold.' Hence, 'the general idea of substance may be grounded on plain and evident reason; and yet it will not follow from thence that it is not ultimately grounded on and derived from ideas which come in by Sensation and Reflection[1].' We cannot, in fact, argue that because certain conceptions and principles are seen to have a rational justification which is logically *a priori*, therefore they have an origin which is independent of all contents of experience. This is indeed the true retort to Kant's remark that knowledge may begin with experience without originating from it.

It is time, however, to turn from Kant's criticism of Locke's empirical derivation of the categories to his own treatment of them. The great value of the conception underlying Kant's 'transcendental deduction,' in which he seeks to show the implication of universal determinations of thought in the cognition of objective fact, has already been indicated. But holding that these universals have no intrinsic connection with the content of sensation, he is unable to proceed in this way beyond a few generalities. Ignoring all specific content of experience, he can only show that knowledge involves the synthesis of a manifold into a single objective system, the unity of which is the correlative of the unity of the subject. When we enquire as to the modes in which this synthesis is effected, we are referred back to 'the metaphysical deduction,' in which an attempt is made to derive a list of the categories from distinctions current in formal logic. The futility of this device has been universally recognised. It must be noted, however, that it is no merely accidental feature of Kant's system, but the direct result of his view of the relation of the categories to the matter of sense. The antithesis between the two having now found its sharpest expression, Kant labours to mediate between them. The purely abstract categories are 'schematised' by being applied to the determination of pure time, and thus obtain indirectly

[1] First Letter to Stillingfleet, *Works*, vol. IV. p. 21.

a purchase upon our actual experience, of which time is accepted as a given form. Abstraction being still made from all but the spacial and temporal aspects of experience, the conceptions underlying the mathematical and mechanical sciences are now presented as the sole unifying principles involved in knowledge. It is upon this assumption that Kant's 'proofs' of what he calls the principles of pure understanding proceed, which are all consequently open to the charge of *petitio principii*. Thus, he does not really prove, as he claims to do, that mechanical determination by antecedent conditions is involved in the very possibility of a cognition of objective sequence, but only that some kind of determination is so involved; while of course if we abstract from all other conditions, mechanical conditions are the only ones we shall either look for or find.

The Kantian theory is dominated throughout by the antithesis between the abstract universal as an object of conceptual thought and a mere manifold of sense impressions; and between these two, as thus opposed, only an artificial and external union is possible. This is effected for Kant through the unique position assigned by him to space and time, especially the latter, as at once universal and pertaining to sensibility. Their designation as *a priori* forms of sensibility covers, indeed, a serious confusion; since Kant fails to distinguish between the spacial and temporal character of sensible experience and the space and time which are elaborated on this basis by conceptual thought. The former, which is all that Kant professes to assume, contains in itself the refutation of the view that the content of sense consists of a mere manifold; while the appeal to the latter, which Kant really makes, reduces his attempted mediation to an obvious circle. In Locke's more naif theory, the need of a *tertium quid* to mediate between sense and thought does not exist, since their functions have not been set over against each other in this absolute way. The subsequent development through Berkeley to Hume depended primarily on stripping the Lockian idea of the noetic or thought aspect which, even when simple, it had at least implicitly possessed in his theory; thus creating the *impasse* from which Kant failed to find a real means of escape. An effective answer to Hume must not, however, begin, as Kant's did, by accepting his reduction of sensible experience to a mass of separate impressions, but by exhibiting the essential correlation of the immediate aspect of experience and thought throughout our cognitive consciousness. It must, in this respect, go back to Locke, but to a Locke fully conscious of his own assumptions.

As regards Kant's special views concerning space and time, it is worth while noticing that he, as well as Locke, consciously relates his theory to that of Newton. It was from Newton that he derived his conception of space and time as logically prior to the determination of things in space and events in time, upon which he professed to base his arguments for their subjective origin. The same priority Locke, too, attributes to those 'boundless, invariable oceans of duration and expansion.' So far, therefore, as this priority of the whole of space to its special determinations is concerned, there is no important difference between the two thinkers, though it is not connected by Locke as it is by Kant with the apodictic character of geometry. The metaphysical inference which is drawn by the former is, however, of a very different character from that of the *Critique*. In place of the contention that space and time are forms supplied to the objects of experience by the mind, we have the view that 'in their full extent they belong only to the Deity.' If Locke's theory is undeveloped and crude in expression, it at least avoids both the subjectivism of Kant and the ascription of ultimate reality to the material system. To object, as Kant does to the similar expressions of Newton, that the theory implies that space and time are conditions even of the Divine Being, is clearly to misrepresent it.

§ 15. It only now remains to sum up our comparison of the main positions and procedure of Locke and Kant. If the latter makes an important advance in his theory of the implication of universal thought determinations in all knowledge, he is hampered by his adoption of a more extreme form of sensationalistic atomism than Locke had ever dreamed of. What is needed to correct Locke is not merely an insistence on the indispensability of the universal for knowledge, but a full recognition of its 'secret' presence in the content of immediate experience. With this recognition would disappear the view that factors essential to knowledge have their source in the mind, in contradistinction both from experience and from the nature of reality, with the resulting theory of the relativity and subjectivity of knowledge, from which Kant, with all his endeavours, is unable wholly to free himself. No longer would the principles of our conceptual determination of objects appear as a fixed and rigid framework, ungenerated by experience and incapable of modification by further experience and reflection. Finally, our method, without sacrificing its logical character, as rendering the universals involved in our knowledge explicit objects of thought, would remain in that close and fruitful contact with experience which Locke above all desiderated.

INDEX